Wake The Fuck Up!

Wake The Fuck Up!

Life Is but a Dream

~~~

Michael B. C. Murray

Editorial Chief: Gloria Hernández
Editorial: Rhodá Uí Chornaire
Design Cover: Sharon Davitt

Published by Michael Murray in February, 2016
Michaelbcmurray.com

Wake The Fuck Up! – Life Is but a Dream
Trade Paper: ISBN: 978-0-9972894-9-7

Edition 1: First Printing: February 20th 2016

Printed in the United States of America

CONTENTS

Introduction

by

Anthony Grey

Massively important, significant, and potentially epoch-making – that is my own considered estimation of this claimed new historical and spiritual information with the profound teachings that follow in this extraordinary book. They call into question in a dramatic way I have never encountered before, many of the core spiritual practices, which over the past two millennia have greatly influenced and shaped the ancient and modern world.

And perhaps most significantly, if widespread credence is given to these newly presented teachings – whether that is sooner or later – great positive changes in spiritual understanding and practice can potentially follow to unite all mankind and influence the ways of our whole world for the better.

This book, in fact, makes it unmistakably clear that this is the key reason for the publication, which is to stimulate a new and destined process of enlightenment and spiritual awakening, not only for spiritual seekers but for people of each and every faith across the world. In that sense, it is highly relevant for all seven and a half billion of us, without any exceptions. Michael explained to me, that this information was given to him very insistently during several years of direct communication and through several different avenues, such as altered states of consciousness, visions, lucid dreaming, and transcendental meditations. The timing of this information clearly enshrines *Wake Up! – Life Is But A Dream's* core ambition; to alert the world that it is time to wake up!

And this is to emphasize to all readers that the process of enlightenment is rooted ineluctably in love, forgiveness, compassion, unity and oneness – and the firm understanding that every human being is in true reality not a physical body but above all an eternal, divine being and equal always to all others whatever their race, gender or creed.

It might perhaps be helpful and appropriate at this point to describe briefly how author Michael Murray received the writings that make up this book. He sets out his own story first in full fascinating detail in the early chapters, The Life and Times of Michael Murray, describing how several near-fatal accidents during the first thirty-three years of his life made him familiar with extraordinary, repeated out-of-body experiences.

During all these experiences he found himself in each case looking down, detached and pain-free from above, at his perilously-injured body. Each time, very remarkably, he recovered, and an inner certainty grew in his mind that his own truest essence was definitely spiritual not physical.

Later he was confined illegally and unjustifiably – sometimes in virtual solitary confinement – over several years at his own home in Letterkenny, Ireland, by corrupt Garda police acting on behalf of a powerful Irish politician and businessman. During that period, Michael struggled desperately to retain his health and mental equilibrium and it was then that he went through other, similar but more extensive 'internal' experiences which then culminated in a very deep and profound spiritual awakening on the night of September 29, 2008, which also happened to be his birthday.

Then in 2009, when Michael reached the awakened state thereafter, he immediately began to give talks about the revelations he received, directly from his newly acquired awakened state of mind. He was already aware of the voice within when writing down the material you are about to read, and then also began to hear this same gentle, internal guiding voice when answering questions at his own public talks.

This same voice also had introduced him to the concept of the Akashic Records, known as the spiritual archives which have long been considered by spiritualists and psychics to exist at an invisible spiritual level, containing comprehensive information about all humanity's past individual thoughts and actions. The word Akashic comes from a Sanskrit root meaning space, ether or spiritual plane. During the next seven years between 2009 and 2015, Michael was guided internally to write this book, "*Wake Up! Life Is But A Dream*", along with his second spectacular revealing book called "*The Metaphysics of the Universe*".

As a foreign correspondent working for Reuters international news agency in Cold War Berlin and Eastern Europe, and later in the China of Mao Tse-tung and his violent Cultural Revolution, I spent my days and nights seeking out new slivers of truths to add to our world's ever-lengthening spiritual search for peace, love and reconciliation, and indeed that elusive state of enlightenment that so many have failed to reach.

Also later, as an historical novelist fortunate enough to produce one or two international best-sellers, I researched and wrote in depth over quite a few years about the war-torn nations of Vietnam, China and Japan in the nineteenth and twentieth centuries. I haunted national archives and libraries in several different countries, looking always with my journalistic eye for previously unremarked historical or spiritual 'scoops' or 'exclusives'.

Very occasionally I felt satisfied that I had been able to dig out something significant and present it in a new and previously unseen light in my novels – at that time hoping that we might learn some important political or military lessons from past mistakes and be inspired or chastened to do something different to change for the better our chronically conflicted and suffering world. But gradually as the years passed, I began to realize that these were futile hopes, and that sadly, historical novels however revealing they might be, were not going to be enough.

Then through having become a small, independent publisher as well as a writer, I encountered Michael Murray for the first time through the good offices of a fellow, London-based *A Course in Miracles* student. And it was in the early weeks of 2014 that I saw for the first time a rough early draft of this book. On reading it, I felt an immediate strong resurgence of optimism that perhaps a single book could, after all, play a vital role in helping our world forward out of its seemingly unending suffering and disharmony.

Many of these revelations are so historically and spiritually profound, and for me, carried the ring of truth and conviction. Convincing spiritual truths immediately began to leap off almost every draft page of the manuscript of *Wake Up!* And I can only say that to be involved in introducing this book to readers, and attempting to help place it in its true place among the world's great spiritual books past and present, feels to me now, like a great honor and privilege.

Wake up! I feel sure, provides vital new understandings we have never had before, it will continue to inspire and without realizing it, we may have already begun to witness the beginnings of a historical leap forward in the growth of a unified human spiritual awareness. It certainly looks like that to me.

And I believe it is not an exaggeration to say that this latest addition to the growing list of inspiring publications, *Wake Up!*, has in itself the inherent power to help accelerate the spiritual evolution and awakening of all mankind. And as I give way to Michael Murray first relating his own remarkable story, I will conclude by saying I trust that you, dear reader, may possibly be inspired too in some way or other, as I have very gladly been, by all the truly extraordinary writings which follow.

Anthony Grey
21st January 2015

Anthony Grey is a former foreign correspondent with Reuter's international news agency in Eastern Europe and China, an international best-selling author of the historical novels Saigon, Peking and Tokyo Bay and the recent non-fiction memoir *The Hostage Handbook*. He also founded the Tagman Press publishing imprint in 1998.

The Origins of This Book

In 2008, I underwent a very profound spiritual awakening, that resulted in a drastic change in my way of life. Prior to this, I was not a spiritual person, nor a seeker of any form of spirituality in any way. I had never even read a spiritual book in my life. I did not know it at the time, but found out soon after, that what I had just accessed and attained, almost all of the entire spiritual community was desperately seeking. That said, even though I was not a spiritual seeker, I was in fact a very spiritual person underneath. Why? Because, I had actually been encountering one spiritual experience after another throughout my life from the age of seven, and without even knowing it.

As a child, just after my first near death experience, I began to see some very strange people and events. It was at my grandfathers wake, just a few years after my first near death experience, when I saw him sitting on a chair just smiling at everyone who was in the room. He did not seem to know that he was dead, but he was in so much peace; it was vibrating from him. I was the only one who saw him. He gave a little wave to me, smiled and then he was gone. I remember telling my sister, but she laughed at me.

Later, as I grew older, whenever I would go to a wake or a funeral, I would see those people who were supposed to be dead. Then, after a while, I stopped going to all wakes and funerals because it scared the wits out of me. I could tell no one because any time I would mention it people just laughed, so I kept my mouth shut from then on.

Then, after my second near death experience, I found that I could astral travel. For a period that lasted about five years, I experienced an out of body event almost every week and I was terrified. This time I told my dad, and he thought I was mad. He suggested a shrink, so again I shut my mouth and said nothing more.

After my third near death experience, I found that I had this very strong inner knowing when something was about to happen, and I was always correct. My intuition had been magnified a thousand times over. This was my inner guide connecting with me through my intuition, which saved me on many, many occasions. And alas, after my fourth near death experience I had this inner knowing that I was about to be engulfed within my shadow self, in other words, I knew I was going to be in hell for the next ten years, and as it turned out, I was one hundred percent correct.

Then, in 2008, I underwent three major shifts in consciousness. My self-awakening happened on September 22nd, 2008, and seven days later I experienced a spiritual awakening on September 29th, my birthday. Four months later, on February 20th, 2009, I experienced Revelation and woke up within my true higher Self. Revelation is described in the book, *A Course in Miracles* or *The Course*, as direct communication from God.

I received all the information that you are about to read in this book, in various forms of communication: Through meditation I can enter altered states of consciousness and within those states I experience visions; I experience transcendence, which is like an out of body experience where I seem to be lifted out of my body and find myself not here. In truth, I am travelling nowhere, I am just experiencing different states of mind that are now open to me.

Immediately following each experience, I began to write down, or sketch what had just been revealed to me. This has been happening from day one, since September 29th, 2008, until the present, and as the years roll by, it is always new information, new teachings, new concepts, new truths, and new revelations.

Everything I have ever requested, I have received. I received all the maps and scales of every universe, of every dimension, and every state of mind. I was endowed with the knowledge of the various archetypes and the structure and contents of every state of mind that there is. I was basically handed the knowledge of everything metaphysical that has ever been. And for the last seven years, this is what I have been teaching on a daily basis.

It is when my mind is the most still that I can transcend my physical body altogether. Then, from time to time I lapse into the consciousness of Pure Awareness and bathe in the bliss of life that lies deep within. To do this I have to become literally lost in my mind. I find that the doors to the inner sanctuary of bliss that dwells within the present moment simply will not open to an intellectual mind. The mind must be free of all thoughts, ideas and concepts. When I can achieve this, I find that I can travel in the stream of consciousness and enter into the realms of higher consciousness that seem to me to be a place long forgotten, but now remembered.

I will refer to only one book an it is called *A Course in Miracles*. It was Helen Schucman, Ph.D., a renowned psychologist, who, over several years, received the internal dictation, and she scribed the words that are contained in the book called *A Course in Miracles*. That book also tells us that words are symbols, of symbols twice removed from reality. While it was Dr. Schucman who transcribed the words of *A Course in Miracles*, I feel very strongly that I was given the task to supply the symbols that are beyond the words written in *A Course in Miracles*. From what I know today, I feel that this is what my entire life experiences represented, this is what all my near death and out of body experience were for; a lifetime of preparation for me to do the things that I do today. In fact, you could say that my life required that I learn through personal spiritual experiences, rather than from spiritual books, or readings about other people's experiences. It is not until you have a direct experience of your own that you will wake up.

My most important goal and only incentive in writing this book, and the second book that will follow, *"The Metaphysics of the Universe – The Theory of Everything"*, is to help in the awakening of the universal collective consciousness.

In the first section of this book I will talk about my past one last time. This is not to condemn anyone, nor to seek for the punishment of anyone, but only as a means to demonstrate that no matter how much pain we are in, or how much suffering we experience, there *is* something we can do about it. There is another way. I only write my past experiences to show you that way, and so that you too can experience the bliss of life, that is within you and everyone at this very moment. My suffering led me to the final surrender, and it was in my final surrender that my awakening was born.

In the second section of the book I will focus on the teachings I have been endowed with and on how we can "turn the other cheek" so that we may look at life in a different way. Thereby, finally transcending all pain and suffering once and for all. There are new tools, new spiritual messages, and new revelations – complete with my original diagrams. Some of these teachings you will have much resistance to, some will seem quite unbelievable, and some you will find enlightening.

All I ask of you, the reader, is an open mind as you read this material because a closed mind will simply not wake up. I have a rule in life today: I reject nothing, good or bad, right or wrong, and I accept everything. Why? Because our heart will only hold what is true, and everything else will dissolve. While the intellect will reject and judge everything you see, hear, or read. This part of you, the intellect, is the ego, and throughout this book you will read a lot about the ego that it might not like because the ego has many defenses against the truth.

About the Author

Today Author Michael Murray spends his time living between Los Angeles, California and in Dublin, Ireland. Michael travels the world extensively teaching workshops, seminars, spiritual conferences and many more similar events. In a few short years, since 2008, Michael has gone on to become one of the world's foremost experts on metaphysics, consciousness and spiritual psychology.

Michael was born in the town of Letterkenny, in Co Donegal, Ireland on the 29th of September 1964. Throughout his life, up until 2008, Michael had many interesting professions such as a builder in construction, as caregiver in health services, as a property management consultant, and finally as a poker player, and, as he would say with a laugh, not a very good one at that!

In 2009, a few months after his awakening experience, Michael founded the non-profit organization called *A Course in Miracles-Ireland – The Foundation for Inner Truth.* The Foundation today is being run by a full board of directors, and an executive committee that oversees the day to day decision making process.

The Foundation was established to promote the teachings of *A Course in Miracles in Ireland* and to help those who seek another way to live in this world that is without fear, anger, hate or any form of separation whatsoever.

The primary aim of the Foundation is to provide a spiritual home for students and teachers alike in Ireland, for the integration of education and spirituality with study, practice and application of *A Course in Miracles*. *The Course* itself, as a spiritual path, rests heavily on the study, learning and application of its thought system. To understand this Course is to live this Course.

The Foundation's motto is education – which literally means to lead out of. And its primary purpose is to learn and apply how to remember what we forgot – our True Self – and to forget what we remember – our false self. The process of education that this Foundation will pursue, therefore, will help lead students out of the darkness of illusions and into the light of knowledge, which already dwells within.

Namaste!

What is *A Course in Miracles*?

A Course in Miracles, or *The Course*, can be anything you want it to be. Ask and you will receive. It can be a holy book; it has all the Christian symbols and Jesus clarifies a lot of what he said in the bible, which will intrigue all those who still love what is good about religion.

The Course is a spiritual book; it has some unbelievable revelations concerning the levels and degrees that cover the entire spectrum of all forms of spirituality that are currently in this world.

The Course is also a psychologist's dream come true, and the revelations that are applicable to modern day psychology are staggering. This is a holy grail of all books for any psychologist who truly wants to know how the entire structure of the mind works and is applied.

The Course is also one giant tool box and it reveals with clarity all of the ego's tools that keep you regurgitating the same pains, the same fears and the same sufferings over and over again. It also has a second set of new and profound tools that will lift you out of the darkness and bring you into the light. And finally, in my opinion, the most important feature in this book is that it is a book that provides the Ascension Codes to wake up.

The Course itself is the world's first holographic book that reveals the entire structure of the mind, as well as the road map home. It is a self study book that will simply help you wake up. If you wish to wake up in this life time, then this book will help you achieve that. Up until this point in our spiritual evolution, everyone who has awakened has done so through the dark night of the soul.

As I will discuss in this book, the path of the dark night of the soul is a very dark, isolated, victimized path to choose. Not everyone makes it on this path because it gets so dark that many would rather kill themselves, if they do not have a good reason to live. However, *The Course's* path to wake up is a gentle letting go, rather than having everything get taken from you at once.

A Course in Miracles is a truly amazing psychological, theological and spiritual book to be embraced. And yet, I stress, it is only one of the very many ways to wake up!

PART I

The Life and Times
of
Michael Murray

CHAPTER 1

~ ~ ~

I Did Not Die!

I have little time for the past these days, it is a place where I rarely venture into. However, I feel that I should give a brief recount as to how my past has brought me to the unbelievable place where I am today. I should also mention here that I, in no way, hold any grievances for those who seemingly did me wrong, and I offer them only my deepest gratitude and eternal thanks, for if it were not for them, my life today would not be the bliss-filled life that it is.

I was born in the north-west corner of the Irish Republic, on the 29th of September, 1964; the youngest of eleven children. My maternal grandparents lived with us, which meant that in total there were fifteen of us living in a little farmhouse just outside the small town of Letterkenny, in County Donegal. Life was very tough in those days. Money was scarce and my mother and father had a lot on their plates looking after all of us, and also managing the farm.

For me, life started to become a bit of a struggle from around the age of seven onwards. From that time, through no fault of my own, I was somehow introduced to some very, very unusual experiences.

One day, while I was out playing on the farm, I fell and hurt myself quite badly, cutting both of my knees. In those days, if you felt ill or had any kind of injury, it was widely believed that the best cure for everything was an aspirin tablet. It did not really matter what the ailment was, an aspirin was thought to cure everything. I remember running into the farmhouse with tears running down my face and my grandmother was there, as she always was, with the cure in her hands: the aspirin tablet!

However, with so many of us running under her feet, my grandmother made what turned out to be a grave error that day; she forgot to give me a drink of water with the tablet. For that mistake I was going to pay a high price because that tablet lay in my stomach for the next few days and we were totally unaware of its effects on my stomach lining.

The next morning, I woke up feeling very ill. My temperature was quite high, so I was kept away from school and sent straight back to bed. As the day progressed, I became weaker and weaker, and by the evening I started to feel very sick and went to the bathroom. While standing over the sink, I started to throw up for what seemed like an eternity. It was pure blood that was coming up, and although I don't remember it, I was told that I quickly collapsed to the floor. I was rushed to the hospital. I have no memory of the trip, but I remember very clearly transcending my body and being in a place of unbelievable peace, joy and love.

Then several days later I woke up from this inner bliss that I experienced, and was thrust back into the trauma in my body and its first near death experience. As I came to find out in the years to come, this was not to be my last.

Back in the hospital I looked at my body and I was shocked to see that there were so many needles, tubes and drips about me that I didn't know what was going on. The pain was unbelievable; I could not believe that this was happening to me. Also, I discovered later that the aspirin tablet had burned a hole right through my stomach wall and into my spleen. I had been bleeding internally for over two days and I was lucky to have survived. I also learned that at one stage, the doctors had given up hope that I would ever regain consciousness. Somehow I did. And although I did not know it then, I was going to spend the next five years being readmitted to the hospital for treatment and emergency operations for severe stomach pains, stomach cramps, gastrointestinal bleeding and abdominal adhesions. Not until the age of twelve did I return to living a normal, enjoyable life that included playing football, which I really loved.

Five years later, at seventeen years of age, I left school and started working in a local factory that made frozen potato chips. One day, as I was working high up on a load of wooden pallets, I slipped and plunged down about thirty feet, head first, onto a concrete floor. My skull was badly fractured. However, something interesting happened at the moment I hit the floor: in that same instant I found myself standing right next to my body, watching it lying on the floor with blood pumping from the back of the head. I could see that my head was badly damaged and I should have been in excruciating pain, but it appeared that since I was not in the body I did not feel any pain.

Then, as my body was being taken to the hospital, I went with it all the way, just hovering above it in the ambulance. At the hospital, I seemed to lose sight of it and found myself in a long, black corridor like a vortex with a circular door at the end. There was a very bright light shimmering around the edges of the door, and the same shimmering radiant circle of light was reflected all around me. As I found myself going towards that incredible circle of light, I remember sheer terror rising within me. I felt petrified of that light and what lay beyond the door but I could not understand why that light caused such a threat to me. However, it was this sheer terror I was experiencing, this almighty fear that drove me back down and out of the vortex, and the next thing I knew, I was back in the hospital.

I remember being high up against the ceiling in the corner of the operating theatre looking down on this battered body lying on a table with its head cracked open. I saw the doctors and nurses were working vigorously on the back of that guy's head. Poor, miserable sod, I thought. In that same instant, I realized it was me who was lying on the table! The very second I realized it was me, I found myself zapped back into my body. It was then that the sheer pain of the fall hit me. I was in agony. I didn't feel a thing while I was outside the body, but the instant I returned to the body, the pain was agonizing. As I came around from the operation, I remember telling a beautiful nurse that I thought I was dead. She looked at me, laughed, and said, "We thought you were a goner too, but thankfully you are okay now". With that she smiled and walked away. It took some time, but somehow I eventually recovered.

Things returned to normal for a few weeks after this incident. Then, as I was drifting off to sleep in bed at home one night, I heard a strange ringing vibration noise in my head. It was like a very resounding vibration, which continued to intensify. In a flash, I found myself out of my body again, and once more, I was terrified instantly, because I did not understand the experience nor could I control it. This experience occurred nearly weekly over the next five years. I always became more frightened as I got further away from my body, but on every occasion, although I would always return, I did not know how. These out of body experiences always happened as I was drifting off to sleep, and no matter what I did, I could not prevent them from happening.

After about five years, one night I managed to wake up just before the vibration began. This vibration, I knew, was always the predecessor to another out of body experience. At the time I always hated these experiences and wanted them to stop. This night was different, and by waking up just before the vibration kicked in, I seemed to have deactivated the out of body experience from happening. It was the first time that I was able to stop it and I was over the moon! I was ecstatic because until then, I felt dread that this might keep happening to me for the rest of my life. The only person I ever told was my father, and he said that if it continued, he would have to send me to see a shrink! I remember him asking me a few months later if it was still happening. I said "No", but I was lying. I certainly did not want to see a shrink so I kept quiet about it all and just decided to deal with it myself.

The out of body experience recurred in 1996. I was thirty-two years old, and I had gone on a holiday to Ibiza with a dozen football friends to enjoy two weeks of sun, sea and all night parties. We had all been taking part in a crazy poolside team quiz with other tourists, in which the rules said that you had to jump into the water as you gave your answers to the quizmaster. Nobody knew that I could not swim, as I had never wanted to admit it to anyone. We had often played pool-volleyball together, but for reasons of pride and ego, I had always stayed in the shallow end where I could stand. As I hesitated after answering my question, a friend rushed up, and amid great hilarity, pushed me head first into the deep end. Needless to say, I instantly sank to the bottom like a rock. All of my friends thought I could swim, and when I did not surface immediately, they thought I was staying underwater as a laugh just to make them panic.

I remember lying on the bottom of the pool looking upwards, and seconds later, I began to lose consciousness, but not awareness. Strangely enough, this was one of the most tranquil and peaceful experiences I had ever had up until that time. I was not gasping for breath as I expected I would be, and it all felt quite blissful. And again, I felt my consciousness leaving my body - I was having another out of body experience! Once more, I found myself back in that same identical vortex with the same identical door, and the same circle of light at the end of it. And again, I was petrified as I found myself going towards the light. However, it was again fear that drove me back out of that vortex,

8

and I returned to my body, just as I was being pulled out of the swimming pool.

After all the many out of body and near death experiences I had one very clear knowing: *I was not my body.* However, I did not know what I was. At the time, this was a concept that I, almost unconsciously, would deny and suppress in my mind. But the question still remained. It would be some years yet before I would get the answer.

In December 1999, my life took a dramatic turn for the worse. I experienced my fourth near death experience, where my femoral artery was severed. I again experienced the same vortex, and the same fear drove me back once again into this world. I spent the next six months recuperating, and soon after I entered a period of ten years where I was increasingly embroiled with corrupt Irish policemen, and a very questionable politician. The decade from 1999 to 2009 was in fact to become a period of my life, which could be accurately described as "the dark night of the soul". Yet like the out of body experiences I have previously described, it has become clear to me that the events of this period played a crucial contributory role in my progress towards acquiring the extraordinary experiences that were about to take place; experiences that I never expected in all my wildest dreams.

CHAPTER 2

~~~

The Dark Night of the Soul

The dark night of the soul perhaps sounds like an experience that should be avoided at all costs. In my opinion however, everybody sooner or later is likely to pass through some kind of period of "darkness", either in this life or in lifetimes to come. It is said that many seekers of enlightenment search for this experience very deliberately to aid their advancement towards a state of higher consciousness.

In my case, I can say that I certainly did not. I was not at that time in any way a spiritual seeker, or a spiritual practitioner. I was not even religious. I had lost all faith in formal religion at my secondary school that was run by Catholic priests. Almost daily at that college I was beaten, threatened, bullied and harassed by these so-called representatives of God, to the extent that I left school at sixteen, having learned very little. At that time, I felt that if these "chosen" people, who could be so abusive to mere children, represented God, then that God was somebody I had very little interest in.

One priest, who shall remain nameless, taught me Irish and deliberately humiliated me every single day for three years. In front of my peers, he constantly called me by the Irish term Amadán, which translates as "stupid" in English. Consequently, I left school in 1981 at the age of sixteen, making a solemn vow on two issues: firstly, I would never utter another word of Irish in my life and secondly, I would never attend church again.

Thereafter, I tried to keep both of those promises. 'However, I say 'tried' because in 2008 everything would change for me. The way I see it now, at no time did I walk away from God, instead, I only walked away from the "god" that these people represented. In the meantime, from the day I left school onwards, every time that I was asked about going to church or "mass", as we call it in Ireland, I pointed to my chest and replied, "my church is inside me, and my God is there also". To tell the truth, I did not really know what that phrase meant at the time, but it made me feel really good.

I should perhaps mention that the experience of the dark night of the soul does not, by any means, happen in just one night. The "dark night" in question can represent a period of intense pain and suffering that varies greatly for every individual. As I have already said, my own dark night lasted almost ten years. And it was indeed a lengthy period in my life in which there was a profound absence of peace, love and happiness.

In my case, the way my dark night of the soul came about had its roots in the family I was born into, which was one steeped in politics. My grandfather was one of four people who established the Irish political party known as Fianna Fáil in 1926, in my home county of Donegal. After the British left Ireland, Fianna Fáil emerged from a split among members of the Sinn Féin Party, who rejected the Anglo-Irish Treaty of 1921. The Fianna Fáil party is generally recognized as a centrist to center-right and conservative political party. Having been in power over sixty years since its inception, Fianna Fáil generally represents a range of people from all social classes.

Given this political background, it was hard for me not to become entangled in local political plots and other intrigues in Letterkenny – which ultimately led to the very serious consequences that were to follow.

In essence, between 1999 and 2009, I was subjected to a form of what can best be described as part-time illegal house arrest, and virtually full time acute persecution and intimidation when outside my home by corrupt members of the Garda. Friends, family and almost everyone I knew eventually shunned me, and I became completely isolated in my hometown. I was effectively confined for much of the time in my home through the direct actions of the local corrupt police force – the local Garda Síochána – who were following the instructions of an unscrupulous local politician, who used his connections, political and otherwise, to enhance and protect his business ventures and his personal power. I will not disclose the name of this politician, but will refer to him as the Politician. He was a long-standing close family friend, and I was therefore, on good terms with him for many years. Not only was he involved in national and local politics, he also had substantial business interests.

In my early working life, I had benefitted personally in many ways from his help. He first used his behind the scenes influence to find me employment with the local health authority. Later, he helped me again in quite a different way. I had foolishly obtained money from a local bank, which I was not entitled to, by manipulating accounts. I was charged in court, but through the Politician's interventions, I only received a suspended sentence. In 1991, he used his influence in securing a post for me in the maintenance department at the local Institute of Technology-- from a list of 94 applicants. I held that permanent post for some ten years - until the Politician and I parted ways.

The parting between the politician and I occurred due to what he considered a betrayal on my part. My crime, according to him, was that I intended to open a nightclub that would run one night a month. When he found out, he immediately became hostile towards me and used his connections with the local Garda to force the closure of my opening night before it even began. These corrupt Gardaí used intimidation and threats against the owners of the local nightclub venue where I had booked my night. Their tactics worked as the owners pulled the plug on my opening night. In addition, the Politician was instrumental in having me removed from my job, the very same job that he had helped me get years before.

It may appear incredulous that one man should have such powerful influence. However, at that time in Ireland, many politicians and those holding authority could act without fear of being held accountable. Garda corruption was rife in the whole of County Donegal throughout the late 1990s and continued up until 2008. In fact, the corruption was nationwide. In 2002, a major tribunal, the Morris Tribunal, was set up to investigate the problem of police corruption where I lived in County Donegal. It was to cost in the region of €100 million, and it set out to get to the bottom of many allegations that had been made during that time of unacceptable and abusive activities by Gardaí. Amongst its many cases, the Morris Tribunal reported on one particular man who had been wrongly framed by Gardaí for murder, and this innocent man later received €1.5 million in compensation. In another case, it was revealed that another innocent man was framed by rogue Gardaí who had planted drugs on his nightclub premises. As a result, he received a four-year jail sentence. This unfortunate man described his experiences as, "a tormenting saga of imprisonment, estrangement from family, loss of business, public and professional ignominy and despair." He was later found to be totally innocent, and received €4.5 million in compensation.

The Morris Tribunal concluded its public hearings in December 2007, and its final report was issued in October 2008. In formal terms, it was a public inquiry "to address allegations of corruption and dishonest policing in the 1990's and early 2000's against the Garda Síochána, the national police force of Ireland".

Mr. Justice Frederick Morris stated in his summary: *"This Tribunal has been staggered by the amount of indiscipline and insubordination it has found in the Garda force. There is a small, but disproportionately influential, core of mischief-making members who will not obey orders, who will not follow procedures, who will not tell the truth and who have no respect for their officers. These are the people we pay to stand between us and the criminals. Maybe we should reconsider. Maybe we need to pay criminals to stand between us and the Garda. Maybe, there isn't any difference![1]*

Several senior Garda officers were found guilty of a litany of offences that included: victimization, harassment, assault, intimidation, planting of damming evidence, cover- ups and even perjury. Just about anything you could name, they were found guilty of it. In 2008, during his summing up, Mr. Justice Frederick Morris posed the question, "Could such things ever happen again?"

Well, such things were not only going to happen again, they were in fact happening to others and me during the six years that the Morris Tribunal was in session. Unfortunately for me, the Politician was protected from any involvement in the Tribunal, by the terms of reference that were applied to the Tribunal, no politician could be held to account for anything. It was reported that the Morris Tribunal was the biggest internal investigation into police corruption ever held in Ireland's history. In my view, it was not only the biggest internal investigation, it was also the biggest internal cover-up in Ireland's history.

The saga of my dark night of the soul really began in early 1998, when I tried to open up that first nightclub in my hometown. To illustrate how the whole story unfolded into a nightmare, it is necessary to tell the entire story in detail. In planning my nightclub, to start the ball rolling, I did a deal with a local nightclub and bar manager who was also a good friend of mine. He agreed to rent me the club that he managed for one night a month for the following twelve months. A deal was struck that he would get all drink sales from the nights in question, and I would get the door admissions. It was also agreed that I would bring in my own DJs and sound equipment.

On the day leading up to the scheduled opening night, several Gardaí arrived at his premises, at the behest of the Politician I presume, and threatened him. They warned him that he would be forced to close the premises if he didn't cancel the contract with me. He refused and the police promptly left. One hour later, a senior police officer arrived and again made several threats to my friend in an effort to thwart my opening night. My friend again refused and once more the police left the scene.

However, just one hour before my night club was to open, the manager received a phone call from the proprietor of the premises, whose brother was a Garda officer in a nearby town. The proprietor instructed the manager to cancel my contract. It became apparent that friends of the Politician within the Garda Síochána had put pressure on the proprietor's brother to take this course of action.

It was clear that the Politician had wide ranging influence far beyond my hometown. Once his perception of me changed, to that of someone who he felt "betrayed" him, he did not stop at stopping my club night from taking off. Now he was going to do all within his power to destroy me. I knew from personal experience that this is how he dealt with anyone who he felt had crossed him.

As I said before, he was not at all happy that I was trying to open a nightclub that he saw as competition and after he closed it down, he did not stop there. At that time, I had another business in town. It was a café-bar with pool tables and amusements. Shortly after the nightclub was forced to shut down, the same corrupt Gardaí began to harass my customers on a nightly basis and also began laying siege to my premises. Some of my customers were arrested, some were assaulted, and most were scared off by these thugs in blue uniforms with badges.

Eventually I had to close my café-bar. From this time onwards, the Politician made sure that every Garda in Donegal was out to harass me for whatever reasons they could find whether they were legitimate or fabricated. I soon discovered that I was under constant surveillance by Garda plain-clothes detectives, and was, from then on, regularly stopped, harassed, victimized, and then searched by the drug squad. I began to make complaint after complaint to the Garda headquarters in Dublin, but I got nowhere, and it was clear that nothing was going to stop the unlawful and unjust behavior of these thugs.

At this point, the only thing I had left to generate an income was my day job in the college and a few hours overtime. At the time of my appointment, several senior managers were also appointed by the College through the Politician's interventions. Thus, the Politician was able to call in favors from those who owed him their job; in return they agreed to help make my work life unbearable for me. One day, a number of Gardaí arrived at the Institute and began to investigate my work dealings. I was informed by the Human Resources Section at the College that I was to face a number of serious charges relating to a fraud that had taken place some years earlier.

Needless to say, these charges were false and have never seen the light of day. Nevertheless, I was suspended from work on full pay for a year, and eventually was sacked early in 2001. As I was unfairly and unjustifiably dismissed from my job, I sought legal advice with regard to suing the College. However, I was informed by reliable sources that the barrister that I hired was approached by the College's Human Resource Management, who promised to retain my barrister for the College's future legal work if my claim could be sabotaged. And that is exactly what happened. My barrister and solicitor ensured that my case saw delay after delay, and eventually ran out of time and nothing was done.

Constant betrayal, deceit and oppression by people whom I had considered close for over a decade was affecting my mental state and wellbeing, and I felt ostracized. For all such activity, the Politician used a phrase called "The Squeeze". He used this expression in the context that if there was someone he wanted removed from a position of power, he would use all manner of means to "squeeze" that person out. He used this same tactic with all rival businesses, using his local henchmen within the Gardaí to harass other local nightclub owners into submission.

In using this form of harassment and intimidation, the Politician had a hand in closing down several other nightclubs all over Donegal throughout many years. I know this because during the time I had maintained a friendship with him, I had the opportunity to witness how he would handle his competition and saw how he would "squeeze" others out of the business. At this time, he had successfully "squeezed" me out of two businesses, and used his friends, whom he had appointed in the college, to "squeeze" me out of my job.

The Politician was never satisfied with just getting his own back, he always wanted to make those who he believed crossed him suffer further. He once said within earshot of me, "I don't just want these fuckers removed from their jobs, I want them buried as deep as possible in the ground." As I found myself without a job and a source of income, all that remained for me was my social life, and that was about to be hit next.

By early 2000 I found myself under constant surveillance by Gardaí who were close to the Politician. I was stopped and searched regularly, and often arrested on trumped up charges. Everywhere I went the Gardaí followed – but before long, things took a more sinister twist. For a period of around six months, I found myself being barred from almost every pub and nightclub in my hometown. As I would enter an establishment, the owners would take me to one side and tell me that I was no longer welcome. Some owners quietly admitted that the Gardaí had threatened to scrutinize their businesses if they refused to bar me. In addition, soon afterwards I discovered that I was also now being labeled a drug dealer of the highest caliber – despite the fact that I was well known in Letterkenny and Donegal at that time as a sportsman.

At the time of the smear campaign, I had played football for over twenty years, and naturally, as a sportsman, I had never been involved with drugs in any way. Those who knew me well were aware of this truth. Those who did not know me well perhaps chose to believe the Garda, either way, they had no choice. One local man commented to me, "If a Garda says it, it must be true".

So I headed off to the local Garda Station and made another complaint about this smear campaign. I was seen by the Chief Superintendent who simply appointed another Garda to investigate my complaint. At that time, there were no independent investigators of formal complaints against Gardaí. This was, and still is today, the root cause of all Garda corruption. The force itself is policed by itself, and my case was not any different. In Ireland, the Garda even illegally secretly listen in and record private phone calls between those arrested and their legal teams in almost every Garda station in Ireland. Therefore, my complaint in regards to the smear campaign against me was never investigated properly, and it was covered up just as quickly as it began. From my earlier friendship with the Politician I was aware that he had several high-ranking Garda on his books. Thus, I began to see that my complaints were unlikely to be acted upon. Nonetheless, I kept trying in hopes that someday someone would listen. So every time the Gardaí acted against me illegally I made a complaint, hoping that sooner or later I would be listened to. But alas, that has never happened.

In early 2000, the shit hit the fan for the Garda in Donegal. Garda corruption again made big news headlines and several high-ranking Gardaí in Donegal were investigated for a litany of criminal offences. Those offences included: the forgery of a murder confession, the planting of bombs by Garda officers, the harassment and intimidation of several nightclub owners and the planting of drugs on them, the planting of firearms on a civilian, and instances of false arrest and imprisonment. The most senior Garda involved in the bomb making and corruption was also a very good friend of the Politician. The Politician had leverage on the senior Garda, as he knew everything about the bomb making and all those involved. The senior Garda was courting the Politician, seeking for political favors to help him on his promotions up the ladder to the top job of Garda commissioner.

As news broke of the national inquiry into Garda corruption, the Politician began to pull back from his friends in the Garda somewhat, and he started the process of severing his links with several high-ranking Garda officers, but still continued to use low-ranking Garda officers to harass and intimidate me on a daily basis. He needed to keep me quiet at all costs as he knew that I had knowledge of his collusion and dealings with these corrupt Gardaí. And the best way for him to do this was to destroy my reputation, and ensure that no one would ever believe anything I said!

Thus, for over ten years, the harassment, intimidation and pressure continued, -- despite the ongoing investigations of the Morris Tribunal -- and it worked, it really worked for him. As a result, by early 2001, I was effectively an outcast in my own hometown. I was barred from just about everywhere, and any time I went to another town to socialize, I was followed by the Gardaí and promptly barred from any establishment I visited. So, eventually, I had nowhere to go and no one to turn to. As a result, I just began to stay within the safe confines of my own house.

Some friends continued to call on me at home, where we would share a few drinks and play cards. However, this ended as my home was under constant Garda surveillance, and Gardaí stopped and searched everyone who visited me as soon as they would leave my home. Who could blame my friends for not wanting to visit me anymore? It was absolute torture for them! To overcome this situation, I moved home a few times to different areas of the town, but each time the Gardaí would find me, and set up camp outside my house to keep my friends and everybody else away from me.

Although this was very hard to endure, I did not give up the struggle. In 2002, I started another new business, a property management company. I opened the new office very quietly and kept my head down as much as possible. Even so, for the next four years when I would be going to my office, I would run the gauntlet of the Gardaí who were always waiting nearby. I was still under surveillance, even during work hours. As soon as my office closed at 5pm, I retreated home, as I was unable to socialize anywhere in my hometown. From that time onwards, there was one Garda in particular, for reasons best known to himself, who took a new and special interest in me. He began to harass me on a daily basis. He was not one of the Politician's men as far as I knew, instead, he was corrupt, it seemed, all by himself. But I am pretty sure that this thug was being used by another Garda who was loyal to the Politician. He appeared to be something of a psychopath who broke all the rules whenever and however he wanted. And to be fair, I was not the only person in town that he was terrorizing. I won't give his true name here, let's just call him Callaghan. As I made official complaint after official complaint about the actions of the local Gardaí, a senior Garda in Letterkenny sent Callaghan after me in a big way.

You see, the problem was this, my persecutors were falsely labeling me as a drug dealer, but there was no evidence to back that claim. I was never caught in possession of drugs, I was never with anyone who was caught in possession of drugs, nor was I ever in a place where drugs were discovered. And this was a big problem for the Gardaí, as I continued making complaint after complaint.

Then something happened that just about saved my life. The corrupt Gardaí had a plan that somehow I saw through almost straight away. One night, on my way home, I was stopped and searched. As usual, I was asked to stand at the side of the road while the Garda searched my car. This time in particular, I sensed that something sinister was happening, but I could not put my finger on it.

It was not the usual stop-and-search that I had become accustomed to. Somehow it felt very different. As usual, they did not find anything, so I was told to drive on to my home. But, although I could not put my finger on it, something kept bothering me. All during that evening at home I felt that something was wrong … that there was something which remained elusive and did not seem quite right. This feeling stayed with me even after I went to bed. But while I was lying in bed, it hit me! At first I thought, "no, they could not possibly stoop that low to pull a stunt like that." Then, I immediately jumped out of bed and went straight outside to my car and began a search. I had noticed previously, during the Garda search that day, that one Garda in particular had been paying unusual attention during his search to an area in the back seat of my car. He had not really seemed very interested in any other place, which I thought at the time was very strange.

So when I reached my car, I searched the area to which I had seen the Garda pay the most attention. And sure enough, I found what I was looking for stashed craftily under the seat at the very back – a big bag of ecstasy pills. So I quickly removed the drugs, and immediately threw them in the fire as soon as I went back indoors.

I knew exactly what was going to happen next. On the following day, I was pulled over again in town by two different Gardaí. My car was searched once more, and of course they both knew exactly where to look -- and boy did they look! They ripped the whole back seat out of my car, and I watched them turn to each other in disbelief because they could not find what their partners had planted. They appeared highly exasperated, but were forced to let me go. However, this was not to be a one-off. The exact same thing happened on two more occasions, and each time I was able to find and destroy the planted drugs before they came back to search me.

Finally one day, while I was in the center of town, the man I thought of as "Psycho Cop Callaghan" stopped me and began another thorough search of my car. Of course, he didn't find anything because I had already removed what had been planted there on the previous night. However, Callaghan went ballistic when he found no drugs and began shouting loudly in front of two other Gardaí. When he finally calmed down, he took out a little plastic bag and reached down onto the floor of my car and began lifting out dust and other bits of dirt, which he placed in a bag and sealed it. I knew exactly what he was going to do, he would later contaminate the contents of the bag with traces of some drugs. So I got into my car and went directly to the Garda Station to make a complaint and ensure that there was a record kept of what I had just witnessed. At the time, I was assured that what Callaghan had done was not lawful and nothing would come if it. But alas, that was not to be the end of it.

Two years after the Callaghan incident in which he collected dust from my car, I was driving home one night, and once again I was pulled over by a Garda. Without reason to suspect anything illegal he searched my car and found €5,000 I had with me from a car I had just sold. He decided to take this money and, to cover his theft, he falsely arrested me for drunk-driving, even though I had not been drinking at all. When I appeared in court for this citation I found that the Garda had falsified the report of my supposed drunk-driving arrest to cover the evidence of his theft and, furthermore, the plastic bag that

Callaghan had removed two years earlier from my car was now produced in court.

In open court, it was alleged that definite traces of drugs had been found within that sample. From my point of view, I now had proof that they were fabricating evidence against me, and I knew without a doubt that Callaghan had planted drugs in that sample to be used against me in court. In total, I spent four years in court fighting that case, until eventually the evidence was termed 'inadmissible' and thrown out by the court thereby granting me a victory over the case. Furthermore, the Garda who had falsified evidence was found to be lying under oath, as his colleague would not support his perjured testimony in court. Needless to say, the money was never returned to me.

Regardless of how often the Gardaí failed to find legitimate reasons to arrest me or how much time would pass, I started to feel that it was impossible to abate their constant harassment. Other examples of their tireless oppression included the time when my office was broken into and money was stolen. Despite apprehending the culprits, the Gardaí never returned my money. It does not take a genius to work out what happened to it.

Even more frustrating was when my office was again broken into and despite the fact that my office manager identified the culprit, the Gardaí failed to investigate the robbery at all. The final straw, however, came late in 2006 when one day Callaghan arrived at my office as I was about to leave and he arrested me. He illegally forced me to stand outside of my office, handcuffed and in full public view, while my clients witnessed the incident. He then assaulted me several times en route to the barracks, and when we arrived at the Gardaí station he viciously pushed my head into a wall. This left my head badly gashed and bleeding. I was in disbelief when I learned that Callaghan had charged me for loitering outside my own office!

Fortunately, when the case went to court it was thrown out by the judge who could not believe that a member of the Garda could do such a thing to somebody who owned his own business in town. I could have easily filed a case against Callaghan and the other Gardaí involved for unlawful arrest, assault and battery -- but by this stage, I simply could not take the abuse anymore.

I was systematically being broken by a corrupt political system that was enabling individuals like the Politician and thugs like Callaghan and others to harass and intimidate people as it suited their personal interests and corrupt whims. I was exhausted and broken and I had had enough. Life had become a painful struggle since no matter what I tried to do I could not improve my situation in the least and it had deeply affected me professionally, personally and emotionally. I just wanted to give up. So, as 2006 came to an end, I handed the keys of the office to the manager and walked out of my property management office for the last time. I was mindful that this was my third business in a row that these local corrupt Gardaí had been instrumental in closing down.

What followed for me then was a period of total isolation. I seldom ventured out of the house, except to do a little shopping, and whenever I did venture out, I was constantly harassed and victimized by these same people. I was now, for all intents and purposes, living fully under a strange, nightmarish form of

28

"house arrest". I could leave - yes-, but I had nowhere to go. I could not ask friends to come and visit me and run the Garda gauntlet that was always nearby. I could not go and visit them, because if I did, I would have a Garda escort and they would remain outside of my friends' homes.

So I stopped going to see anyone because it was not fair to bring them under such intense surveillance. It was I who was being hounded and harassed, and I could not bring that to their doorsteps. So in 2006, I began a period that was to last an additional three years or so, where I was totally socially excluded from society. I felt severely isolated, and I feared that it would never come to an end. The Politician appeared to have succeeded in isolating and silencing me, so that nobody would ever believe anything I said. His tactics were working!

For me, my extended illegal "incarceration" led to numerous psychological consequences. These were amplified by the stresses of living effectively in a state of exclusion from normal civilized society. The imposed isolation forced me to retreat deeply into myself, trusting virtually no one, living alone in quiet desperation. I suffered an impaired sense of identity, cognitive dysfunction, irritability and chronic depression, interspersed with anxiety and panic attacks, and an overall deterioration in my physical and mental health.

My former way of living was taken from me. I was thrust into a new, painful, solitary existence. Looking back now, I really don't know where I got the strength that brought me through that period - but it came from somewhere, possibly somewhere within. If I had been sent to prison with a known time limit, I could have handled that more easily. However, I received this unlimited, undefined sentence that did not have an end date. This was the hardest thing of all to grasp and get my head around.

My mind was in agony as the days passed, with no peace, love or happiness in my life. My life became a living hell. I was in a "prison" with no bars, no walls and no justice. I did seek help via solicitors, barristers, newspapers, and even made appeals to politicians, but all to no avail. I went to the Garda headquarters in Dublin, and told them what their officers were doing, and asked for my case to be investigated. I was told that it was being investigated, but in reality my harassment investigation was also being cleverly quashed.

I continued to do everything possible to bring attention to my case, but no one listened, no one wanted to listen. No one was interested, and no one seemed to care, and I soon realized that nothing was going to be done. Even though I knew this, I still kept trying and trying. Sadly, in Donegal, there were no rules for the police. They did what they liked, when they liked, and how they liked. They knew that they were going to be protected, like they always had been, and still are today.

I was absolutely alone, and it would take the next few years of loneliness and isolation for me to finally realize the true nature of this gift I had been given. I was forced to slow down, I was forced to look within, I was forced to find another way, and for this, as strange as it may be to say, I will always be eternally grateful to those people who perpetrated those perceived injustices. The Politician, as I would find out, would be my greatest ally and savior. He literally was sent from God to help me, to help me to wake up.

The subtle and effective psychological damage inflicted on me by my detention was not merely a by-product of torture by state agents. It was a deliberate act to debilitate me, as I have said before, to discourage anyone from ever believing anything I had to say. The intention of those torturers was to render me incapable of having a voice. Who would believe anything I ever said again? As my sense of alienation and isolation intensified, I felt totally alone, abandoned and rejected by society. I agonized at how human beings could treat each other in this way.

Looking back from my final state of ostracism and isolation, I realized that I had often thought, "if I could only get this thing I would be happy, or... if I could only get that I would be happy". Well, in some ways, I did get a lot before my strange disaster struck, but I realized I had never found that elusive state called happiness. To me, I realized, happiness had always been just around the corner – alas, it was a corner that I had never been able to turn! Happiness, it seemed, had always been just one step ahead of me. It had been so close at times that I had felt I could almost taste it, but I never did.

Then I found myself in a strange "prison without bars", a prison that was not sanctioned by any legal authority, where no sentence had been handed down by any judge. It was an unlawful almost invisible prison, run by corrupt, rogue police officers, and I felt myself completely stranded in my isolation and suffering. I could function well enough at an ordinary level, but each day was a hollow choir of nothingness – no dreams, no motivation, nothing but despair and loneliness. I was alone, but not wishing to be, unable even to express myself to those who initially chose to hang around. At the beginning, as I have said, a few close friends had stuck by me. But as time moved on, so did they. I finally came to a time of sovereign solitude. In this bizarre state, I looked at my possessions and everything material that I had ever owned, but nothing stirred within me. I was losing hope as each day passed. Nothing had worked for me. I had not found the happiness I craved, and, increasingly, a certainty was growing in my mind that nothing was going to work for me in the future either ever again.

There were nights that I lay awake pondering the existence of a God. Who was he? Where was he? And how could he not care? Then these thoughts passed. I deserved it, I told myself. I deserved to suffer, a small internal voice seemed to tell me – and I eventually came to believe this small voice that appeared somehow to have been with me all my life. In early 2007, I began to seek help, reaching out to a doctor friend who suggested I talk to a psychiatrist. Over the next six months, I saw several psychiatrists. Each psychiatrist prescribed drugs, and increasingly more mood altering medication, when all I really wanted was simply to talk to somebody. I never did find that person to talk to, but I did amass a large number of prescriptions. From the time I handed my property management office keys to my manager, I was forced to live on social security, although I had some small savings.

After a year or so, finding myself in deepening emotional pain, I turned to alcohol. I needed an escape from the pain, and drink made that escape possible, but only just for brief periods. The pain always came back with a vengeance. Therefore, I had to keep drinking every day to dull the ever increasing suffering and turmoil that was going on inside my head. Before long, I was drinking a bottle of vodka a day, and on weekends, this often increased to two bottles. Altogether, I was drinking around nine to ten bottles a week. On top of all that, I was taking Valium, Zimovane and Xanax to relieve my anxiety, and Lustral for my depression. I felt that these drugs did not help, so I turned to even stronger and stronger drugs. In reality, all I was doing was killing myself, and I knew it.

By this time, my body weight began to fall at an alarming rate. By the end of the summer of 2008, I had dropped from 76 kilos to just under 45 kilos. I was emaciated, gaunt and I appeared to be reduced to skin and bones. An alcoholic and a drug addict, I had basically stopped eating, except some days for a banana, maybe a single yogurt, and some milk. Eventually, I began to suffer regular heart palpitations. With my heart missing beats, I was in effect just waiting for the end. In fact, before long, I was indeed praying for the end to come – and soon. One evening, as I sat alone deep into the night, I wrote the following poem. This poem was written on the 22nd of September 2008. One week later my life was never to be the same again.

The Darkest Night

Now upon me is the darkest of the night.
All hope has been relinquished, no one to call.
Surrender has come, the end is in sight.
A man beaten, I am ready to fall.

My tears, my fears, no longer linger.
The flame in my heart is all but out.
My soul, my love, is all but a stranger.
Mercy and compassion, there is no one about.

My sentence is long, a life I must pay.
The law has erred, and many will flee.
The door is open, but I must stay.
My prison is transparent, all can see.

They judge me, they don't know me.
Love, light is so very far away.
They hate me, they never met me.
Head bowed and broken, I fail to pray.

The world is cruel, I am ready to atone.
A journey is certain, to where I don't know.
The path is dark, I advance it alone.
The end is near, it's time, and I must go.

CHAPTER 3

~ ~ ~

The Surrender

On the 22nd of September, 2008, after ten years of living a solitary life, I felt I had reached the end of my road. All my efforts had come to nothing. There was nothing more to be done, nowhere else to turn. There was nothing more to feel, nothing more to think, nothing else to do, and nowhere else to go. I finally accepted defeat. For me, the struggle seemed to be over. This was the lowest moment of my entire life; this was rock bottom. I could feel absolutely nothing, and I felt helpless, totally helpless and completely alone. I felt that if things stayed the way they were, I could not handle the situation any longer. How did I get to this place? How could this happen to me?

I went into my mind searching for these answers. I thought about suicide, but I dismissed the idea almost immediately whenever it came into my mind. I could never do that to my family, especially to my children. This emptiness that was inside of me, however, was vast; it was a bottomless pit of nothingness.

I had now just attained the state of complete emptiness. Something, I found out much later, that every spiritual seeker one day must attain. However, I was no spiritual seeker – in fact I had never read a spiritual book in my life at this point. And attaining complete emptiness was not my conscious goal in life to achieve. However, here I was at the most pivotal point of my life and I did not even know it.

I did not go to bed that night. Instead, I sat up staring at the roaring fire in my fireplace that was my only friend. Searching deep within my mind, a strange new thought suddenly came to me, "I did all of this to myself". Overwhelmingly, I felt that everything I was going through was self-inflicted. At first I thought this was preposterous. I thought I knew how innocent I was. I was sure about all those who were breaking the law and victimizing me daily, persecuting me, and forcing me into a prison with no walls. I was totally sure of their guilt.

However, I stayed with this new thought somehow... *"I am doing this to myself".* Somewhere deep within me I felt that, however crazy it sounded, I was sure I was doing this to myself. I was absolutely positive. At that moment something stirred within me. There was a shift within my mind – and I knew it was a release of some kind. Some years later, I read a quote from Carl Jung which said; *"There is no coming to consciousness without pain,"*[1] which I now know means, there is no "waking up" except through pain. I realized that I could not endure my suffering any longer. No matter what I did to alleviate it, no matter how much I suppressed it, it was going to intensify and grow in that darkness in my mind. So that night, I simply got down on my knees and surrendered. This was a total surrender to what is, without conditions, agreements, or reservations.

My surrender did not transform my situation, my situation had transformed me. Therefore, because I changed, in that moment everything changed. If I had tried to change the situation, another situation would have emerged to take its place. Instead, because I changed, my entire world changed – in that instant! I accepted that I was not in control of my destiny, my ego was. And at that moment, when that fresh thought surfaced, it was so very profound that I realized that all my pain and suffering was self-inflicted. I realized I was doing this to myself. This was a brand new way of looking at my existence, and for the first time, I realized that I had played the role of the victim from the time I was born. I had been the perfect victim of circumstances and events outside of my control.

Paradoxically, however, I realized that, on some level, I had always been in control. I was in control of how I looked at things. I was in control of how I perceived other people. I was in control of how I perceived myself. I was in control of my mind, but forgot that I had that control. It was not the situation that caused all of my problems; it was my thoughts about the situation that was the problem. I could have at any time, looked at things differently, I had a choice, but forgot that I had a choice. The other mistake I continued to make was that I wanted always to be in control of everything external to me. I now know that one can never control anything outside of oneself; you can only control what is inside one's own perception. And when people or things were not the way I wanted them to be, I would refuse to accept that. This would then create my perceived problems, and that was my biggest mistake.

Next, I began to question who I was. As I sat that night with my aloneness -dejected, fearful, isolated and rejected and abandoned by society- I started to look at something that I had long ago buried away in the back of my mind. I had never previously examined these thoughts, because I was so afraid of them. I started to look back on my life as it was then, but more importantly, I looked deeper into the past, reviewing all of my near-death and out-of-body experiences. But, this time I was doing it from a new belief, that I may be the cause of my experience. And so I began the self-inquiry. In each of these strange experiences, I had found myself looking at my body from a different perspective.

I reasoned that if I was looking at my body, then I could not be my body. If I was not my body, then who was I? Or better still, what was I? Who was the body, and what was I? Also, I remembered that in each near death experience, I never felt more alive. The closer I came to death, the nearer I came to life. I never felt more alive than when I was almost dead. I remembered the expansiveness of being outside of my own body; I remembered that I felt like I was the universe and everything that was within it. I pondered these profound questions for what seemed like hours that night. I remember thinking that this all seemed so ridiculous at the time. In one sense, I was so sure that I was my body. Everything told me that I was my body. Then it hit me like a flash of light – it was my body that was telling me that I was a body!

Every physical sense that I had was telling me that I was my body. So I left that inquiry just there on that memorable night. But later I was to return from yet another new perspective. I would look at all this on a much deeper level. But, for now, in that moment, I felt a sense of release. My pain threshold had been reached, which in turn activated a complete and total surrender within me. The war was over!

At that moment, I felt a surge of peace come over me. It was not like anything I had ever experienced before. I felt that something old was gone, and something new was beginning. It was late by this time, so I went to bed. I knew without doubt that something had just come to an end, maybe the dark night was over, maybe not, time would tell. Something was going to change, and something was already changing within me. It was 6:00 am before I fell asleep that morning, my mind had started to rest and for the first time in years I could sleep a truly restful sleep.

I awoke around 10 am that morning, and I reflected on my musings from the previous night. I was looking back, realizing that it was my surrender that was bringing me this wonderful gift of peace of mind. It was my surrender without conditions, agreements, or reservations; a surrender without demands, needs, expectations or desires.

My surrender was not transforming my situation, it was transforming me. And now because I changed, everything around me changed. There will be no going back, I thought. I am going to accept this wonderful gift that was being given to me. I pondered more on this. And I understood that my surrender did not mean that I was going to let people walk all over me. It meant that I was going to discern without judgment. By using discernment and choosing to be non-judgmental I could then know when it was appropriate to say "yes" or "no" to any given situation. Why? Because, I had no investment on the outcome of any situations. We only judge people because we have a vested interest in how we wish to perceive them. We want to see then guilty of something, anything. The difference is that now I would be coming from a place of acceptance and not judgment. I also knew that my pain and my suffering had become so intolerable that I simply could not stand it anymore; it was this way because I was always trying to either force an issue or resist an issue. This meant that I was not accepting what is. Acceptance of what is, is freedom. By accepting what is, I was free from the frustration of not always getting things my own way. However, my surrender did not mean that I was going to give up. It did not mean that now I was not going to take action. Instead, now I was going to stand back from every situation and take another look. And most importantly, always take a closer look at myself and how I was perceiving any situation.

I knew then that my pain and suffering could only come from me perceiving with a negative mind-set. My surrender meant giving up that mind-set, and looking at the situation once again in the present moment. I thought, *"If I can do this, I can also see that there is a positive situation in every negative situation"*. Another thought came to me, *"Every situation, with no exceptions, had duality within it, and that means that there are positives and negatives involved in everything and in everyone"*. I looked closer at myself. I had believed that great injustices were perpetuated against me, and I demanded justice. I expected those who were responsible to be held accountable and to be punished. I needed someone to understand that I was a victim, and my desire for revenge was blood-thirsty.

And because I held these thoughts every day within my mind, my suffering intensified and the pain became more intolerable. This lasted almost ten years; ten years of enduring so much pain that on that last night I just said to myself, *"enough is enough"*. The overwhelming pain that I had put myself through all of those years finally motivated me to consider that I could choose differently. This brought me into the present moment, into the here and now, to try something that I never tried before – I could choose again.

Now, in this space of the here and now, I was without judgment, of myself and every other person involved. It was only then that I surrendered; it was only then that I could have surrendered. I surrendered my demands for justice. I surrendered my expectations for punishment. I surrendered my need for understanding. I surrendered my desire for revenge. It was in that moment that everything changed within my mind. A peace so deep encompassed me that I was now able to see it was me who has the choice in every moment to choose between peace and pain. I could see clearly that my suffering was self-created; I was responsible for my thoughts, my thoughts produced my actions, and my actions had ruined my outlook on life.

It was really extraordinary. It was like a great weight being lifted from my mind and my body. As the stillness settled in my relaxed mind, my body became more and more relaxed. I now know that all tension in the body comes from the mind-set that we are in. I could literally feel the flow of energy stream through my body, something which I had never experienced before.

The energy flow in my body had become so blocked and rigid because of the incessant tension that was in my mind from not getting things my own way. And now, because of my surrender, I was able to stand back in a space and see clearly what action I could take. I had to let the past go. At that moment in time, I knew that my holding on to the perceived injustices of my past were the detrimental components of my continuing pain and suffering. In that moment, I was able to let all of those so called injustices of the past go, and in that instant I became free. If I could do this with just a few issues that I had carried with me, I knew I could do this with all the issues of my past.

That first morning after my surrender, I decided to take positive action. I was going to bring into awareness everything from my past and let it all go. I found that the longer I insisted on seeing things my way - which was all the time - the more unconscious I became. And the more unconscious I became, the more I suffered. On the other hand, I quickly found that the more I surrendered, the more conscious I became, and the more conscious I became, the more I woke up. This resulted in more peace in my life, in my world and throughout my entire being. No contest, I thought, no contest!

True Peace of Mind

As I was about to jump out of bed, I also noticed for the first time in many years that I was aware that my mind was quiet and tranquil. The usual incessant chitter-chatter had vanished, as my mind indeed was still, it was very still, and the silence was refreshing. My mind seemed filled with a soft mellow light, and I was at peace. This was a new kind of peace, a peace that I had never experienced before. Something was different, *I was different.* I jumped out of bed, which was something I had not done for years – it had always been a labor to get up – but today was different; I found something new.

As I skipped down the stairs and into the kitchen for a cup of coffee, it hit me... fear – there was no fear anymore! ...no worries, no apprehensions, just peace. My sense of dread and my old fearful self were gone. Over the following seven days, a great stillness arose within me. It was a peace I had never experienced previously. I was at peace with myself, and I was at peace with the world. I looked at everyone around me very differently; in fact, I started to see the world differently. I had until then been the most opinionated person in this world, but I found suddenly that I had no opinions anymore; no judgments on myself, no judgments on other people, no judgments on the world.

There was nothing but a calm outlook on everybody and everything. In this state of peace, it was as if I had been transformed from within, as if somewhere deep inside my mind there had been a shift and that internal shift had transformed my internal and external worlds. It seemed all conflict was over and my internal war had subsided for good.

A few days later, while I was still in my new state of mind and living in peace, I was sitting alone contemplating life and what living is all about, when a thought arose in my mind, *"nearly dying changes nothing, dying changes everything"*. After several near-death experiences nothing really had changed within me, except the profound realization that I was not a body. I had experienced life outside of my body, so therefore I knew for a fact that I was not my body, I was something else. I did not know what I was, but I knew I was not a body. But I still didn't know what that something else could be.

I figured that if I had actually died, I might know this by now. Unbeknownst to me, I was about to find out much sooner then I expected.

Much earlier in my life, in each of my out-of-body experiences, there had been a very high audible vibration, like a high-pitched tone in my head. I knew this tone well. Every time I experienced this tone, I knew that I was going to leave my body. I had really hated these experiences. Frightened was not even close to how I felt.

Rather, I experienced sheer terror. I always thought that it was fear of the unknown. Just seven days after my experience of surrender, in fact on the night of my forty-fourth birthday, on the 29th of September, 2008, everything changed; indeed my entire world changed that day. I was sitting at my desk listening to music with a headset, while my son sat on a couch behind me watching television.

Out of the blue the old familiar vibrations started. However, unlike every other time I had felt the oncoming of the vibrations that I knew would lead to the old terrifying out-of-body experiences, I did not resist them nor did I feel afraid any longer. Instead, with my newfound attitude of surrender and acceptance of what is, I embraced the experience. This time, strangely enough, it was to be very different.

The Awakening

On the night of my birthday, the 29th of September 2008, exactly one week after my surrender, as I mentioned above, I was sitting at my computer with ear-phones on, listening to music. My son Jason, who was fourteen at the time, was sitting behind me watching television. Then something happened. In my mind, there was a strong sense of something stirring. I immediately remembered this feeling – it was the frightening vibration to which I had become so accustomed to many years before. I did not move a muscle.

But curiously, there was no fear within me now. I was at peace, and in fact, this time I welcomed the vibration. As the vibration intensified, it happened. I began experiencing another separation of my mind and body. I was back in my mind, out of body, in that old familiar corridor-like vortex, going towards that very same door again, going towards the light. This time there was going to be no retreat on my part, as had happened several times previously.

As I reached the door, the light all around it intensified; it was blinding. However, again, no fear arose within me. This time, I even welcomed the opportunity to walk through that

45

door. I had an inner knowing that if I walked through that door, it meant some kind of death. It was this fear of death that had always prevented me from going anywhere near it before. However, my years of inner suffering had brought my fear of death to an end only one week earlier, and I now found that I welcomed whatever it was that lay beyond that door. It could not be any worse than the hell that I had been living in.

All fear within my mind had dissolved, and I was at peace. As I reached the door, the most peculiar realization dawned on me. This was not the door that I expected. From a distance, this door looked like a solid steel door, but up close, it turned out to be nothing of the sort. It was mist, like a cloud of dark fog that in reality was nothing. So I found myself moving calmly through the fog, into the light beyond.

That was the moment that my entire world changed – and it changed forever. The light was everywhere, there was no place without light. The warmth, the stillness and the love were all-encompassing. My being was fully submerged within this magnificent universe of light. In that moment, a new realization came to me. This light was everywhere, there was no separation between myself and the light. *I was the light.* The unspeakable splendor of sheer, pure bliss filled my every sense. This wasn't like anything I had ever seen or experienced before, yet, somewhere deep within my mind, I knew that I had. The feeling of total unconditional love surrounded and encompassed every part of my essence.

As I experienced this eternal illuminating divine light, I felt certain that I was in the presence of God Himself and I was in awe of this Divine presence. In this state, there was no separation of anything from anything, because there were no things, it was pure Oneness; there was just total unity within the light. I could feel that I was a witness to my own and everyone else's true nature. I knew that in essence we are all an extension of this perfect creation of love.

The foundations for this experience were all laid before me. It had been my own intense personal suffering, I knew, which had brought me to my moment of total surrender. And it was just after my surrender that I experienced the most tranquil state of peace in my mind. I now know that my resistance to surrender intensified my suffering. I now understand that surrender means relinquishing all suffering. Surrender means relinquishing your need to control other people, your need to control all external circumstances and your need to control all events. Surrendering means relinquishing every belief you have, or have ever had, about yourself and all others.

I had just surrendered and relinquished the "self" who I thought just had to be in control. I had relinquished all material, physical and psychological needs and desires. I had dropped all my physical, emotional and psychological attachments. It was through my attainment of peace that the ground was prepared for this experience to manifest itself.

Then it was over. My consciousness brought me back into my body, and there I was sitting at my computer again. My son Jason was still sitting behind me, watching television. I burst out crying. Streams of tears came rolling down my face. Never in my life had I cried like this. But I knew it was not the experience of being "in the presence of God" that made me cry. It was the discovery of my own true nature – the discovery that I and everyone else, without any exceptions, are wholly innocent, no matter what we believe we have done or not done.

It was this certain knowing that humbled me. And I did not just believe it, I now knew it. I realize that this experience is unfathomable to understand. Words alone appear inadequate in explaining the experience, and every time I have tried to use words, I have found those words have totally devalued my experience. And every time I repeated it in my mind, streams of tears ran down my face.

I must have cried for two hours that night, never once looking back at my adorable son sitting on the couch. I did not want him to see me like this, but at the same time, I wanted to shout it out from the rooftops, *"This world is not our home, this is not who we are! We are so much more than what we think we are!"* Yet, I suspect most people will never believe this until they experience it for themselves. Many people might believe that I am delusional and will not believe me.

I also asked myself this question and the answer rather surprised me. The test to see if someone is delusional or not lies in Oneness – they will feel an absolute Oneness with everyone and everything that they encounter. Someone who is delusional, will re-enforce that they are separate, special or unique in some way. Someone who is delusional and going insane will have very low regard when it comes to other people's feelings and emotions, however, someone who is truly awake will have a much higher sense of Oneness, towards themselves, and all others.

So I was not delusional, I thought, because in my heart I had an unbelievable abundance of love for everyone and everything. I could truly see that my best interests and the interests of all others was the exact same. If I really wanted to help myself, then my mission now was helping everyone else.

I went to bed that night and knew that my world would never be the same again. I awoke the next morning early. It was 6:00 am, and I jumped out of bed. To be truthful, I really did not sleep that night. I could not sleep, and as I was lying in bed pondering the mystery of life, I heard this very clear and distinguished voice say, *"It is finished"*. I did not know it then, but I would be hearing a lot more of this voice as the days, weeks and years were to pass.

Transcendence

The next day was the 30th of September 2008, and I found myself very different. It was as if I were seeing for the first time, and everything looked and smelled differently. All my inner conflict was gone. My thinking was different, and my hearing was different. My thoughts were now clear and pristine, but the most telling part was the silence. I could transcend the normal chitter-chatter of mental activity. In one fell swoop my sense of wellbeing and self-esteem had not only returned, but had increased a million times over. However, this was also different. It was not egotistical cockiness; it was a confident surety of self.

There was no frustration, no anxiety, and no sense of failure any more. I felt that I could achieve anything I put my mind to.

The War Is Over

I felt that the 30th of September, 2008, was a day that was to be the start of the rest of my life, and for the first time in years, upon waking up in the morning, I did not hurry to the drug cupboard for my daily drug supply, nor did I reach for a bottle of liquor. In fact, I went shopping for some healthy food supplies so that I could have my first proper breakfast in years. It felt so good to be able to enjoy a healthy meal, to have no drugs in my system and to have a mind at peace, that, in fact, I felt like a new man.

At this point in my story, I need to refer to happenings outside of my home. As I mentioned earlier, I had been under the constant surveillance and harassment by the Gardaí for about a decade since 1998. At about the same time as my surrender and awakening and, by a seemingly extraordinary coincidence, the Gardaí abruptly stopped harassing me.

The Morrison Tribunal, which had sat for six years, had concluded its hearings in December, 2007. Between that time and the 30th of September, 2008, a report on the findings of their investigation had been drawn up. It had recently been announced that the findings were going to be published in October, 2008. It seems that as the publication date was imminent, the Gardaí decided to withdraw all surveillance and to end all intimidation and harassment tactics. I cannot say exactly when this momentous change occurred as I was distracted by what else was happening for me at the time.

As I was saying, I felt like a completely new man, and after breakfast, I headed straight to the drug cabinet to gather every drug from the cabinet and from the rest of the house. By the time I finished, I began to laugh at the amount of drugs I had amassed. There were hundreds if not thousands of pills, now all sitting in a big bowl on the table. With great gusto I threw the lot into the trash can. Ever since that night, I have not taken a single tablet, absolutely none. I have never even had a headache since. I then did the same with my alcohol stash. I poured every drop down the sink, and I did not have a drop of alcohol for the next three years.

Today, I may have a glass of wine with dinner, three or four times a year, or possibly, a glass of Guinness once or twice a year. But that would be the sum total of my drinking now. I just never feel the need for it, but I can enjoy it in a social situation, if the occasion arises. The medical term 'withdrawal' refers to the physical and psychological symptoms experienced when reducing or discontinuing a substance that the body has become dependent on. Symptoms of withdrawal generally may include anxiety, irritability, and intense cravings for the substance with severe nausea shortly after.

As the days passed, I was waiting for the withdrawal symptoms to arrive but as each day passed nothing happened. I had no sweats, no anxiety, no depression, nothing. It was like I had never taken a drug or a drink in my life. My strength was now coming back and my weight began to climb. In a matter of weeks I was back up to over 64 kilos and feeling great, feeling strong, and feeling alive like I had never felt before in my life. By Christmas 2008, my weight was back up to 70 kilos. I was just so happy all the time, and for no reason whatsoever. I was walking this world in a blissful daze of lucid dreaming.

My mind was elevated to a heightened awareness of seeing, thinking, and being. My experiences defied physical description, and can, at best, be only hinted at. During these experiences I came to such clarity of knowledge, insight, awareness, revelation, and illumination that it was beyond the grasp of my thinking mind; in fact, beyond any sense of intellect I have ever known. These experiences were fleeting in linear time, although, in the moment, they also seemed to be eternal. During the daytime some lasted a few seconds, some perhaps up to ten minutes. But at night, when my mind was quiet and settled, some lasted for more than an hour, or perhaps as long as two hours. I was now living life like never before.

It is almost impossible to describe this in words, but after my awakening I was so sure of who I was that I did not have to prove anything to anyone. My faith now was not a reverence for traditional formal religion or a mere intellectual belief in who I was. Instead, a very profound conviction and an all-encompassing trust had swept away all doubts as to who I really am. I now knew myself, I had just found myself. I know now that there is no "I" in me. It is we. We can choose to either experience ourselves all as One in Spirit or all as individuals, separate and alone in the world. I had found something within me that I knew for certain had always been there. It was a treasure trove that I had carried with me all my life, without knowing it. In fact, I now know that everyone carries this great wealth within. It is placed carefully within each of us and when the time comes to claim it, it is there – just waiting. The tragedy is that most people will never claim this treasure, their true inheritance.

Therefore, most people, sadly, will die in poverty. To die in poverty is not dying penniless. You can die with ten million dollars in the bank, but you will die in poverty if you do not claim your real inheritance. To claim your real inheritance all you have to do is remember who you really are, not who you are pretending to be. Imagine living your life never having to worry about anything ever again. This is not only possible, but inevitable, because if not in this lifetime, there will be a future lifetime in which you will eventually choose to remember who and what you truly are. Remember who you really are and everything is yours.

A HIGHER SELF AWAKENING

My story now moves forward four months – to Friday the 20th of February, 2009, when I was at home with my cousin, Diahann. We were both sitting on the sofa at my house, listening to some beautiful meditation music in front of a big open, roaring fire in the fireplace. We had been talking for hours as we usually did. It was cold, windy and rainy outside, a typical Irish winter's night. It was just after 10:30 pm, and as we were talking, I felt a very subtle vibration in my head, and after a few moments, it started to increase in intensity.

I grabbed a hold of Diahann's hand for I knew what was about to take place. Then it happened again. I felt a full-on vibration in my mind- another shift in consciousness. The walls of the room disappeared, and the last thing I remember seeing before I entered full consciousness was the couch I was sitting on and the roaring fire. Then in that instant, I was having another out-of-body experience.

I had this indescribable feeling of being swept up and guided by an unrivalled superior power, a powerful spiritual force that seemed to lift my 'Self' out of myself. This was accompanied by another sensation of separation of mind and body consciousness. The awareness of my body was lost and it seemed to be on the verge of eliminating itself. This state intensified until "I" finally disappeared and became immersed in pure consciousness, contentedly floating as it swept me from one state of mind to another, and then another. I felt close to another dimension and another world altogether, travelling in an intense golden stream of light. At its simplest, my experience of attaining such high states of consciousness was that my inner "Being" transcended the limits of my ego self, which represented my lived world experience, and moved me closer to the very Source of Being itself. I was in Heaven and I was about to meet God.

Here my consciousness of "Being" was conscious only of itself. This was a state of pure consciousness. It was expansive and all encompassing. There were no objects to measure it. The expansiveness was one of light; the light of awareness. It was not like artificial light that is found in a room, but rather, it was an intimate experience where *I was* the light. In this state, my body did not exist, there was no awareness of my body whatsoever, no awareness of anything emanating from my body's sensory apparatus.

I wanted to stay, I really wanted to stay, but I felt compelled to return. There was something that I had to do. I did not know what, but I felt strongly guided that my "mission" would unveil itself when the time was right. Then, the light seemed to fade almost immediately. At that point, very slowly, the world began to reconstitute itself around me. At first, some faint sensation of my body and surroundings returned, subsequently, some sense of where I was and what time it was followed. Then some sense of my person and my physical senses also returned. The world, it could be said, at last returned to me, and was organized and constructed into all the layers of awareness that make up our ordinary sense of reality. Yet, I was left with a sense of renewal, of having thoroughly absorbed the blissful nectar of a timeless realm immersed within. At that moment, my whole body and mind experienced a rush of euphoric joy and unbelievable wellbeing.

At that point, my consciousness brought me fully back into the room with Diahann. It was only then that it hit me – I was back in the cold, bleakness and darkness of this world. It was like being lowered into a dark and cold cave. I then saw Diahann, not as a body, but as light. It was the most beautiful image I have ever seen in this world. Diahann was a body of light, the most beautiful colors of the spectrum you could only imagine. The light emanated and glistened from her head to her toes. I was seeing Diahann as she truly is.

And then it was over, and I felt squashed as my consciousness took me back in my body. I looked at Diahann, as I was readjusting my physical eyes so that I could see and I noticed that Diahann looked stunned as she stared into my eyes. I was speechless as we sat just staring at each other for what seemed like an eternity.

And then I spoke and revealed some details of my experience to her. I could not easily put into words everything that I experienced that night. It all seemed so "out of this world". I told her I had been transported to Heaven. Once again, it is impossible for me to describe my experience accurately because the words I use cannot do justice to what I had just experienced. It was like experiencing every ounce of love on this planet, every moment of ecstasy, every second of joy that everyone has ever had or ever will have here. It was like experiencing all that can possibly be imagined and all of this was pouring into my very essence, into my very being, all at the same time!

This was "Bliss" like I never thought was imaginable. As we talked, I said to Diahann that I had not wanted to come back because I really did not want to come back to this place at all. But something within me had compelled me. Now, there was something I knew I had to do here. I did not know what, but I had an inner knowing that something of great importance had to be accomplished here before I could return to that extraordinary other realm. I then went on to say to Diahann that I wished I could have stayed there longer because only a few moments there were not long enough.

Diahann looked at me and said, "What do you mean – only a few moments? You were in a trance for an hour and half!" I could not believe it- it seemed like such a fleeting experience. It could not have possibly been gone that long. Then I looked at the clock. She was correct, it was well past midnight!

Perhaps the best way to provide an objective description of this is to let Diahann describe the experience from her own point of view. In order to do this, I asked her, not long after the event, to write down her recollection of what she saw. Here is what she wrote:

"Michael and I were just sitting talking about life in his sitting room. Both of us were on his couch, listening to some meditation music. As we were talking, Michael grabbed hold of my hand. I was a bit startled and looked hard at him. Right away I knew something was up. His eyes were just staring into space, and he looked to be in some form of trance. I held his hand and just sat there staring at him not knowing what to do or say. So, I said nothing. I did nothing. But I knew instantly that he was having another 'experience'.

"As the seconds ticked by I continued to look at him, knowing that wherever he was, he was not in that room with me. His entire physical face had changed; he looked nothing like himself. He was transfixed and in a total trance. After about an hour, I began to get a little worried, and so I spoke to him. I said, "Are you okay?", but I got no reply. He said

nothing, so I just sat and waited. I kept looking at the clock. After about another half hour I began to get really worried.

"Panic was just about to set in when at last he began to move. His breathing came back to normal, and he subsequently moved his head and opened his eyes and stared straight into my eyes. He just sat for a long moment, looking at me, and then very slowly, he began to reveal exactly what had just happened. I was stunned, relieved, and delighted for him. I will never forget this experience. Michael physically changed right in front of my eyes. It was an indescribable experience for me to witness. I will never forget it as long as I live."

After Diahann left that night, I went to bed, and could not stop thinking about what had just happened. I told Diahann that I was receiving all this information, but I had no idea what it meant. She said to write everything down, and to keep a journal on everything that I received from then on. I could not sleep, so I went downstairs and began writing down everything that I had just experienced. I did not sleep that night at all, and the following day, I was so full of energy that I could not ground myself. I was literally electrified with energy. I could not sit, eat, or settle down. So I went for a walk, and as I walked, I was still receiving all kinds of insights and information. It was download, after download, after download of material and insights.

Liberation

I walk this world today a free man, liberated by the truth of life. I walk this world every day knowing that, how I see you is how I see myself, what I do for you, I do for myself, and how I make you feel, I will feel myself. The freedom and liberty from knowing this, not believing it, but knowing it, brings me such an explosion of unconditional love outwardly and onto everyone, and then it comes right back to me again. When this happens, it is like a moment of sheer bliss that I never thought even existed. And these moments never leave me. I can, at any time, step out of these moments, but I can also step back in again at will. These moments can be accessed by stillness, in the absolute silence of our mind. Beyond all thoughts and images, there is an ocean of peace, love and happiness that is never changing and never ending and is accessible to everyone.

Revelation

As I read the book *A Course in Miracles (The Course)*, some months later I was dumbfounded as my experience was explained just perfectly in this book. It said, "*Revelation induces complete but temporary suspension of doubt and fear. It reflects the original form of communication between God and His creations, involving the extremely personal sense of creation sometimes sought in physical relationships. Physical closeness cannot achieve it . . . Revelation is intensely personal and cannot be meaningfully translated. That is why any attempt to describe it in words is impossible.*"[2]

The Course goes on to say, "*Revelations are indirectly inspired by me because I am close to the Holy Spirit, and alert to the revelation-readiness of my brothers. I can thus bring down to them more than they can draw down to themselves.*"[3]

After each of these experiences, my mind and inner being were filled with a sense of overwhelming joy and ecstasy that sometimes felt almost unbearable. As each experience passed, I sensed a newly-gained knowledge within myself, a knowing that the mysteries and purpose of life had just been revealed to me. Over the next seven years, I would share and teach what these experiences revealed to me.

Visions

In the days and weeks after this experience, I began to witness a number of visions. I remember telling Diahann, and she suggested once again that I write them all down, and that I add sketches also. She said that there must be a reason why I was seeing all of these visions. I soon came to learn that this new form of consciousness was accessed through my silent state within. When all my thoughts and dream imagery, with all its mental content were eliminated, there was an ocean of peace, joy and love within. In this place, there were no desires to be desired, there was only an ocean of pure consciousness of a deep and contented silence. My ego self was silenced, but my higher Self was still able to see, because this Self, I learned, is everything that exists and there was nothing distinct from it to see.

The Self, I found, was conscious of nothing within or without. This is the base from which I was able to access these states of pure consciousness. Once I accessed this transcendental new state of mind, I was able to be aware of the experience itself. My experience always characteristically took a symbolic form in revealing itself to me. These experiences were much more abstract and had heightened sensory aspects to them. There was a quality of limitlessness to them.

As the days passed, I learned that as I became more and more centered in stillness all thoughts disappeared. I was left in a state of pure inner silence. All familiar boundaries that defined who I was: the false sense of self who I thought I was, was fading from my awareness and dissolving altogether. I was so awake in this new state of pure awareness that there was nothing else to even consider. I was everything, and everything was One. No traces of thoughts, ideas, concepts or images entered into my awareness in any way whatsoever. My inner Being was now completely, inwardly fully awake. In short, *I was Awake!*

Within a few months of this last experience I began teaching the most unbelievable manuscript on truth, life and the secrets to enlightenment. The purpose of *Wake Up!* is to reveal to the world the symbols and their contents that are contained in spirituality including *A Course in Miracles*, the only holographic book in this world. You can see that *A Course in Miracles* is holographic because no matter what page you open, it will literally talk to you, right where you are at that moment.

The teachings that follow in this book I have been teaching now since February 21st 2009, since the night of my experience with God in revelation. Every year for the next seven years, I would receive several hundred revelations that would come in the form of visions and out of body experiences. The nightly visions over many years revealed to be the structure of the ego thought system in its entirety, along with the entire structure of the mind, and all the levels of consciousness and awareness within it. The purpose of this book *Wake Up!* is only to share these revelations with you, the reader.

Spiritual advancement is crucial if we are, as one people, to move into the higher states of consciousness. The world as a collective consciousness is not ready to wake up just yet. However, the good news is that you do not need millions upon millions of people to join in your awakening. It is a solitary inside job to be done and achieved by just one person – You. If this is your quest, then you may just find that this book will be of some help to you. If your journey is to attain peace, joy and love, that is real, blissful and eternal, then read on, you have come to the right place. So what is Spiritual Advancement?

PART II

The Teachings
of
Michael Murray

CHAPTER 4

~ ~ ~

Spiritual Advancement

"What if you recognized this world is an hallucination? What if you really understood you made it up? What if you realized that those who seem to walk about in it, to sin and die, attack and murder and destroy themselves, are wholly unreal?"[1]

People get stuck in a given belief system and prematurely commit themselves to what they "believe" as the ultimate truth, instantly stunting their spiritual advancement. True spiritual growth is an unconditional, universal commitment that is not attached to any one philosophy or any organized religion. A person becomes universal in shared interests when they make a commitment to view humanity as one brotherhood. The person who advances to this mental state is no longer stunting their spiritual advancement. Those who are spiritually developed are capable of having spiritual knowledge without having to make a constant reference to literature, persons, or other people's misinformation. They will speak knowledge in their own words because it is within the ability of their inner Higher Self to do so. No one is excluded or exempted from this, if they only have the desire and will to know.

When humanity learns to think for itself and it begins to silence its mind, abstaining from all mental noise and mental pollution, the "Voice" within will emerge on its own and it will respond and become a person's internal guide and teacher. In this mind-set a

> *Only love and patience will slowly change the individual to the point where, through the demonstration of love, there will be a change of mind.*
>
>

person unequivocally recognizes the established Truth because the Higher Self already knows Truth. When spiritual knowledge and love are understood and shared, great things can be accomplished because of mutual awareness and understanding of shared interests.

What is in the best interest of everyone is in the best interest of each individual. Humanity is straddled between the two planes of awareness, physical and spiritual. In our daily lives we experience the mental stresses and conflicts of two conflicting thought systems, which are love and fear.

Most people may not be aware of this condition because of a lack of awareness. There is also the problem that many people in this condition may be unwilling individuals who prefer to stay in this state of misery. This type of person cannot be forced to understand this condition. Only love and patience will slowly change the individual to the point where, through the demonstration of love, there will be a change of mind. Then, and only then, can they change the condition for themselves. Assistance can only be extended to them if they are willing to accept it. This is the eternal quest of humanity and it will continue without cessation or interruption, from physical consciousness to spiritual consciousness and then to Oneness and beyond.

Spiritual development and growth is impossible and un-imaginable to the conditioned mind-set of the ego. Immortality, as unbelievable as it may be, is very real and not based on fantasy. It requires willingness, desire, effort and a training of the mind in order to relinquish the separated self, and rise above the immutable thoughts of ego. It is not an easy path to walk upon because it requires proper mind training, which means changing and discarding our outdated and useless belief systems that have been pounded into our minds through conditioning, not to mention the daily barrage of negativity from the ego mind. However, all this noise can be shut out and eliminated from the quiet mind and that alone will bring a profound change. This is a first step toward spiritual development and growth. The person who walks upon this path will experience resistance from the difficult old habits of the mind which they have created. But in the end, the rewards reaped from their efforts will, by far, outweigh the greatest rewards known to this world. No person can understand this truth unless they have walked this path themselves: understanding comes only from having the experience.

Spiritual Growth

Your spiritual growth depends on the choices you make. Your greatest lessons are the ones that you have learned during the toughest times in your life.

Remember what some people say "what does not kill you makes you stronger". This is so very true in all walks of life. In all experiences you have grown spiritually taller through the

> *Your greatest lessons are the ones that you have learned during the toughest times in your life.*
>
>

roughest times in your life. Depending on the choice you have made at these points in your life, you will either move on to another crossroads in life, another set of lessons, or those lessons unlearned will be repeated once again until they are learned. The choice is always yours, you have free will, and you always have the power to choose. If you are stuck in life where similar events always seem to be happening, then you have failed to learn your lessons, and you are not making the correct choices that can ultimately bring you peace. You will continue to make deliberate and sometimes unintentional wrong choices, until one day you will get so fed up that you will consider that there must be a better way.

When you reach this point, you will become more motivated to make the correct choice and it is pain that will be your greatest motivator. When you have suffered enough you will sit up and start to pay attention to life. It is at this point that you will become more aware of how you interact with everyone around you, and how you will interact with the world itself.

This material world you appear to be in seems to be solid and it is experienced exclusively through the body's senses. It is currently the dominant motivating force in your life. You will always seek to please the body through these senses with a comfortable home, a car, other possessions, wealth, fine clothes, a fit body and possibly even drugs and alcohol. All of these illusionary needs must be met because of the lack that you are experiencing within. This lack will always be experienced as long as you identify with the false sense of

> *The more you fight to change something, the more resistance you will encounter.*

self you believe yourself to be. This false separated self has many needs and expectations, and when these needs have not been met it leads you to depression and anxiety. You can only experience depression through the perception of lack, and lack can only be experienced with the ego. Spiritual growth depends on awareness, the awareness to not put up with anything that does not bring perfect peace to you.

Change Through Awareness

Change can only happen through awareness and understanding, not by conflict. The more you fight to change something, the more resistance you will encounter. Make peace with yourself; find the middle way, the balance. When Buddha became enlightened he did so by finding the middle way, the balance of life.

In his journey to enlightenment Buddha led a life of sacrifice, poverty and destitution after he first experienced a life of splendor and abundance. He just went from one extreme to the other and clearly neither worked for him. Buddha found the middle way through awareness by valuing what he was trying to attain, when compared with what he already had. Like him, you are not asked to give up anything, you are not asked to give up your jewels, your money, cars, homes or anything material. It is only the attachments to our ego thoughts that we are asked to give up. Buddha lived in a palace, and had great wealth, but he did not value it. He also tasted destitution and poverty, and again, he did not value that. He then found the middle way, by recognizing that on the road to enlightenment, it matters not whether you are rich or poor, male or female, young or old, educated or uneducated.

Buddha realized that enlightenment is simply not choosing a side because there is no right or wrong, guilty or innocent, nor good and bad. He found understanding through the awareness that all of these dualistic concepts did not truly exist. He found the middle way.

By gaining understanding though awareness you will find that middle way when you look at the true value of what you have versus the value of what you are trying to attain. The more you value something, the more you will fight to keep it, the less you value something the easier you will find to let it go. What has true value to you, whether you are aware of it or not, is peace, happiness and love.

The road to happiness begins with peace. Bring peace into your life and you can be sure that it will lead to happiness. To give up all things that take your peace away, first you must be aware of them. You must begin to dissociate from the you who you think you are, and become the You who you truly are. You are not who you think you are! If you could, just for a second, stand not outside yourself and observe your mind, observe your thoughts, you would experience yourself as someone else. This someone else is the Observer. It is our attachments that take and keep us away from our true Self. Once we are attached to anything external we are outside ourselves and we cannot observe our thoughts. The more we can observe our thoughts, the more awareness we will have. The more we do this the more we are dis-identifying with our false self.

If we are unaware of what we are thinking there is not much that we can do about it and thus, we must learn awareness. It is a must. When we are unaware we are like robots that are pre-programmed and conditioned. However, we are not robots, we are limitless, powerful and extremely enlightened beings who simply have forgotten who we truly are. The best question we could ever ask is 'Who am I?' Or better yet, 'What am I? What is this thing I call self?

We may have asked millions of questions in our lifetime, but did we ever ask the most obvious question of all, 'What am I? We may understand quantum physics, black holes, and computer science, but do we understand who or what we are? Once we find out what we are we will begin to wake up. Awareness is the key. Who is thinking the thoughts that you think? You think it is you, but it is not you. So, if it is not you, then who is it? You are not your thoughts, you are choosing the thoughts you think, but these thoughts are not you.

Watch your thoughts for the next thirty seconds, and look at the thoughts that are in your mind. You have good thoughts, and you have bad thoughts, where are they coming from? Are you producing these thoughts? The answer is no. So where are they coming from? This is the next step in discovering what you are. You are not your thoughts, you are not the thinker, rather, you are unconscious and believe that these thoughts are your thoughts. These thoughts belong to the ego thought system and are not yours.

There are two thought systems, two minds, each belonging to its' own exclusive set of emotions. In one mind you will experience emotions such as fear, guilt, anger, annoyance, and lack. In the other mind you will experience emotions such as compassion, abundance, peace, joy and bliss. You do have a choice as to which mind you choose to live in. Are you making the correct choice? Which mind do you believe you dwell in? Which "I am" are you?

The Two Rooms

As we have already discussed there are two selves within each of us, which means there are two versions of the "I am". There is the true I am, which is *"I am that I am"*. Then, there is a second I am, which is our false self, or the separated self. One I am is wholly without any form or identity, while the other I am is very identified in form. The separated self's identity kicks off straight away the second we are born. We are born separated into a body that exists only in duality. Within duality there are contrasts, such as light versus dark, good versus evil, those who are innocent versus those who are guilty. There are also polar opposites, such as north versus south, east versus west, etc.

The moment we are born we develop two spaces in our minds, let's call these two separate spaces the two rooms. Everything we like goes into the good room, and everything we hate goes into the bad room. So, the second we are born

> *Everything we like goes into the good room, and everything we hate goes into the bad room.*
>
>

we hate it, because we have just been separated from the bliss. As infants we were in a state of bliss in the womb, and we are then thrust out into a world of contrast and lose that bliss the very second we are born. As a newborn child, the very first thing we hate is bright light.

Children who cry a lot are very uncomfortable with the lights they are thrust under the moment they are born. You see, in the womb there were no contrasts, there was no bright light or dark space to be aware of, it was a state of being, it was a constant state of unawareness. Yes, there will be some outside noise, and interference, but nothing like the contrasts that are in store for this newborn child when it leaves this heaven inside where all needs are met. Then to leave that oneness and be pulled into a world of contrast, a world of right and wrong, a world of good and bad, a world where we are going to like things, and we are going to hate things, is very confusing. We have a lot of sorting out to do, and we will spend the rest of our lives doing that.

As children, two energies will now arise within us, one is dark, everything we do not like, and the other is light, everything we do like. We will feed these two energies now for the rest of our lives. We begin with hating the light, so we will project that hate out in the form of crying. Next we will ether like the food we are given or we will hate it. We will put some foods into the good room and some foods into the bad room. So the second we are born we begin to fill up these two rooms. We put the light into the bad room when we are born because it makes us feel uncomfortable, so the light becomes our enemy. But after a few weeks or months pass, we get used to the light and now the dark becomes our enemy. We begin to hate the dark and it makes us very fearful.

You see, the moment we choose one that we like we will automatically hate its opposite. If you begin to love the light, you will automatically begin to fear its opposite, which is the dark. For everything you love in life has an opposite, and being so, it is conditional. In conditional love there will always be things that you find fearful. All conditional love will carry fear and hate within it. *The Course* tells us that there is no love in this world that is without ambivalence. As children we do this with foods, colors, sounds, tastes, touch, all before we are able to even think properly, or understand anything.

People we like go into the good room, and those we do not like go into the bad room. We do this every day; we are constantly filling up, and emptying these two rooms. Things we like today go into the good room, then, when we do not like them anymore, either tomorrow or another day, they then go in the bad room. People we used to like but now hate reach the same fate, they all go in the bad room with the other bad things in our life. We also do this with religion. The religion we choose, or that our parents chose for us, goes into the good room while the other religions, every single one of them, go into the bad room. To recognize this, know that in this process there is no order of level of preference. There is no hierarchy of illusions; to decide which room something should go in, a mild dislike would be the same as a murderous thought about something.

We spend our entire life filling up these two rooms in our minds, regurgitating the contents of these two rooms over and over again, until the day we die. As long as you give energy to these two rooms, your mind will remain split, and a split mind is an unconscious mind that is asleep. We as human beings are on our sixth stage of human evolution. The Neanderthal man, who went extinct around 40,000 years ago, only had one room in his mind. He was at the fifth stage of evolution. He did not know right or wrong, or, what was good or bad because he simply had no imagination. We needed a good room for our imagination to awaken.

When Homo sapiens evolved around that time, this was the reason why they could thrive. A new breed of man evolved that had two rooms in his mind. Now humanity began to grow and evolve, because these two rooms helped us to become sociable, settled and educated. These two rooms led to art, literature, philosophy, religion, science and specialness. Without these two rooms, mankind would have never evolved to reach the heights we have achieved today. We need to have two rooms to activate our imagination.

The Neanderthal man went extinct because he could not imagine anything. He could not objectively stand outside himself and ask himself: "Was that thought I just had true or false?" Having only one room to work with he could not consider the concept of true or false. In fact, he was not self-conscious that he was a man, instead, he was like any animal, bird or fish. No animal has self-consciousness, if it did, we would know about it. A bird cannot stand objectively outside itself and know that it is a bird; it needs self awareness for that. Art and literature go hand in hand with self-consciousness, and we know that no animal has self-consciousness because no animal has ever written a book or painted a picture.

The famous missing link was never between man and ape, but between Neanderthal man and Homo sapiens. It was the introduction of the split mind – the two rooms – 40,000 years ago, that elevated our rapid human developmental growth. This only occurred when the human brain was ready to interpret the split mind.

We know exactly when these two rooms came into our awareness, because new tools, new art, and new shifts in consciousness, new ideas began to surface around the same time. This was mankind's first step into self-consciousness and these two rooms were vital for that to occur. Now that we could contemplate more complex thoughts and concepts, we could begin to organize our lives in such a way that we could evolve and become more civilized.

As I mentioned earlier, we are at the sixth stage or our evolution. The seventh stage is our last stage, and it is our natural evolution into spirituality. It is the age of perfect man, where man and spirit become One. So, if your plan is to wake up then you must make these two rooms one room again. The important difference this time is that we will be doing it consciously, not

Your mind is kept split because you are separating and dividing everything that is in this world, and putting it into one of these rooms.

unconsciously like Neanderthal man did. These two rooms keep your mind split, which is the true game here for the ego. Your mind is kept split because you are separating and dividing everything that is in this world, and putting it into one of these rooms.

As long as we keep these two rooms intact, we will experience separation and the ego will remain alive and well. And as long as your mind is split, you will remain unconscious because a split mind will never wake up! Your goal, and every spiritual seeker's goal, is to know that these two rooms are an illusion. You will only know that when you begin to truly observe what you are doing with these two rooms in your daily life. A thousand times a day you give attention to these two rooms, either the good room or the bad room. To the ego it does not matter which because as long as you see separation and contrast it keeps the ego alive. You give attention to these two rooms by labeling people good or bad, right or wrong, guilty or innocent.

Every relationship you have, you give attention to the concept of the two rooms. Your task is to look at the attention that you give to people, and the room you put them into. Then, you must correct that by reinterpreting these two rooms. We put them into a room where everyone is equal in every way, and we do this with our thoughts. It is not a physical experience. You still might be a little doubtful about the truth of these two rooms, but one thing is for sure, you feel the effects of these two rooms every day in your awareness.

Effects such as fear, guilt, shame, unworthiness, hate, anger, irritation, annoyance, and every negative experience you have come from this place. If you are experiencing any of these emotions, and I am sure that you are, then there has to be a good reason for it. You probably have spent years dealing with all of these effects, and may have even resolved some of them, but you will find that the fix was only temporary yet you have never been able to solve them once and for all. The reason is that fixing an effect, does not truly fix anything. Although you may not have known the cause of your problems before now, you must realize that the only way to solve anything is to fix the cause and not the effects. Only then will you be able to accomplish a permanent fix. However, effects have great importance because they will show us the road map to the cause. So, let's look at some effects and bring them to the cause.

The Effects

The effects that you may experience from any of these two rooms go something like this. We always put other people into the bad room, because we want to be in the good room and we do this by using guilt. Every time you put someone into the bad room, you put yourself into the good room. And we always want to be in the good room, because we hate the bad room. Every time you put someone in the bad room, however, you will eventually become fearful in the good room. You cannot place guilt onto someone, put them into the bad room, and then escape from fear yourself by going into the good room. Further, as long as you keep making some people special, you will always have someone to hate, and therefore you will always need to have the two rooms; you cannot avoid this.

Whether we know it or not, accept it or reject it, we are all one and each one of us is connected to one another. Everything here in this world, and all that is in front of your eyes is *you*, and as long as you keep seeing differences between people, your mind will always be split, because you are, in reality, splitting yourself. This is the cause of your suffering and *you* always pay the price for that, not anyone else because there is no one else, just you! The ego always gets paid. Remember that. Every time you dance with the devil, you must pay a coin.

The coin will always be pain, suffering, lack, unworthiness, shame and many, many more negative emotions that are profoundly experienced. These dark and heavy negative emotions feed the ego, and you cannot escape these emotions as long as you keep filling up these two rooms. This is how the ego is sustained in energy- by your energy. It is in these two rooms that the ego gets all of its energy from you. To live a life in which you see any difference among people is equivalent to being at war with someone while you are supplying that other party with all of its guns, ammunition, missiles, etc. All of the ego's weapons come from you, and if you did not do this, transcending the ego would be as easy as taking candy from a baby.

So stop feeding the ego, especially if you want to wake up. That is what we are all doing. We are all giving our energy to the ego, and then the ego is crucifying us for it. It is insanity at best, and suicidal at worst, because we will die. Only those with a mind that is split will taste death. But death truly means being reborn to do it all over again, with no memory of this life or any other past life. You begin your next life, just as stupid as you began this one. We are all born in ignorance of the meaning of life, how our minds really work, and how this world truly works. There are many who will choose to come back for another physical experience; they are not ready to go home just yet.

The Illusion of Free Will

It is also these two rooms that hold the great illusion: the illusion of free will. You believe that you have free will, and this is where you believe you have it. You are constantly choosing between these two rooms, selecting what is good for you, and rejecting what is bad for you. You are constantly choosing what you think is right and wrong, or, what you think is good and bad. This is the greatest illusion of all, because it matters not which room you choose, you are still choosing the ego. The ego cannot lose because what you believe is good and right, is an illusion of what is good and right.

The same goes for what you believe to be bad and evil, they are illusions of what is bad and evil. You are constantly being conned while the ego is on a win-win game here, and it cannot lose. True free will means choosing between the internal and the external, everything else is an illusion of free will. Both of these rooms are external because they separate and divide everyone around you, and thus, keep you separate from everyone, including God. We must become one with each other first to become one with God.

Here is a new spiritual insight: There is only room for the past and the future in these two rooms. The good room has our future, the bad room has the past. There is no present in the two rooms; there is no space for the Now, as long as you are attached to the thoughts of right and wrong, or good and bad. You cannot be at One with God, and not be present, in the Now. So, you can see how clever the ego was when it made this mind set; it did so to keep out the awareness of the present moment, which keeps out the awareness of God. Being attached to these two rooms keeps everyone separate all around you, because you see everyone as either good or bad, and right or wrong. You make people different and separate by being attached to this mind set.

You cannot be one with God and be separate from everyone else. As you ascend in spiritual awareness you will find that there is a space within you that has just one room, and in this room everyone is equal and everyone is One with everyone else. There are no separate interests that anyone will have that are different from anyone else's interests. There is only oneness in this room, and when you find it, you will be amazed at who you really and truly are.

Remember the golden rule: "*Do to others as you would have them do to you.*"[2] In reality, there aren't two rooms, both are totally made up and are of the ego. Another name for these two rooms would be the persona and the shadow, or the ego right mind, and the ego wrong mind. All of these names are just symbols of the ego's thought system. Learn them well, for it is the way out. And the quickest way out is to do it through first understanding this concept and then becoming the Observer.

The Observer

You will have heard me by now say that you have two selves; you as a separated self, and you as your higher Self. The you who is reading this book is the separated self, or your false self, while the you, that is still unknown to you at this time, is your higher self. Another name for the false self would be that of the thinker - the thinker is the actor in the dream. Meanwhile, another name for the higher self would be the Observer. The Observer observes and the thinker thinks, and it is here that conflict seems to appear. The Observer is without judgment, ridicule, condemnation, attack or defenses. He is peaceful, loving and joyful of life.

The thinker is an actor playing a role in the movie of life. He can be judgmental, defensive, aggressive, pushy, violent, hurtful, and fearful with a sense of sin and guilt. Or, he can be sweet and eager to please people, but with anger and hate hidden within. The actor plays many roles all at the same time, but he is never aware that he is playing a role. The actor/thinker is the ego, while unconscious. The ego could make the statement, "I think, therefore I am!" While the higher Self could make the statement, "I think, therefore I am not" The thinker is the false sense of self, it is the ego self-image personified. If there were no thoughts, there would not be a thinker. Thoughts created the thinker

> *The ego could make the statement: "I think, therefore I am!" While the higher Self could make the statement, "I think, therefore I am not".*
>
>

and if there were not a thinker there would not be an Observer, because there would be nothing to observe.

As long as the thinker is thinking, there will be an Observer observing. All conflict seems to be between these two opposing forces. The thinker does not allow the Observer to observe, and the Observer does not see what the thinker sees, nor does he want to. You see, the thinker always sees two rooms, while the Observer has just one room. The thinker is always using judgment in deciding which of the two rooms to put things into, while the Observer has just one room, which is, what is only what is true. It is only when thinker and Observer become one that this seeming conflict will end. The Observer could make the statement, "I think, therefore I am not". The Observer is the Observer of all thoughts, all emotions, all words, all deeds and all actions fully without judgment.

There seems to be a sense of conflict between these two forces that are vying for your attention. The reason for this is that you believe that your false self is at war with your higher self, or the thinker is at war with the Observer, but this is not so. The higher self does not engage in conflict with anyone, especially with the false self that it knows does not exist. No. In truth, the thinker is at war with itself.

The illusionary good self that we all believe ourselves to be and that we have put in the good room is at war with the illusionary bad self that we also all believe ourselves to be and that we have put in the bad room. In other words, the thinker is at war with itself. This war will continue as long as you are unaware of the two rooms, and how you are using them. The use of these two rooms keeps your mind split, and as long as your mind is split you will be in a state of conflict. The only way out is through being the Observer.

So, how does the Observer operate in this world? How do we really know that we are truly the Observer, and not the ego pretending to be the Observer? The first thing that you must understand is that we live in duality, which means that we live in a world that has both right and wrong, good and bad, and innocent and guilty. Everything you see in this world has an opposite. No matter how many books you will sell, if you are an author, there will be a percentage of people who will love them, and there will be a percentage of people that will hate them. That is the way that this world is and how duality is made up. Therefore, to understand the concept of the Observer, you must first understand duality.

Every drama that you see in this world has both good and bad within it, depending on whose perspective you are looking at it with. Are you looking at it with the thinker's perspective or the Observer's? For example, it is in our nature to always stand behind the victim, and in all dramas there will be victims. When we make the choice to sympathize with the victim, what we are really doing is

The Observer does not pick a side, does not choose who is right or wrong, nor who is good or bad.

we are unconsciously attacking the victimizer. In *The Course* we learn that to defend means to attack. If we defend the victim, we must attack the victimizer, because in this world, all defenses mean attack. So, as long as you keep defending, you will keep attacking. When you do this, you are not the Observer.

The Observer does not pick a side, does not choose who is right or wrong, nor who is good or bad. The Observer observes without judgment, and that is what Jesus meant when he said, "become passerby"; be without judgment. The Observer will never be drawn into anyone's drama, or stories. However, the Observer will also never judge the drama as good or bad, or right or wrong, because the Observer will know that it is only in dramas that we learn our biggest lessons, and we all need to learn our lessons; it is the way we all grow spiritually. Learning to be the Observer is also a lesson, and the lesson as the Observer is always to remain neutral. Becoming the Observer is the easy part, remaining the Observer is the most difficult part, herein lies all lessons for the Observer. The lesson is to live your life without judgment.

So, what does it mean to live your life without judgment? To live without judgment is to love unconditionally. That is what the Observer does. As the Observer, you will have relinquished any needs, desires, expectations and demands that you would have on anyone or anything. You will become attached to nothing external to you. It is only our attachments that keep us attached to the actor in the dream, the false self.

The Observer is attached to no one and nothing external to itself. This does not mean that you do not have relationships and or seek for things in the world. It means that you are not attached to the outcome of anything you do in the world. To live a life as the Observer is to live a life completely detached from all the drama of your body, other bodies, and the entire goings on in this world. You will not become embroiled in any disputes as to the rights and wrongs or good and evils of anything in this world. You will be wholly without opinion on who is guilty or innocent and who is saintly or who is evil. You will know that such things come from the ego trying to pull you into people's stories and dramas. If you get caught up in the dramas of this world you lose the office of the Observer, thereby losing conscious awareness of who you truly are which means that you will get annoyed and even angry at the drop of a hat. Vigilance is vital if one is to remain the Observer.

If you lose your peace over anyone or anything you can be guaranteed that you are becoming attached to that object, person or event, which means that you have just lost your status as the Observer. Maybe, the reason you become attached to something is because you picked a side as to who was right or wrong, good or bad, either in your own drama or in someone else's drama. Perhaps you picked someone who was right or wrong in an argument. Maybe you judged who is guilty or innocent in a crime. Maybe you endorsed someone who you thought was either good or bad in attitude.

If you fell into the trap of choosing a side you will lose all peace. Fear will rise and anger will follow, all because you now have become attached to the drama and you lost sight of yourself as the Observer – a state of being that brings so much peace and bliss to your life. Attachments and the Observer do not go hand in hand, one cancels out the other. If you become attached to anyone or anything, you lose your Observer status; on the other hand, when you learn to observe, you will let go of your attachments.

So how does one practically operate in the world and remain as the Observer? The answer is easy, but you must first understand how judgment works. You cannot live without judgment, unless you know how judgment works. You see, living in a world of duality also means we live in a world of opposites, and that means that we all must judge. When you judge something as good, you keep it. And when you judge something as bad, you also keep it. In your mind, when you judge someone or something as bad, you believe that you are rejecting it, you believe that it has no value, therefore it matters not to you. But the opposite is true, everything you reject, or judge as bad, you label it and therefore you keep carrying it with you. You have just put them into the bad room. Just imagine all those terrible people you have judged as bad, wicked, or evil, you still carry them with you at all times in your mind because they are in your bad room. This is the past that we all carry with us. We carry all the judgments of bad, angry, guilty, evil people. There is only one way to transcend all of this, and that is to transcend time all together by becoming present in the now. Here in this place you are without judgment, therefore you have once again become the Observer.

To become and then remain the Observer we must first understand that every time we seek outside ourselves we activate the separation all over again. It is as if we are entering into the "Matrix", or the ego thought system. In itself, there is nothing wrong with seeking outside ourselves because we live in a world where everything is external to us, even our own bodies. The problem, however, arises when we become attached to what we are seeking outside. In fact, not only do we become attached, we will also defend it and attack anything that could negatively impact our attachment.

Let's say you see a news story about a stranger who is being victimized and you react to it by feeling sorry for them. You could think that it is just terrible what that poor person is suffering. What you have just done is you have become attached to the person in the news story, and in doing so, you now attack whomever you perceive to be the victimizer of this poor soul. You have defended someone, so you lose the status of the Observer. That is how easy one can fall into the ego trap and become lost once again. You see, every time you defend someone you must attack. That is what all defenses mean - defenses mean attack.

Once you have taken a position you are no longer the Observer and you will lose your peace of mind. Please note, I am talking about your thought process here and not what you do in form. If you see someone who is getting physically attacked on the street, then by all means do defend that person when appropriate. Or if you see someone who is being bullied by all means do take action as you deem appropriate. What I am talking about here is how we constantly condemn people in our minds. We do this within our relationships, our family, our friends, when we hear about news stories, and even when we see fiction being portrayed in movies.

When you defend you attack and when you attack you condemn – this can only be done by the thinker. The Observer never attacks because it never defends. Instead, the Observer accepts all as is without judgment. In every case, you, as the Observer, will do this in full awareness of the truth, that we are all One. There truly aren't any bad people, there are just people who are very afraid. It is these people who will give us our biggest lessons and will help strengthen our ability to remain the Observer.

Another way of saying that the Observer never attacks, because the Observer never defends is to say that the Observer never judges knowing that judgment is rejection. The Observer never rejects anyone or anything because the Observer knows that everyone and everything is a part of itself. Every time you seek outside yourself, you must judge, so do not judge yourself for judging; simply, as I mentioned before, do not attach yourself to any of those thoughts of judgment you believe you are making. These thoughts are not your thoughts; they are the thoughts of the ego thought system.

When I am doing things in the world, I set a goal, but I never become attached to that goal. If it works out great and if not I see it as an experience that I needed to learn from. For example, when I am setting up talks, arranging conferences, doing classes and courses, both live and on line, I am actively and knowingly seeking outside of myself. I know I am in judgment, because I am using judgment to accomplish what I am trying to achieve. However, while I am in judgment I never take any judgmental thoughts seriously or personally, and after a little while all of these thoughts disappear. It is only when we attach ourselves to these judgmental thoughts that they stay with us. So, how do I keep my peace and remain the Observer while I do things in the world? I never become attached to the outcome of anything I do.

Everything I do externally to me is always unconditional because this leaves me free from becoming attached to anyone or anything. I do not lose my peace over the outcome of anything, whether it is in relationships, events, talks or conferences. They are all lessons for me to learn from.

Another way I keep my peace and status as the Observer is that I am always vigilant for any demands, expectations, needs or desires that I may have of myself or other people. These are all little traps that will get you attached to someone, or something and I am always very observant for any of these. And the best way to be extra vigilant is to watch for the loss of peace.

If I lose my peace over anyone or anything, I will know that I have become attached. In that case I will deal with that attachment almost immediately, and let it go using simple forgiveness. See Chapter 10 – *True Forgiveness*.

How Judgment Works

A great man once said, *"Lead me not into temptation"*. Another way of saying the same thing is, *"Let me not seek outside myself"*.

The thoughts of judgment work on three levels. If you do not understand these three levels, you will never understand judgment. These three levels are on three different levels of consciousness, and awareness. Level 1 is the unconscious level of the split mind. Level 2 is where you begin to wake up. Here you are spiritually awake, which is a much higher state of awareness than that of the separated self on level 1.

Then on level 3 is where you have become conscious; you are awake within your higher self. So, while you are on level 1, you are unconsciousness and you will be judgmental because everyone who is unconscious is still actively seeking to have their needs met through external means in the world.

Here is the key, if you are on this level: do not judge yourself for judging. It is only when you judge yourself judging that it has an effect on you. When you do not judge yourself for judging, judgment has no effect on you. Instead, simply be aware that you are in level 1 and that you are in judgment and ask yourself if you want to remain there. As long as you don't do anything you will remain there and the price will be very high in terms of pain and suffering because all judgment is ultimately self-judgment.

Level 1 is judgment; it is the ego thought system talking to you. You will hear thoughts and judgments of how bad certain people are and how rude some people are. You will condemn everyone you judge simply because you believe these thoughts and judgments are yours. After all, this is the ego's objective; to deceive you into thinking that you are a bad person for making so many awful judgments against so many nice people. The ego will remind you over and over again what a terrible person you are for being so judgmental.

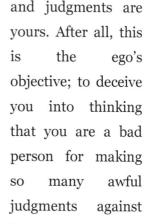

If you spend your life constantly seeking outside yourself and constantly being attached to external stimulus, then you will be very judgmental.

Now you will be on the look out to see who else is being judgmental, all because you would rather see someone else as being judgmental, rather than owning up to the fact that is you who is being judgmental. We use projection to do this. Once we get to this stage, we lose all sense of what we are doing, because being judgmental, and then denying it, causes us so much stress and upset that we will become sick. This is the price we pay for not knowing how judgment really works. If you spend your life constantly seeking outside yourself and constantly being attached to external stimulus, then you will be very judgmental. There is no escaping this. The only way out is to now look at this a different way. You must detach from the judgmental mind and move to level 2 by becoming non-judgmental.

Level 2 is non-judgment, and being non-judgmental means you are seeing what everyone else sees, but you are not choosing a side. In other words, you are seeking for things in the world, but you are not attached to the outcome of anything you do in the world. Now you are aware that you are in judgment and being judgmental, but you are not judging yourself for judging. In level 2 you now know that these are the thoughts of the ego thought system and not your own, and therefore, they have no effect on you.

Since you are now letting go of seeking outside yourself, you are also letting go of your demands, expectations, needs and desires because as long as you keep any of these you will be judgmental. This is just a step in the process and although letting go is going to be really hard for you it will be very worthwhile because the objective here is to reach level 3, which is living a life of being without judgment. The ultimate goal for any spiritual seeker is to live life without judgment, because this is the realization of your enlightenment and the end of conflict.

Level 3 is being without judgment. Being without judgment means that you are not attached to anything external to you. You choose to see neither the rights nor wrongs of this world because you know both are traps that will keep you involved in the dramas of this world. You see neither the guilty nor the innocent because you know both are one and the same in content. It is only in form that we seem to differ.

This is a state of mind, not a state of denial. This is where you will spend most of your nights and a few hours every day in deep meditation. In this place you seek for nothing either internally or externally, you will just be, wanting nothing, desiring nothing, expecting nothing and needing nothing. You will live in the bliss of your true nature, which is everyone else's true nature for that matter. Being without judgment is a state of mind that dwells in Oneness and, in turn, encompasses you in bliss!

This is cause and effect at work; the cause of the bliss in your mind is your willingness to be without judgment, to be the Observer. This means that in your mind you must be willing to walk away from any event, circumstances or relationships inside seven seconds without hesitation or guilt of any type. Being awake means being free with no attachments whatsoever. Being awake you will know that there is nothing and no one that you are not a part of, and so you truly never leave anyone.

Keep in mind that to remain free in this way is a state of mind and only your willingness is required to give up anything that is external to you. If you can understand duality and judgment, you will understand who the Observer is. Then, it is only your unwillingness to live a life without judgment that is standing in the way of untold riches and success for you. But remember this: what is in the way is the way. When Jesus said, "turn the other cheek," he meant, can you look at this another way?

Whatever obstacles are in your way, your task is to look at them from another perspective. If you can look at any block you have from the perspective of the Observer, you will see the answer to that block. Look at it without any attachment to the outcome. Look at it without demanding anything from it, no matter what it is, or who they are. Look at it without needing or desiring anything from it, or them.

If you can train your mind to look at everything in this way you are learning to observe, you are becoming the Observer. Becoming the Observer is the easy bit; staying the Observer is the hard bit. You may have had that state of mind many times throughout your life, but maybe you never knew what it was. It was one of pure tranquil peace of mind. It will always be something you are attached to that will take the status of the Observer away from you.

All you have to do is become vigilant for absolutely anything that takes your peace away and let it go. Then one day you will wake up, and you will have a peace that never leaves you. You will have a joy within your heart that depends on no one and nothing external. You will be happy for absolutely no reason whatsoever. The effects of the emotions of peace and joy together are what will bring the bliss of life into your awareness. Peace plus joy equals bliss! And you will have it on tap anytime, any place, and wherever you want it, it will never leave you. This is the treasure that awaits you, this is your inheritance, and it is within you in this exact moment, right now, in the Now. When Jesus said the kingdom of heaven is here now, this is what he meant. The kingdom of heaven is here, in the Now. Heaven is a timeless place, there is no past or future, there is only eternity. Eternity exists only in the present moment, in the Now.

If you want to taste what Heaven is really like then live your life without judgment. Live your life as the Observer. Do not choose who is right or wrong. Right and wrong do not exist. Truth has no opposite. If anything has an opposite, it is of the ego and it is an illusion. Do not choose who is saintly and who is evil, both are traps that will pull you into the dramas of right and wrong. Let all demands that you have upon yourself and others go, these demands are costing you bliss. Look at the needs and desires of both yourself and others, and let them go; you do not need to need anything from anyone.

> **If you want to taste what Heaven is really like then live your life without judgment.**

The ego itself is a thought system of judgment, victimization, brutality, and death. So let us take a look at what the ego is, and how it greatly affects your life in every nook and cranny. The ego is the pain body. It is wrong-minded thinking; it is that little voice in your head that keeps telling you that you are worthless, that you are guilty, and that you should fear this world and the people in it. Every time you have experienced fear, guilt, anger, hate, revenge, it has always been the ego that is directing your thoughts. Every emotion that you have ever felt within the body is more than likely to have come from the ego, than from God. So, what is the ego?

The Ego

When you have achieved true emptiness, when you overcome and dissolve the separated self, you have overcome the ego. Here, at this place, you enter into the vortex and bathe in the bliss of life.

What Is the Ego?

The term ego means different things to different people. What you will believe the ego to be depends on your level of consciousness. The higher your level of consciousness, the more clearly you will be able to define the ego. Everyone has an ego, because there is only one ego, and if you spot it, you got it. The ego is a level of consciousness we all share, and if you believe in the concepts of right and wrong, good and evil, then you are in the ego thought system. The ego itself is a dualistic thought system that believes in right and wrong, and good and bad. This world is not dualistic as many believe. But the reason why it appears to be dualistic is because we are attached to the ego's split mind of right and wrong and good and evil. It is this ego split mind that we all identify with, and then project onto the world causing us to experience right and wrong, and good and evil.

While asleep and unconscious it is impossible to exist in this universe without the ego's awareness all around you. However, by becoming aware of and understanding how it works it is possible to live outside of its power and influence over you. To reach this state it will take a great deal of willingness, astute awareness, and dedicated vigilance. But to achieve this state that will bring you total inner peace, radiant joy and tranquil living, you must first recognize what the ego is and reinterpret it.

The only way to transcend and defeat the ego is by reinterpreting it, not by attacking it. To try to control your thinking, your life and your destiny is futile, because the more you think you are in control the less control you really have. You see, the ego has always been in control, you have not. You have always had the illusion of control, because you have always been choosing the ego. Every time you choose who or what is right or wrong, you choose the ego. Every time you see someone or something as good or evil, you are choosing the ego. A big trap that most people fall into is this: They try to change the world according to what they believe to be right and wrong with the world because they believe that they know what is good and bad. This is well and good if you are not trying to wake up, because this will keep you asleep since all that you are doing is energizing the ego's thought system.

There is a beautiful line in *The Course* that says: "*Therefore, seek not to change the world, but choose to change your mind about the world*".[3] As long as you keep trying to change the world, you keep choosing the ego. In this world it seems that whatever you seem to see, hear, smell, taste or feel, can be judged as good or bad, and right or wrong. It is this way because you believe that this world is a world of duality; it is not.

Rather, it is our dualistic mind that, as individuals, we project onto the world that makes this world seem dualistic. This is a trap, because if you keep choosing between these concepts you keep the split mind of duality in place. *The Course* also tells us that this world is wholly neutral. In reality there is no right and wrong, nor good and bad; these concepts are pure ego. The split mind is a controlling device that the ego uses to gather energy from you and to keep you in a state of fear.

The ego quite simply is just a thought system. It is the voice in your head that you think is you. It is the thoughts you think you think, except they are not your thoughts.

If, and you know this well, you are controlled by your ego for most of your life, then you will experience so many ups and downs that will repeatedly lead you to disappointment that you will eventually see no purpose in this life. All sense of hope will fade and deep sadness will overcome you to the extent that you will no longer have a will to live. This is the ego's ultimate goal for you: death, and you will never know why you feel this way as long as you remain identified with the ego.

The ego quite simply is just a thought system. It is the voice in your head that you think is you. It is the thoughts you think you think, except they are not your thoughts. It is the ego's thoughts that judge, attack, hate, murder, condemn, seek specialness, and it is the ego's thoughts that are prideful, jealous, fearful and many more that ultimately stem from fear. The ego is the voice of all negative thinking. The ego just loves for you to play the victim.

The ultimate goal for the ego is for you to become a victim in every relationship you have. This enables it and you to justify all attacks and blame everyone else for how miserable you feel and how miserable your life is. Everything we feel, all of our emotions come from our thoughts, and it is these thoughts that rule our lives. However, they are not even our thoughts, because these thoughts belong to the ego. Hence, the ego truly runs our lives and bombards us with thousands and thousands of thoughts that we seem to have no control over.

All of our judgments come from the ego and, as a result, someone who complains a lot and who judges other people a lot has given their power over to the ego. It is not who they really are; instead, it is the ego who is making those harsh judgments and not them. When they identify with this thought system they think that it is them who are thinking these thoughts. They become the thinker; in fact, they become the ego.

Always remember this: It is the ego who is the intellectual, and it is the ego who is the thinker. Many have tried to outthink the ego, and all have failed. Do not try this, for it is the biggest mistake you can make. You can only transcend the ego's thoughts with right-minded thoughts but you cannot try to outsmart it at its own level. You are not the person who is thinking these thoughts.

The ego will disguise its thoughts as your thoughts; it will disguise its feelings as your feelings. The ego will make you believe that the you who is identifying with these thoughts is the real you, but all along, it is the ego that is disguising itself as you. Everything bad that has ever happened to you has come from your allegiance to this thought system. You are not the thinker; instead, you are giving your power to the thinker who you mistakenly believe is you.

You give it power by reacting to its instructions, and by attacking others as well as yourself. You give it power when you react emotionally to the thoughts that it throws at you. You give it power every time you believe a thought that is just not true. You will literally die for your ego, without ever knowing that you have been fooled.

If you could just realize how much you feed the ego by identifying with this thought system you would be in disbelief. Whenever you give it power over you, it will hound you and harass you for more and more power. Whenever you feel bad about yourself you have always given the ego power over yourself. When you feel victimized by those around you, or feel victimized by the world you live in, you have given power to the ego to be your ruler and to be your tormentor, and you have done this without knowing that the ego's goal for you, at all times, is pain, suffering, misery and death.

Once identified with the ego, people will protect it to the point that they will lie, cheat and kill to preserve it, not knowing that the greatest enemy that they have ever had is deep within themselves. In fact, the ego's greatest defense is that not only do you not know that it exists, but that you do not know that it exists within you! The ego is a prison that keeps you chained to a life of suffering and misery, and most people do not have a clue that this is the real cause of all suffering and everything that is wrong in their lives. Do not believe everything you think that you think, period!

The ego has lied to you from the very beginning. When you lie to yourself you are not really lying; you are allowing the ego to tell you all sorts of things and then the ego will make you believe it is you who is lying. In religion the ego manifests itself as the devil, because once we believe that the devil exists, we can blame everything on the devil. You may say, "the devil made me do it", when all the while it was the ego.

The ego invented the devil to make everyone believe that evil existed externally, not internally. However, the ego *is* the devil, and everyone has an ego. There is no such thing as an external enemy, no matter what that voice in your head is telling you. The real enemy is always within you, always. All perception of an external enemy is the projection of the ego onto that enemy. Your greatest enemy is you; it is your own thinking.

The more you relinquish the ego's thoughts, the more peaceful you will become. The more peaceful you become the more you will begin to enjoy life. This transition is a process and it will take time and great discipline. This is because the ego will not want to disappear and it will fight to keep its power at all costs. When you become aware that you are not that silent destructive voice in your head, and you are not your daily thinking you will become more conscious.

The more conscious awareness you hold, the less power the ego will have over you. The ego needs to feed itself with negativity, or specialness, and, therefore, it will seek out many ways to trap you. I can tell you, while you are unconscious, the ego is very cunning at best and quite vicious at worst.

Remember, the ego can only survive as long as you believe in it and the only way that you could possibly believe in it is if you continue to

The more conscious awareness you hold, the less power the ego will have over you.

believe that you have separated from your Creator. And so the ego can only survive as long as you believe that you are an individual separate from everyone and everything else. Therefore, the ego's objective is to survive and this can only happen as long as you continue to see yourself separately from other people.

For example, it wants you to be more spiritual than anyone else and more knowledgeable than anyone else. This is specially true when it comes to *The Course* because as long as you focus only on intellectualizing the deep truths in *The Course*, you are less likely to bring them into your heart and apply them. The ego wants you to be number one, richer, better, and more successful than anyone else. The ego loves fame and specialness and wants you to stand out from the crowd.

However, beware, the ego also wants you to be number one at being depressed, poor, sick, victimized, etc. You see, the ego does not care if you are happy, miserable or working hard at being at either of these two ends of the spectrum, as long as you see yourself as special and therefore different and separate from everyone and everything else.

When you look in the mirror who you see is not you. You are more than just a body that looks back; you are a silent consciousness that bathes in bliss. You are a compassionate, loving, sharing, and humble eternal light being, ascending back into the light. All of these attributes are who you really are. If you can experience this, you will feel a sense of oneness with all of creation; you will feel a sense of oneness with all life. Every living thing will have value to you. All life will be very precious to you. You will reach a state of constant joy and no matter who you are with or where you will be, you will be the real you. You will be as you were created to be, and this new sense of life will be so fulfilling that you will seek for nothing else, because you will have everything. You are everything. This is your higher Self and this is the real you.

The Ego and Enlightenment

Incredibly, the ego wants to be in on the act of enlightenment. The ego wants enlightenment more than anything else, and if it can't have it, it will make sure that you don't have it, at all costs, even unto death. If you happen to die before you wake up in this lifetime, you will ensure the ego's survival by coming back to the physical universe once again. The only way you can stay up is to wake up! You must remember that everyone is already enlightened and so there is really no need to spend your life trying to become enlightened. All you have to do is stop un-enlightening yourself, and you will automatically be enlightened. It is the ego that keeps enlightenment unconscious and hidden deep within the minds of every single person on this planet.

Ironically then, it is a shock to discover that the ego itself also wants to be enlightened. This, however, will cause you problems because you must separate yourself from the ego or else you will not wake up. The ego is often motivated to seek higher consciousness and, thus, give itself a greater ability to dominate you and your environment. Not always, but often, it is the ego within that most eagerly pursues higher consciousness. It wants to be in charge of the enlightenment journey; it wants to manipulate events and make life work out more to its own selfish satisfaction. The ego wants to be enlightened and it will use many unsuspecting seekers along their spiritual path, which will become a great hindrance for those seekers.

However, what people do not realize is, it is themselves that they must relinquish. The seeker of enlightenment is the ego, hence, the seeker must be relinquished for you to wake up. But, as long as the ego dominates your journey, it is on a collision course with your true nature and your higher consciousness. There's going to be a showdown, and it could get bloody. There has to be a confrontation sometime soon if your higher Self consciousness is ever to emerge. You may, instead, have a highly developed ego which is sure that it is causing the events of higher consciousness to unfold bit by bit. Your ego, after all, can be very interested in the attributes of higher consciousness, in meditation and its association with enlightened beings. The ego feels personified gratification and satisfaction when moving up the path towards higher consciousness.

The ego may also have the opinion that, because of its grasp on matters, it will one day establish or — by its thought process and feelings —bring about its enlightenment and awakening into pure Awareness, God consciousness. The ego believes that one day it will mirror and reflect our true Creator. The ego is convinced that it will achieve higher consciousness and a divine awakening of its own.

The ego is convinced that it will achieve higher consciousness and a divine awakening of its own.

This is ironic because the ego itself is the main obstacle; it is the obstruction of the light of consciousness. You cannot bring darkness into light, and the ego is a thought system of darkness. And if you are still attached to the ego, and you try to wake up, you are really trying to bring darkness into the light. This process will scare the living day lights out of the you, which is really the ego as long as you do not know who you are. You will feel great fear if you try this, so you must separate yourself from the ego first. This is really important.

The ego can fight a very lengthy battle if it fears it is going to be destroyed, and will try to destroy you before it will give in to something so much greater than it knows itself to be. The one thing that holds back seekers of enlightenment more than anything else is that they don't know how to let go of their egos. They can't separate their true self from their ego self. To do this they must take some very radical steps. They must begin the process of relinquishment. They must relinquish the separated self and all of its defenses.

The ego wants to bring about higher consciousness and enlightenment by its own dramatic means. Certainly, it doesn't want to be granted fulfillment by a power outside of itself, so it tries to do this by using the persona, the false right mind, rather than the true right mind. Once you have gained knowledge of all there is to know of these parts - the ego thought system, the separated self, its defenses, its coping mechanisms, and its attachments, - you now begin the process of letting it go. You first separate the separated self from the ego thought system, and then you dissolve the separated self itself, which is your false sense of self.

If you have reached this point, having fulfilled its part, the separated self is now weak and about to be dissolved and your transformation into your higher Self now occurs instantaneously. Now, with your higher Self awakening within you, you have let go of your false sense of self. You now know yourself to be a different person than you thought you were. You, while unconscious, were merely the manifestation of the ego itself. Every thought that you have ever thought, came from and still belongs to the ego. You now have a complete set of new thoughts, and new emotions as a direct result of this transformation. When all relinquishments have been successfully achieved, when all ego attributes have been let go, what is left is how God created you: divine, immortal, and eternal, forever loved and forever loving. This is the real you!

If you are continually at war with your ego, then stop it. Stop it because you are giving it unbelievable energy when you do that fight with your ego. So what is the correct thing to do? You can only transcend the ego, not fight it. The ego is on level 1 of consciousness and that means that the only way to beat it is for you to transcend to level 2. However, that is not going to help you if you have no idea about the levels of teaching and learning. These levels are not only for *A Course in Miracles* students and teachers, but for every spiritual seeker out there. You cannot jump from level 1 to level 3 like most people in spirituality are attempting. You must confront the shadow, the persona, the ego, the separated self. And you can only do that from level 2, not level 1. So what are the levels of learning and teaching?

There are five levels of consciousness, I will first discuss all five levels and then concentrate only on the bottom three, because that is exactly where the work is that we have to accomplish. You see, it is our job to get from level 1 to level 3. Level 1 is asleep, and unconscious. Level 3 is awake and conscious. The key here for every person who wants to wake up is level 2; you must learn how to get there and know what to do when you get there.

The Three Levels of Learning & Teaching

If you are familiar with my teaching method you will be aware that I teach on three levels. This is because in this world there are three types of people: there are those on level 1 who are spiritually asleep, those on level 2 who are waking up, and those on level 3 who are awake. In truth there are five levels within *The Course*, and also in our spiritual ascension, whether you are a student of *The Course* or not. However, I am only really interested in the bottom three, because after that, everything is automatic; you are no longer in charge of time or direction when you reach this point. However, until you reach this point you are in charge of time. The awakening on level four will be on its own accord. So, what are these bottom three levels and what does it mean to learn and teach from each level? Let's start with level 1.

LEVEL 1

Most, if not all, spiritual seekers and students of *A Course in Miracles* set out from level 1. Dr. Kenneth Wapnick was probably the master teacher of this level in *A Course in Miracles*, and in the last fifty years, in my opinion, no one has surpassed his direct style of teaching. Ken was ruthless with the truth in his teaching style, and that is exactly what is needed to transcend this level into level 2 awareness.

Level 1 consists of three elements, which are the world, the body and the split mind. The spilt mind is the mind of right and wrong, of good and evil. If you are attached to these concepts, you are attached to this level. No one can transcend to level 2 and be attached to the split mind, which is just another name for the persona, and the shadow, or the yin and the yang, or the good room and the bad room.

There is an old saying, if you are in hell and want to get out, it is best to find someone who has been there, and found a way out. In other words, it is best to find someone who has been there and actually knows the way out. If you want to transcend level 1 and move on to level 2, you really want a teacher on level 2 to take you there.

If you wish to transcend level 1 there are three things that you must do. First, you must reinterpret the two rooms of right and wrong, of good and evil, into another two rooms, which will now be termed, what is true and what is false. Second, you must transcend all personal identity you have with the body and its image. The body image itself, along with gender, family, nationality, and religion must all be transcended. Thirdly, you must undo the three layers of the ego defense system, which are: our attachments, our coping mechanisms, and our ego defenses.

This work must be done in conjunction with the following correction: You must use the tools of the true right mind, or true right-minded thinking. It is a fact that as long as you continue using the ego's tools you will remain a slave to the ego. To help you reinterpret the ego, there is another set of tools that originate in right-minded thinking, and these tools will bring you into level 2. These tools are called: advanced true forgiveness, complete forgiveness and self-empowerment.

These three tools, if properly understood, can be used in any spiritual philosophy to transcend level 1 into level 2. You see, there was a missing link in most eastern and western spiritual philosophy; it can now be understood as is called level 2, right-minded thinking, and right-minded detachment.

Most spiritual seekers in this world are on level 1, and they are trying to jump to level 3. What they are really trying to do is this: They are trying to avoid looking at all the self-hate that has caused them so much pain. Instead, they must learn that one must truly look at all the most horrible hate in this world and make it conscious. The way you make it conscious is by claiming it back as a

Making the shift from level 1 to level 2 means you are taking responsibility for everything in your life.

denied thought of your own mind that you are attached to. In owning this responsibility, you can detach from that thought and it will never bother you again. However, if you do not claim it and take full responsibility for *all* of your thoughts, you are stuck on level 1 and in hell for a long time yet. Making the shift from level 1 to level 2 means you are taking responsibility for everything in your life. This is the price of admittance to level 2. So, what is level 2?

LEVEL 2

Level 2 is the true right mind, or as *The Course* calls it, the Holy Spirit. The true right mind is a mind that lives in constant *peace*. When you choose this mind to interpret your world rather than the ego right mind, you will also find that elusive true peace of mind that depends on nothing external. This mind is also home to a constant *joy* that dwells within.

LEVELS OF LEARNING

Level 3

AWAKE

THE SPLIT MIND

Level 2

The Ego
Ego Right Mind
False
Unreal

P

Holy Spirit
True Right Mind
True
Real

THE EGO SPLIT MIND

Level 1

The Ego Wrong Mind
The Shadow
Bad/Wrong Room
Past

P

The Ego Right Mind
The Persona
Good/Right Room
Future

However, this joy relies on nothing external; you are simply happy and joyous for absolutely no reason whatsoever. *Love*, in the true right mind, is a love that is so deep and profound, that you will simply just get totally immersed and lost in it. This love cannot be found externally in another person or in anything that you believe is separate from you. When you add all three together – peace, joy and love – you enter a state of mind that you will remember because you have been there; it is the state of Being. The state of Being is another name for the state of bliss, and that is who you are: bliss. You were created in bliss, and you will live in bliss for eternity.

However, there is a long way to go to get there from level 2, because what I have just described are the attributes of level 3, but you must become stationary on level 2 to ascend onto level 3. This means that from the moment you connect to the true right mind on level 1, you will be spending most of your time, up and down between both level 1 and 2. The key to speed this process up is learning that you can collapse time at your will at any time. The way you can speed this up is to learn three things very quickly: Learn how judgment works, how projection works, and how forgiveness works, and then you can do this very, very quickly when you apply these concepts on a regular basis. In simple terms, learn and know this: everything that pisses you off or presses your buttons shows you something that you are attached to. Learn to detach from it. Everything that gives you joy and happiness externally, detach from it. See both ideas and concepts for what they truly are; see them now as true or false, rather than as right and wrong.

You cannot correct an error at the same level of awareness where the error was created, which means that to solve level 1, you must look at it from level 2. Albert Einstein once said, *"The significant problems we face cannot be solved at the same level of thinking we were at when we created them."*[4]

So this means that the problems on level 1, the ego mind of right and wrong, of good and evil, can only be solved on another level, in another min-set, which is level 2, with the mind that is called in *The Course* the Holy Spirit.

LEVEL 3

When you land permanently on level 2, and no longer are attached to level 1, you will transcend to level 3. Here, you will be awake. Here, there is a new set of rules to live by and from. However, you will not need to learn these new rules because you are these new rules, they will be automatically applied by you. This is where you literally become your higher Self. And, as your higher Self, you will live by the nature of God.

At level 3 you will seek for nothing outside yourself that you cannot detach from in one second flat and with no effects on you. Here you will seek for nothing except the truth in every relationship, in every person, in every situation, and in every aspect of your life. Here you will tolerate no exceptions when it comes to the ego and its own selfishness. Here you will be in total service to all others in everything you think, do and say. Here your knowledge will come from God rather than from this world. Level 3 is the highest state of knowledge in the world of form and at this level your perception will be true at all times and you will have attained vision that will free you from all unconscious projections. Vision means understanding. You will perceive everyone and everything through the lenses of Oneness rather than separateness. Vision means seeing the truth rather than illusions. You will remain here at level 3 as long as you are guided to. Then, without any direction on your part, you will transcend to level four and in the same

> *Vision means understanding. You will perceive everyone and everything through the lenses of Oneness rather than separateness.*
>
>

instant you will wake up in Heaven on level five.

When you ascend to this place, you have now left all controls behind, and in your new state of pure Awareness, you will have merged into your true nature of Being, and you will have awoken the Christ that dwells within and you will have remembered that you are One with God.

So, one of the main ingredients of level 1 is the separated self, also known as the small self, the ego self, or the delusional self. But no matter what name you call it, it is you, the you that is reading this book. So, what is the separated self, and what makes it tick, and more importantly, how do you dissolve it? Let us see...

CHAPTER 5

~~~

The Separated Self

Part 1
What Am I?

For some particular reason, since my awakening, I have been drawn to psychotherapy, especially that of Sigmund Freud and Carl Jung. If you have studied either of these two acclaimed academics, you are in for a treat in this chapter, as we will be discussing the teachings they both left behind. The ancient Greek philosopher, Socrates, once said, "Know thyself" and this is what he was referring to: There are two of you, you as your true Self, and you as your separated self. Only one of these selves is real, the other is an illusion.

You have probably only ever known yourself as your separated self. The separated self is the part that is in constant contact with the ego thought system. When you, as a separated self, are spiritually asleep and unconscious, you automatically become the manifestation of the ego thought system itself. You become the ego. Everyone who is unconscious has this ego manifestation. It is not until you wake up that you now become aware of the separated self and you will know that you are not an ego manifestation anymore; you will now be aware that you are a separated self. You are about to become self-conscious. You are about to wake up to the truth of who you thought you were. You see, we have to come to a point of knowing who we are not, before we can truly know ourselves. It is here that we will understand what it means to *"know thyself"*.

Who is it that is reading this book? Have you ever asked yourself or questioned the "who" who is thinking these thoughts? The "you" who is reading this book is the one we are going to discuss now. You are not who you think you are; you are pretending to be someone. There are three parts to you: a personality, a persona, and a shadow. The personality is "who" you chose to come into this world as, to experience yourself as a physical human being. There are countless personalities that you can choose from, but we will cover that shortly.

The persona is, as Carl Jung described, the packaging of the ego.[1] It is the mask we wear. It is how we want to be perceived in public. We cultivate our persona to be liked and loved by other people. We all like to be around like-minded people whom we just adore. What we are doing is projecting our own persona onto them. We all love our personas, and hate our shadows.

Which brings us to the last part of our separated self which is called the shadow. This is the part of ourselves that contains all of our self hatred, all of our guilt, all of our fears, and all of our shame. The shadow is the part that we are constantly trying to get rid of. We do this by projecting it onto people, and especially onto people we do not like.

We will go further in depth on these three aspects of ourselves, but I am still not finished with the separated self, because there are three more layers all around the separated self that protect it and keep it separated and within the ego thought system. These three layers

> *The shadow is the part that we are constantly trying to get rid of. We do this by projecting it onto people, and especially onto people we do not like.*

must become known, understood, mastered and then relinquished before you will wake up. It is these three layers that are the totality of the ego defense system. When you can learn and master these three layers, you are free from the ego, and you will remain free for eternity. Free from all fear, guilt, stress, irritation, and just about free from all negativity – period.

The first layer is called our defense mechanisms. It was here that Freud came into his own and really exposed the ego defense system like no other person to date. However, Freud did not get it all right. Freud made the fundamental error of starting at the wrong point. You see, Freud thought that this world was real and that we were in fact human beings, instead of spiritual beings. Freud thought the ego was just one small part of the human psyche – instead, we learn in *The Course* that the ego is the entire separated self and that the universe, and just about everything you can see and not see with the human eye, is all part of the ego thought system. Further below we will expose all the defenses of the separated self in great detail.

The second layer is called our coping mechanisms, and again

The purpose of any true spiritual seeker then is this: to bring the three components of the separated self into awareness as One.

Freud came to the rescue and exposed our entire ego's coping mechanisms. We need tools to cope with being separate. So, if you want to remain separate, then you will need these tools to keep you reasonably "sane". This is not an easy task to achieve. However, if you're on the journey to wake up, then these coping mechanisms must be learned and then replaced with new coping mechanisms.

The last and final layer contains all of our attachments. This layer contains all of our relationships including the ones we love and the ones we hate. It contains all of our emotional, psychological and material attachments. This also includes attachments to our bodies. You will know you are attached to your body if you judge it in any way either as awful or beautiful, as too skinny or too fat. The biggest attachment you have will always be to your body, your self-image, and your reputation. There are people who might even want to kill you if you tarnish their reputation. What they are defending is their ego's self-image. That is what a reputation truly is.

The purpose of any true spiritual seeker then is this: to bring the three components of the separated self into awareness as One. This means that the constant goal of getting rid of your shadow must be relinquished and the shadow must be claimed as your own. We claim our shadow back by this method. If we react to someone or something with judgment, we acknowledge that what we see in another is a reflection of how we see ourselves. We then take full responsibility for this reflection, and claim it as our projection. Then we correct it and hand it over. We simply bring back our own projections of our own shadow. So by bringing back our shadow projections we become one with our shadow.

The same with the persona. The constant needs and desires to be liked and loved must now also be relinquished because it never really worked anyway. Finally, we must also be willing to let our reputation be torn to shreds. Our reputation is enshrined in our personas. It must not be defended anymore because, if it is, you are protecting and defending the ego persona, all the while you are trying to undo the ego itself.

So you can see the conflict of issues that arise during this process. However, once all three parts of the separated self become one, the journey really begins, and there is still great work to be undone. The three layers that surround the separated self must be re-interpreted and then relinquished. But, first they must be identified and that is what we are going to do now; we are going to find out what makes you – You.

Even though these teachings are from *The Course*, everything I talk about here in this chapter is not new. It is all around you, and has been for decades. You will find everything I talk about here on any Internet website that contains Sigmund Freud's or Carl Jung's works. However, what I have done with Freud's work in particular, is that I have re-interpreted it now according to *The Course*.

Know Thyself

Spiritual seekers have been searching in vain for the true meaning of "know thyself" for centuries. Many have believed that to know thyself is to know thy true self. This, I am afraid, is not the case. Before you can come to know thy higher Self, you must come to know thy lower self, or as I call it, the separated self.

When you are spiritually asleep, you become the manifestation of the ego thought system itself.

The separated self is a complex concept that has many parts, many defenses, coping mechanisms, and attachments. In this chapter we are going to explore, for the first time, every single component of the separated self, or as many other scholars call it, the ego self. Throughout the entire book of *A Course in Miracles*, you are reminded over and over again that you are not the ego, and this is for good cause; because you are not. Rather, what you are is a separated self within the ego thought system.

However, when you are spiritually asleep in that thought system, you become the manifestation of the ego thought system itself. In other words, you become the spokesperson for the ego and its entire defense system, and believe me, you will defend it until death. Many have done so, and many more will do so again and again.

The Three Layers of the Ego's Defense System

As we now know, and have already discussed, we all have two selves: our higher Self, or our true Self, and our separated self, or our ego self. This means that you must now begin separating your separated self from the ego thought system itself. This is simple, but not easy. To do that you must first know thyself.

As mentioned before, the separated self has three parts, which contain the personality, the persona, and the shadow. We will look at and begin the process of dismantling the separated self. However, there is more to this than meets the eye because there are three layers that keep the separated self separate. These three layers, consist of the following: The first layer is what we call our defenses, and as long as we remain asleep, we become these defenses. The second layer is what I call our coping mechanisms, and as long as we wish to be separate, then we will need these coping mechanisms. It is not easy being a separated self, and we need coping mechanisms to cope with the stresses and strains of being separate. The last and final layer is called our attachments, and as long as we are attached to our attachments we will remain asleep, separate, in pain, and we will suffer. The price we pay for our attachments is our peace of mind, and can we afford to pay this price?

You see, in this world, our peace usually depends on getting everyone out of the house for the evening, or maybe going to an Ashram for a few weeks. As long as you are trying to find peace by moving all the seeming external people and places into place, you will never find true and lasting peace. Yes, you may find peace for a short while, but in the end you will always lose your peace to your attachments. That is the price of all attachments, the loss of peace in your life. But for now let's start with the separated self, and namely, the part called the personality.

THE THREE PARTS OF THE SEPARATED SELF

As a personality, you were born into a body that lives and dies within time. Your personality, similar to your body, is a vehicle that you will lay aside when its purpose is fulfilled, when the time is right, and when you decide. However, you will continue with life because you, who are spirit, cannot die. The question is, therefore, who is the personality? And an even more important question is, who are you? It is only the personality that can feel anger, fear, guilt, regret, shame and loneliness. It is only the personality that can judge, attack, manipulate, and exploit. It is only the personality that will seek external power. It is only the personality that will love for the sake of being loved, for to love for the sake of being loved is human, whereas, to love for the sake of loving is divine.

The Personality

No matter how much we want to change the personality we can't, it can only be transcended. It is ingrained in our DNA,

124

and as long as you will use the body, you will also use the personality. The personality is the part that reacts to any and all situations that we may experience. It is inclined to get very angry or very depressed at the drop of a hat. As spiritual beings, we choose a personality to come into this life to have physical experiences. The personality will give you the lessons that you have chosen to learn; lessons you have chosen to overcome. Other personalities will also oblige you with many lessons as you go through life, and they are most likely going to be family members that are very close to you.

Let us say, for example, that you have chosen the introverted personality. You will naturally be shy and reserved and will not like to be in the public eye. However, you may have a desire to be a public speaker, but your personality type is a hindrance as you have a great fear of public speaking. Now, your life experience will present you with one of two choices: you can do everything you can to overcome your fear of public speaking, or else, you can adhere to the fear and stay in the background while feeling a sense of not being good enough and feeling unworthy. It will be your life challenge to overcome this obstacle. The permutations of experiences each of us choose are endless, and the greatest challenges that we face in life will always come from the personality type that we have chosen to experience this time around.

It is important to remember that in each life we experience here, we will choose a different type of personality to experience. Thus we will have different challenges in each life. For example, you may have been an extrovert in your last life, and in this life you may have chosen to be an introvert.

I was born as an extrovert in this lifetime, but as you have already read in my own story in the first few chapters, my life experiences and challenges brought me into the energy of an introvert personality. This was quite a painful but very necessary transition for my awakening. This was not by choice; my extrovert personality was taken from me, which in turn forced me to become an introvert. When I say it was not my choice, I am not saying that I did not choose to plan my life in this way. I did. I chose all my experiences before I was born. What I am really saying is that I did not know that I was choosing my experiences at the time it was happening in my life. My freedom, my friends, my family, and my possessions were all forced from me by seemingly external circumstances. However, that I had planned these external circumstances to aid my awakening was not known to me at that time. To this day, I owe all my gratitude to all those who played their parts perfectly in helping me to wake up. But how I hated that switch from being an extrovert to an introvert personality. It was a very painful transition for me. So I know what it feels like to overcome these challenges we face in life. Take a look at the personality types below and discover which one you have chosen.

The following are a small sample of personality types taken from the widely studied theory in mainstream psychology known as The Big Five personality traits, or the five factor model (FFM). The five factors are openness to experience, conscientiousness, extraversion, agreeableness, and neuroticism.[2] These are primary personality types and most people are able to see themselves in one or more of them. Usually there are one or two personalities that each person can primarily identify with. However, this is not an exhaustive list, but merely a general sample, given that each person has their own unique personality. It is important to know not only your own personality but also the personality of the people who are in your primary relationships so that you can find the best way to communicate with them, thereby providing a much deeper understanding in your relationships.

Extrovert and Introvert Personalities

Extroverts enjoy interacting with people, and are often perceived to be full of energy. They tend to be enthusiastic and action-oriented individuals. They like to talk and assert themselves, and many extroverts possess high group visibility. Extroverts are the life and soul of the party.

On the other hand, introverts are less involved in the social world and require lower energy levels than extroverts. They tend to appear quiet, low-key, shy and deliberate. Most introverts are very comfortable in their own company. Introverts' lack of social involvement should not be interpreted as shyness or depression. In fact, they are more independent in their social world than extroverts. Introverts need less stimulation than extroverts, and need more time alone. This does not mean that they are unfriendly or antisocial; rather, they are reserved in social situations.

Examples of Extroverts: I am the life and soul of the party; I want to be in the spot light; I don't mind being the center of attention; in fact, I want to be the center of attention; I feel comfortable around people, as long as the conversation is about me.

Examples of Introverts: I don't talk a lot; I prefer to observe; I think a lot before I speak or act; I don't like to draw attention to myself; I am quiet, especially around strangers; I sometimes have a great fear of talking in large crowds; I usually sit at the back; I am very comfortable in my own skin; and I would rather not be heard or seen.

Are you an extrovert or an introvert? Or maybe you are one of the following...

Open and Closed Personalities

The "Open" personality has appreciation for art, emotion, adventure, unusual ideas, imagination, curiosity, and a variety of experiences. People who are open are intellectually curious, open to emotion, sensitive to beauty and willing to try new things. When compared to closed people, they tend to be more creative and more aware of their feelings. They are also more likely to hold unconventional beliefs. Another characteristic of the open cognitive style is an ability to think symbolically and in the abstract; far removed from concrete experience.

People with a closed personality tend to have more conventional and traditional interests. They prefer the plain, straightforward and obvious over the complex, ambiguous, and subtle. They may regard the arts and sciences with suspicion or view these endeavors as uninteresting. Closed people prefer familiarity over novelty; they are conservative and resistant to change.

Examples of Open: I have a rich vocabulary and love using it. I have a vivid imagination, and spend a lot of time daydreaming. I have excellent ideas and I am usually open to sharing them. I am quick to understand things and help others to do the same. I am intellectual, and love showing my intellect to the public.

Examples of Closed: I am not interested in abstractions, and need concrete ideas that I can grasp. I do not have a vivid imagination, and will not accept others point of view. If I don't see it, I don't believe it.

Do you see yourself as an open or a closed personality?

Conscientious and Un-conscientious Personalities

Conscientious and un-conscientious personalities relate to the way in which people control, regulate, and direct their impulses. The conscientious personality demonstrates self-discipline, acts dutifully, and is highly motivated to achieve. The conscientious personality shows a preference for planned rather than spontaneous behavior. The conscientious personality is common amongst young adults and appears to decline with age. In contrast, the un-conscientious personality has no regard for tidiness or order, they pay no attention to detail, and are never prepared for the expected or the unexpected. They never follow the rules and are always blaming others for any mistakes on their part.

Examples of Conscientiousness: I am always prepared and ready for what life will throw at me. I pay attention to all details, especially the small details that others will miss. I get my work done right away, and on time. I like order. I follow a schedule. I am exacting in my work.

Examples of Un-conscientiousness; I leave my belongings lying around. I make a mess of things. I often forget to put things back in their proper place. I shirk my duties. I blame everyone else for my own mistakes. I pay no attention to detail. I leave everything to the last minute.

Ask yourself this, are any of your friends or family members conscientious or un-conscientious in their personality types? Are you?

Agreeable and Disagreeable Personalities

The agreeable personality shows a general concern for social harmony. Agreeable individuals value getting along with others, and they are generally considerate, kind, generous, trusting, trustworthy, helpful, and willing to compromise their own interests for the interests of others. Agreeable personalities also have an optimistic view of human nature, they would rather look at the positive than the negative.

However, disagreeable individuals place self-interest above getting on with others. They are generally unconcerned with others' well-being, and are less likely to put themselves out for other people. Sometimes their skepticism about others' motives causes them to be suspicious, unfriendly, and uncooperative.

Examples of Agreeable: I am interested in people and will actually listen to what others will say. I sympathize with the feelings of others, and I am always here for you. I have a soft heart, which usually gets broken time after time. I take time out for others, and always put others ahead of myself. I feel others' emotions. I make people feel at ease.

Examples of Disagreeable: I am not really interested in other people. I insult people, because it is who I am. I am not interested in other people's problems, and I do not want to hear what others have to say. I feel little concern for other people's problems and stories.

Are you a bad listener? If you are there is a strong possibility that you may be energized by a disagreeable personality. Likewise, if you are a good listener, there is a strong likelihood that you may be energized by an agreeable personality.

Next come the neurotic personalities, both high and low.

High and Low Neurotic Personalities

Neuroticism is the tendency to experience negative emotions, such as anger, anxiety, or depression, more than others. It is sometimes called emotional instability. Those personalities who have neuroticism are emotionally reactive and vulnerable to stress. They are more likely to interpret ordinary situations as threatening, and more likely to turn a small problem into something hopelessly difficult. Their negative emotional reactions tend to persist for unusually long periods of time, which means that they are often in a bad mood. For instance, neuroticism is associated with a pessimistic approach towards work, and an apparent anxiety linked to work.

At the other end of the scale, individuals who have a low neurotic personality are less easily upset and are less emotionally reactive than the high neurotic types. They tend to be calm, emotionally stable, and free from persistent negative feelings. However, freedom from negative feelings does not mean that they experience a lot of positive feelings, they are just better at keeping their negative emotions and feelings hidden.

Examples of High Neuroticism: I change my mood a lot, one minute I am up, the next moment I am down. I get irritated easily, especially around strangers. I get stressed out easily in ordinary situations. I worry about things a lot more than most people. I am much more anxious about small rather than the big issues in life.

Examples of Low Neuroticism; I am relaxed most of the time, even in difficult situations I seldom feel blue and always look on the bright side of life. I rarely get upset, even when everything goes wrong, in fact, I never over-react to any situation, no matter how threatening. I tend to be calm when everyone else is not. I have the voice of reason; I am the peacemaker in most situations.

So there you have it. You will see at least a bit of yourself in many, if not all, of these examples. What I want you to do next is to look at which personality type ticks all the boxes for you. Give each one a mark out of ten, and then the one with the highest marks will generally be the one that most closely describes you. If you have now selected a personality type that is close to you, you have now come to know a third of your separated self. Before you come to fully know yourself, there are still two other parts that you need to recognize and get to know. There are parts of your personality that you do not like. These are consigned to the shadow part of yourself. This is who you would rather not be. Granted, there may be some good points in your personality that you would keep, but everyone wants to be someone they are not, hence, enters the persona.

The Persona

The persona is the face we put on in public. It is the role we play in the world. It is, as Carl Jung described, "the packaging of the ego". The persona is responsible for advertising to others how you would like to be seen and how you would like to be perceived in the public eye. It oils the wheels for social inclusion. Our social success depends highly on the quality of the persona and its effectiveness in our relationships with other people. The persona that we adopt will always be attracted to the persona of other people. The best persona will be one which can adapt flexibly, comfortably and with ease in many different social situations. However, problems can and will arise within this complicated state of mind.

One of the main problems that may arise is when a personality tries to assume a persona which, for whatever reason, simply does not fit with the personality. We all know, or have known, someone who is trying to be someone they are not. Difficulty can also arise when we identify our self solely with our own persona. That personality is all about itself: me, me, and me! We call this person egotistical. However, as we are all egotistical, it really is unfair to label certain people that way. Absolutely everyone is egocentric.

The persona comes into fruition early in life. It grows out of the need to adapt to the expectations of our parents, teachers and society. We also adopt a persona so that we will be liked and loved by many people. The persona is required for us to fit in and to excel in life. Young children quickly learn that certain qualities are regarded as desirable, while others are not. The persona is who we would like to be.

We look to many people in our lives and try to adopt various traits from these people. These traits are always the things we love about them. For example, we will adopt various role models that will set the standard for the persona. A young girl may see a pop star, a movie star, or a best friend and tries to act, dress and talk like that very special person. A young boy may see a footballer, a movie star or even their own father, and try to be just like them. So, from an early age, we learn to adopt many desirable traits and incorporate them into our personas, while at the same time learn to hide or keep secret those qualities which are not desirable. We banish these qualities to another part of the personality called the shadow, which we will discuss shortly.

The persona, then, is the face and the attitude that you put on and portray to the world every day. The persona may be truthful some of the time, but mostly it is an act, which often varies from your personality's traits. Unlike the personality, which is constant, your persona varies from situation to situation and can be determined by surroundings. An example of this would be in the case of a person with a shy trait in their personality. They may give themselves a loud and outgoing persona to use amongst friends. However, they may refer back to a more discreet persona when in the safe company of their family. People who have been accused of being two-faced have met with this dilemma. They are literally being two-faced: one face is the personality and the other face is the persona. It is the persona that allows us, as humans, to be so versatile, and to function with others so well in various situations. If this was left up to the personality alone, we would probably find it very difficult to function with anyone who didn't share exactly the same personality traits as ourselves. The person you believe that you are is formed by the combination of the personality and the persona. But they are just two parts of the separated self. The third part is the shadow.

The Shadow

The shadow encompasses all of the undesirable qualities that the persona rejected from the personality. The shadow is also almost wholly unconscious, and the majority of people are completely unaware that they have a shadow. While the persona is the public face we show to the world, the shadow constitutes all that we wish to keep secret from others. A successful personality is wholly dependent on both the persona and the shadow working together. However, in order for a successful partnership between the persona and the shadow to continue, the persona must be fully unaware that the shadow even exists. The persona will do almost anything to deny the shadow; it will reject it, hide it, and keep it out of awareness for much of the time. So, just how does a person do this?

We project all the things that we hate and deny within ourselves. What this means is that we unconsciously project the shadow traits that we hate about ourselves, and then we witness these very same traits in other people. Everything you react to negatively in another person you can be sure is your projection of your own shadow onto that person. It is important that you understand that your shadow is truly all the things that you hate in other people such as your family members, your friends, your partners, and more so. It is also what you hate in your ex-friends and ex-partners. The same applies to all the things you hate in this world. These things are also your shadow. In essence, everything you witness and react to with hatred or even with mild annoyance belongs to you.

Thus, what we are doing is blaming others for those things that we hate and are trying to rid ourselves of. To own one's shadow is therefore a painful and potentially terrifying experience, so much so, that we avoid owning it by banishing certain people from our lives. This is not a conscious act of will, but is the inbuilt ego unconscious defense system. We will literally do anything to be liked, loved and accepted by society. What we are really doing is denying our own badness, and projecting it onto others.

As we have discussed, difficulties arise when one becomes solely identified with either one's persona or one's own shadow. If someone becomes too identified with their own shadow, they will really not care about putting a good face forward to show society how

It takes extreme amounts of energy to keep up the pretenses of being a persona, while at the same time denying the shadow.

wonderful they are. Nearly all the behaviors of criminals, dictators and psychopaths are a result of them over-identifying with their shadows to such an extent that they really do not wish to be part of a civilized society. They believe that they have been attacked by society in some way or other and are fully justified in attacking back.

The cost involved in projecting the shadow comes at a very high price. We must stop denying our self-hate, as we are not being honest with ourselves. It is a charade which will come to a bitter end someday. It takes extreme amounts of energy to keep up the pretenses of being a persona, while at the same time denying the shadow. Things usually come to an end when the shadow appears to be attacking the persona directly. Most people then end up in therapy as mental health issues actively arise within the personality. People simply do not know about or understand the dynamics of these three parts of themselves. If you do not confront these issues in your personality, sooner or later, the result will be misery. However, when we are honest with ourselves and come out of denial, we will wake up.

To summarize, the three components of the separated self are the personality, the persona and the shadow. Your personality is who you believe yourself to be in this human incarnation, although it is not the Real you! Your persona is everything you would like to be. And your shadow is everything you hate about yourself.

The persona is attracted to the very same persona it sees in other people. When you say, I would like to meet like-minded people, you are really saying that you really want to meet your own persona. On the other hand, the shadow is everything you don't like in others. Therefore you may say about someone, "I do not like their energy", or something to that effect. Remember that everything you see and hate in another person is really your own shadow because we are all trying to distance ourselves from our shadows.

Now, let's explore this in more depth. The persona hates the shadow and will attack it. The shadow hates the persona and will also attack it. So every argument that you have ever had with anyone is really your persona arguing with your own shadow. The reverse also occurs. Everyone who has ever had a problem with you, and has caused you to react to them, represents your shadow attacking your persona. If you do not react to that person, then you have healed that part of your mind. It is not until all three components of the separated self are brought together that this conflict ends. If they remain separate, this war will last throughout your entire life, and will result in all kinds of illnesses and mental problems.

The shadow is the darkness that haunts you in your sleep. All your nightmares have come from your shadow. Therefore, until the shadow is made conscious, it will haunt you until the day you die, and also follow you after death. It is the shadow that keeps bringing you back here lifetime after lifetime. It must be brought into awareness and relinquished.

Carl Jung said: *"One does not become enlightened by imagining figures of light, but by making the darkness conscious"*.[3] The shadow is the darkness. For one to wake up, it must be made conscious and recognized as part of the separated self. It must be recognized as the projection that it is and should be owned and claimed by the personality and not the persona. The persona, like the shadow, must also be brought back into awareness and made conscious, recognized, owned and claimed as your own. When this happens you are now setting the stage for an awakening.

All three components of the separated self – the personality, persona and shadow – must be brought back into yourself and made one. Only then will the separated self weaken and dissolve. If you keep all three separate on the outside, by seeing them as different from each other, you keep all three separate on the inside. It is this separation that keeps you asleep. This is what it means to know thyself – you must first know who you are not – you are not your ego self. Who you really are, your higher Self, will simply ascend into your awareness all by itself when you first know and then undo who you are not. You are immortal, eternal and the very center of the universe. You have simply denied and forgotten this. Remember who you are, and you will become everything that there is.

Part 2
The Ego Defense System

Three layers make up the ego defenses and keep us attached to the ego thought system, they are: our attachments, coping mechanisms, and defenses. We must bring these three layers into awareness and then relinquish them if we are to become aware of the unbelievably super being that we all truly are. There was one man who explained defense mechanisms better than any other man to date, his name was Sigmund Freud.

THE EGO'S DEFENSES

Defense mechanisms are the tools we use to protect ourselves from things that we don't want to think about, or deal with. Think of the last time you referred to someone as being "in denial" or accused someone of "rationalizing". Both of these examples refer to different types of defense mechanisms. There are many more. We will examine each defense mechanism, so that you may come to understand the defense mechanisms you employ in your daily life. Remember this, defense mechanisms protect the ego thought system but they do not protect you! They keep the ego strong and alive within your psyche. There is no one here on earth that does not use some or all of these defenses.

Sigmund Freud was the founder of psychoanalysis and the psychodynamic approach to psychology. This school of thought emphasized the influence of the unconscious mind on behavior. Freud's theories changed how we think about the human mind and behavior and left a lasting mark on psychology and our culture. Freud believed that the human mind was composed of three elements: the id, the ego, and the superego. In Sigmund

While Freud believed that the ego was just one part of the human psyche, we learn in The Course that the entire human mind or the separated self is the manifestation of the entire ego thought system.

Freud's model of personality, the ego is the aspect of the personality that deals with reality. While doing this, the ego also has to cope with the conflicting demands of the id and the superego. The id seeks to fulfill all wants, needs, and impulses while the superego tries to get the ego to act in an idealistic and moral manner.

According to the theory of *The Course*, the human mind is the separated self, which also contains three elements. As discussed above, these three elements are: the personality, the persona and the shadow. While Freud believed that the ego was just one part of the human psyche, we learn in *The Course* that the entire human mind or the separated self is the manifestation of the entire ego thought system. Freud believed that the ego is the part of the personality that mediates the demands of the id, the superego and reality. He believed that the ego part of our psyche prevents us from acting on our basic urges (created by the id), but also works to achieve a balance with our moral and idealistic standards (created by the superego). According to Freud, the id component made up our unconscious psychic energy, which works to satisfy our basic urges, needs and desires. I call this part the personality. Freud stated that the superego component was composed of our internalized ideals that we have acquired from our parents and from society. The superego works to suppress the urges of the id and tries to make the ego behave morally rather than realistically. I call this part the persona.

Let us take a look at the relationship that each of these parts has with each other and individually. **The Id, Superego and the Ego.**

The Id – The Personality

Freud believed that personality was composed of three key elements. The first of these to emerge is known as the id. The id contains all of the unconscious, basic and primal urges. While Freud believed that the personality was composed of three key elements, I disagree, because two of them did not belong to the personality. Two of these three elements belong to the ego thought system, and have nothing to do with the personality. While spiritually asleep, the personality becomes the spokesperson for the ego itself. Let me explain!

The Superego – The Persona

Freud also believed that the superego is the final aspect of the personality to emerge and it contains our ideals and values. The values and beliefs that our parents and society instill in us are the guiding force of the superego and it strives to make us behave according to these morals. The superego would be the Persona in this reinterpretation. In truth, they are the same thing, because in my theory, the persona is the ego thought system in self-creation. You see, the ego wants to wake up, and the persona is the way it is going to achieve that. Everyone on the path to enlightenment, or to wake up, is coming from the persona. However the persona is what creates the shadow as it tries to deny everything it does not like about itself. Therefore, it is the driving force of everything that we fear.

The Ego – The Shadow

In Freud's theory, the second aspect of the personality to emerge is known as the ego. This is the part of the personality that is being constantly rejected by the persona, or the superego. What I have discovered is that when Freud is talking about the ego, he is talking about the shadow. In truth, they are the same thing, because in my theory, the shadow is the ego thought system in total unconsciousness. You see, the ego wants to wake up, and through the persona – superego – is the way it is going to achieve that. Therefore the persona will ruthlessly discard anyone and anything into the shadow to achieve its own perfection.

Initially, everyone who is on the path to enlightenment, or to wake up, is coming from the persona. They are trying to get rid of everything that is not holy, that is not spiritual, and is not right or good. As long as you keep trying to get rid of anything, you are supplying ammunition to the shadow, and it will come knocking at your door very soon, if it has not arrived already. The very act of trying to get rid of the thing, is giving the very thing energy to attack you. If you are in fear, then this is the reason why. The shadow is in constant war with the persona, because the persona is constantly trying to get rid of the shadow. This is the eternal conflict that we all experience. It is literally the ego fighting with itself while it is trying to wake up, and you are dead in the center, getting it from both ends as you are the personality.

To simplify all of this, I now want to reinterpret the teachings of Freud, and bring them into line with the teachings of *The Course.* Freud correctly identified the three components of the separated self; the only problem inherent in Freud's theory is that his starting point was wrong, as he did not understand that the entire human mind, the entire separated self, is illusionary, as is the world that we live in - it is entirely fictitious. Freud thought that this world was our true reality. Therefore, in thinking that this world was real, he then believed that our true identity was that of a human being, and not a spiritual being. Numerous spiritual philosophies have taught us that we are spiritual beings; none more so than *The Course.* Freud simply got everything upside down. What Freud believed to be our conscious mind is really our unconscious mind. And what Freud believed to be our unconscious mind, is really our conscious state of being. Thus, Freud had things totally inverted.

According to Freud, we will all eventually reach stages of great anxiety when the ego cannot deal with the demands of our desires, the constraints of reality, and our own moral standards. Anxiety is an unpleasant inner state that most people seek to avoid. Anxiety acts as a signal to the ego that things are not going right. As a result, the ego then employs a defense mechanism to help reduce these feelings of anxiety.

While defense mechanisms can be unhealthy for a normal person who is unconscious, or unaware in the world, they are also very necessary for that person to function normally in society. However, difficulties arise when a person avoids dealing with problems within their lives and then over use any, or all, of these defense mechanisms. They may then seek help. In psychoanalytic therapy, the goal may be to help the client uncover these unconscious defense mechanisms and find better, healthier ways of coping with their anxiety and distress. This may be appropriate for those who are 'asleep' in the world. The problem arises for those who have the desire to wake up because they will remain in a state of conflict – between waking up and staying asleep – if they do not recognize, correct and deal with all defense mechanisms. Let's look at each one, reinterpret them, and bring them to the truth.

There are three layers of security that keep us separate: attachments, coping mechanisms, and defenses. So, let us start at the inner layer, called our ego defenses.

FIRST LAYER - DEFENSES

A rationalization is our way of explaining the experiences and emotions that we are feeling. We will know when we rationalize, because it will be an external excuse or justification for an internal problem. One of the most powerful tools the ego uses as a defense is called rationalization.

Rationalization

Rationalization is a defense mechanism that involves explaining our unacceptable behavior or feelings in a rational or logical manner, thereby avoiding the true reasons for the behavior. In other words, rationalization is where we tell ourselves fictitious stories, over and over again, and then end up believing them to be true. For example, a person who is turned down for a date might rationalize the situation by saying that they were not attracted to the other person anyway. Another example is when a student blames a poor exam result on the teacher, rather than on his or her own lack of preparation. When success is attained, people tend to attribute their achievements to their own qualities and skills. However, when confronted by failure, people tend to blame certain other people or outside forces. Rationalizations are excuses, period.

Freud argued that rationalization not only prevents anxiety, but it also protects self-esteem and self-concept. I agree, but this is a short term fix with no lasting effects, as using this defense mechanism will keep you in a perpetual state of fear and guilt. It will lead to further suffering in the long term. Therefore rationalization does not successfully operate to prevent

146

anxiety, as Freud thought. Instead, it simply defers it. Anxiety will emerge once again and lead people to great distress, sometimes resulting in therapy for extended periods of time-even years.

On the other hand, rationalization does protect the ego, as it protects self-esteem and the self-concept. Thus, we might think that rationalization is working, when in reality, one problem is simply being converted to another! We all have many fears deep within ourselves, and we rationalize those fears every day. We can see rationalization working in those who say that they have a fear of flying. The fact is that they are not actually afraid of flying, but convince themselves that they are. They project their internal fear onto an external object. All fear is already inside them, and has been for a long time, and now their egos will look for ways to say that the fear is outside of them. We do the same with many other fears that we have. However, the truth is that the cause of all fear is always inside you. In essence, rationalization is always looking for an external excuse to an internal problem.

The answer to this defense mechanism and all of these ego defenses lies within the concept called complete forgiveness. See the Chapter 10 – *True Forgiveness* for these answers.

Unfortunately, for many people with sensitive egos, for someone who has a high neurotic personality a habit like making excuses comes so easy that they are never truly aware of doing it. In other words, many of us are quite prepared to believe our own lies as the need arises. But take heart; being separate and unaware of the separation is part of the human experience for the great majority of spirits who choose to come here. In fact, there is a great deal of wisdom that is to be achieved through this experience, and an important reason why you would choose it; because this is how you will be able to experience the *opposite* of who you truly are which results in a deep experiential understanding of what you really are. What will eventually lead you back to your true self is the pain

You actually keep every negative emotion that you rationalize, and you lose every positive emotion that you rationalize.

experienced when you are separate. In this you have a choice.

As long as you keep rationalizing your problems and looking for other people and outside circumstances to blame, you will keep your problems and the pain will increase, or, you take responsibility for everything that you experience and react to thereby bringing the personality, persona and shadow together as One.

Rationalization also denies us our health and wealth. Here is how it works. You actually keep every negative emotion that you rationalize, and you lose every positive emotion that you rationalize.

Let us say that you meet this wonderful person and you fall head over heels in love. You will rationalize that the feeling you are experiencing is because you have met this wonderful person. However, after a while, this person leaves you. Where does the feeling go? The feeling evaporates along with them! You lose them, and you lose that feeling of love and bliss that you experienced with them. Why did that happen? Why did you lose the emotion of love and bliss that you felt with this person? It happened because you rationalized it. You projected your own feeling of love and bliss onto this person and when they left, they took that emotion with them. You see, those feelings of love and emotion have always been inside you, and when this person came into your life, they just showed you what was already inside. If you did not rationalize those feelings, by attributing the source of that love to this person, you would not have lost any of them.

All peace, joy, love and bliss are already inside each and every one of us. We do not need other people to experience these feelings.

Nevertheless, other people can help us uncover them within ourselves. The same applies with our negative emotions. Other people will only reflect back to us what has always been inside. If you fell angry with someone, you are rationalizing your anger. You are not angry at this person, you are angry full stop. What is happening is that you are angry with yourself, you have denied the anger, suppressed it, and projected it out. You will always be sure of what you have projected because you will react to it. Therefore, when you are angry with someone, you are really angry with yourself, but you are in denial of that anger. So, as long as you keep rationalizing your anger, you will keep it, and you will always be an angry person. Both the anger and the love have always been inside you; other people will just uncover either for you. You will love the people who uncover love for you, and you will hate those people who uncover the hate in you.

Either way, you are rationalizing both emotions, and as long as you keep doing that, you will always be in a place where you both love and hate people. Sometimes, you will love and hate the same person - that is called the love/hate relationship. However, you do not have to lose any positive emotions that you experience ever again and you do not have to keep any negative emotions either. All you need is awareness; the awareness that these feelings belong to you, and others are only showing you what is inside. It is in this awareness that you will wake up and become the bliss that you seek.

Intellectualization

Another ego defense that we use is called intellectualization. Intellectualization helps to reduce our anxiety by thinking about certain events in a cold, clinical way. This defense mechanism allows us to avoid thinking about the stressful and emotional aspects in our lives and instead, we focus only on the intellectual component.

For example, a person who has just been diagnosed with a terminal illness such as cancer might remain distant from the reality of the situation, and focus on learning everything about the cancer in order to avoid any feelings of distress. Or, people may seek answers to life through different forms of spirituality, and continue to read book after book on the topic, moving from one form of philosophy to another. They will live a life of comparing one form of spirituality with another, always secretly hoping that something will happen to lift them out of the hell they are experiencing as they go through life.

Another example may be seen in the person doing *The Course*, who studies and learns everything in the book about the ego, focusing only on knowledge, in order to avoid the application of the learning. They will recite mantras, read the book several hundred times, intellectualize every word in the book, but will simply refuse to apply the book's teachings. They will

Intellectualization is just another form of denial.

not apply forgiveness, which is the central theme of the book itself. They will even intellectualize what forgiveness is, by reciting words over and over again, without any depth or meaning. Intellectualization is just another form of denial. And denial is the most basic of all human responses.

Denial

Denial is probably one of the best known ego defense mechanisms. The term is frequently used to describe peoples' states of mind, where they appear unable to face reality or admit an obvious truth. Denial is an outright refusal to admit or recognize that something is currently occurring or has occurred in the past. Drug addicts or alcoholics often deny that they have a problem, while victims of traumatic events may even deny that the event ever occurred.

Denial functions to protect the separated self from things that it cannot cope with. While denial may seem like it saves you from anxiety or pain, it does the opposite. Not only does it not protect you from anxiety or pain, it actually prolongs it. Furthermore, denial also requires a substantial investment of your energy. If you are going to use denial then you will need two other components along with it. These are passive aggression and rationalization. Using these two tools we deny our emotions. Remember cause and effect: everything you deny, you suppress, everything you suppress you project, and everything you project, you will react to. So, therefore, everything you react to, you have denied. Simple!

Thus, defenses other than denial are used to keep these unacceptable feelings from consciousness. In many cases, there might be overwhelming evidence that something is true. Yet the person will continue to deny its existence or truth because it is too uncomfortable to face. For the person who wishes to wake up, denial will keep them asleep, because they are denying their true identity. This is the biggest denial of all.

Denial can involve a complete rejection of the existence of a serious situation or a blatant truth. In other cases, it might involve admitting that something is true, but minimizing its importance. Sometimes people will accept the situation and the seriousness of the fact, but they will deny their own responsibility in it, instead blaming other people or other outside forces.

Addiction is one of the best-known examples of denial. People who are suffering from substance abuse will often vehemently deny that their behavior is problematic. In other cases, they may admit that they do use drugs or alcohol, but will claim that their substance use is not a problem.

However, it is important that we all remember that we are all under the influence of addiction. We are all addicts, as we all use some, if not all, of these defense mechanisms, and if we cease to use them we will go into withdrawal, similar to a drug addict coming off drugs. Thus, if you begin the process of dropping any defense mechanisms without replacing them with something else, you will be in big trouble. So please do

Pain is inevitable, suffering is optional.

not do this unless you have proper guidance, and understand exactly what this process really means. Instead of using the ego's tools, there are various tools that we can use, which are described in detail in Chapter 10 – *True Forgiveness*.

Each of the defense mechanisms that you use has a very powerful effect on you. Because when denial is involved you are kept in a state of fear and hate, which ultimately leads to sickness and death. Rather than dealing with all your problems, once and for all, these defense mechanisms suppress and conceal them and they simply return again and again. This is what leads most people to therapy, and will keep them in therapy for most of their lives.

These defenses simply do not work! They are short-term fixes, and they are all designed to keep you asleep and unaware. These are the ego's tools to keep you separate and asleep and they will make you suffer. Pain is inevitable, suffering is optional. We are all going to experience pain in one way or another, it is inevitable. Where you have the option is this, you can deal with it once, or many times. You do not have to suffer. Suffering is where you keep doing the same thing as you have always done, expecting a different result. You choose to suffer if you continue to use defense mechanisms. Fortunately, you have other options, ...there is another way.

We are all in a state of denial if we exist as a body in this world. In this state, we are in denial of one or all of the following: we are in denial that we are one with each other, so we project separateness; we are in denial of our true identity, which is a spiritual being, not a human being, so we project other bodies; we are in denial of our innocence and perfection, so we project guilt, and see it in other people; we are in denial of our own immortality, so we project death; we are in denial of the unconditional love that we have within, so we project conditional love, which is really hate; we are in denial of God and heaven, which is the most profound denial of all, so we project an ego god with heaven and hell attached.

It is very important that we understand the effects of denial which is the projection of self-hate onto other people. In essence, everything that we deny in ourselves, which is all of our own self-hate, will be projected onto others. Thus, we will see in others the things we hate in ourselves. It is only at this point that we have the golden opportunity to forgive ourselves. Everyone is a mirror to us, and when we now see the guilt and hate in another, it is a golden opportunity to let it go in ourselves. If you have reacted to the guilt and hate in another, it belongs to you and you must forgive yourself for it. If you do not react to another, you have already healed that part of your mind.

Projection

Projection is a defense mechanism that involves taking our unacceptable actions and justifying them to either ourselves or to other people. We may act in an unacceptable manner and then justify those actions by blaming someone else for our behavior. This involves an individual attributing his or her

You react to everything that you see wrong in someone else because you have projected it. If you did not project it, you would not react to it. There are no exceptions to this rule.

own thoughts, feelings and motives to another person. For instance, you might hate someone, but your persona, the part of the ego that wants to be liked, tells you that such hatred is unacceptable. The ego will 'solve' that problem for you, by telling you that this other person hates you and it can even go so far as to help you remember past interactions with that person which the ego will help you interpret as evidence that they may have not been nice to you. So now, this leaves you free to hate them.

What you deny you will project, and what you project you will react to – this is cause and effect at work.

You react to everything that you see wrong in someone else because you have projected it. If you did not project it, you would not react to it. There are no exceptions to this rule.

Because you have projected what you don't like in yourself onto others, you still don't like it, even in this other person. If you liked it in yourself, you would love it in another. Our denial is so strong that we are convinced that the ugly characteristics, such as laziness, hate or guilt, that we see in someone else is really theirs. We say to ourselves, "I would never do that, I would never say that". If you are making these statements to yourself, you are in denial, and now because of that denial, you are projecting your unacceptable behaviors onto someone else.

It is very easy for us to blame other people. However, it may be clear to you by now that what we are really doing is projecting all that self-hate and guilt that we deny in ourselves onto someone else. We now banish that person or persons from our lives. This is called scapegoating.

The origin of the term 'scapegoating' stems from an old Jewish custom. In the old Jewish tradition, people would hold a festival once a year called Yom Kippur that celebrates the day of atonement. One of the rituals of this festival was to tie a goat in the middle of the village and everyone from the village would lay their hands on the goat. What they were doing was transferring or projecting their sins onto the goat. At the end of the day, they would kick the goat out of the village and banish it into the wilderness. This was their way of cleansing themselves. They used a goat to rid themselves of their own sins, or they used a scapegoat. We still do the exact same today. We use the tool called projection to cleanse us of our own perceived sins, by transferring them to other people, other countries, and just about anything, and then we banish those people from our lives.

If you do not understand projection, you will never understand life. Denial and projection go hand in hand. The cause of projection is denial, and if you do not deny your own self-hate, you will not project it. The self-hate that I talk about is our shadow, and it is that part of ourselves that we are constantly trying to deny. There is no greater way to deny our shadow than by using projection. There is another way to deal with denial – it is called true forgiveness. See Chapter 10 – *True Forgiveness*.

Repression

As we have previously discussed, every separated self has a shadow. The shadow is the fundamental aspect of the separated self within the human experience that all humans have to face at some stage. The ego thought system has a number of defenses that preserve and isolate the shadow, keeping it out of our awareness. One of the defenses that keeps the shadow out of awareness is called repression.

Repression is a form of defense that keeps certain thoughts and feelings unconscious. It can lead to memory loss of traumatic incidents or events associated with painful emotions. Collectively we have all repressed the thoughts of the separation itself, which is where the thoughts of sin, guilt and fear originate. Thoughts of sin, guilt and fear are the fundamental basis for the entire ego unconscious mind in and of itself. The shadow is everything we hate about ourselves, and we will do anything to keep it away from us, keep it out of awareness. Thus, repression is one way to do this. However, the self-hate will inevitably rear its head one way or another somewhere down the road. Instead, we can deal with the self-hate once and for all by using true forgiveness to undo the shadow.

Let's now move onto the second layer that protects the separated self, the ego's coping mechanisms. It is the use of these coping mechanisms that keeps one in unawareness. The ego's greatest strength against you is that you do not know how it works. Learn how it works, and the ego can work for you. Learn these coping mechanisms and gently let them go so that they can be replaced by new coping mechanisms that will help you wake up and end suffering once and for all.

> *The ego's greatest strength against you is that you do not know how it works.*
>
>

SECOND LAYER – COPING MECHANISMS

A coping mechanism is a tool that we all use automatically. It is an built-in coping device that enables us to deal with all the stress and strains of being separate in a body. The body is like a volcano when energized with the ego's wrong-minded thoughts, and so we need a way of dwelling in that mind. Therefore, the ego introduced these coping mechanisms to not only keep us separate, but also to keep us living in perpetual pain and suffering.

Reaction Formation

One of the main coping mechanisms we all use is reaction formation. Reaction formation reduces anxiety by adopting the opposite feeling, impulse or behavior than you are experiencing. An example of reaction formation would be treating someone you strongly dislike in an excessively friendly manner, like people pleasing. Why do people behave this way? According to Freud, they are using reaction formation as a defense mechanism to hide their true feelings.

Poker players are a prime example of the use of reaction formation. If a poker player has a very strong hand of cards, he will automatically try and hide this fact by acting in a complacent, non-challenging passive way. On the other hand, if the poker player has a very weak hand, and he wants to win the pot, he will act aggressively; he is trying to convey that, "I have a very strong hand and you should beware!"

Reaction formation may also be demonstrated in this way. Let's say that you really do not like someone, such as your boss. However, you need to be liked by him in order to keep your job, and to ensure that you don't get a hard time from him. So, when you are with him, or just meeting him by chance, you will be all smiles on the outside, but full of anger and hate in the inside. You are not being true to yourself, but you will keep your job. This is the price you will pay. Furthermore, the hate and anger inside you will now be projected out onto a less threatening person or object, and this coping mechanism is called displacement. If you use reaction formation, then you will use displacement also.

Displacement

Have you ever had a really bad day at work where your boss has given you a really hard time, and because you needed your job, you unconsciously used reaction formation to hide your true feelings and emotions? However, the down side to this is this, you now have a lot of pent-up anger and you will displace it out onto someone or something.

If in the past you went home and took out your frustration on your family or friends, or the cat! then you have experienced the ego coping mechanism of displacement. Displacement involves taking out our frustrations, feelings, and impulses on people or objects that are less threatening. Displaced aggression is a common example of this coping mechanism. Rather than express our anger in ways that could lead to negative consequences, like arguing with our boss, we instead express our anger towards a person or object that poses no threat, such as our spouse, children, or pets.

> **Displacement involves taking out our frustrations, feelings, and impulses on people or objects that are less threatening.**
>
>

Displacement is you controlling your projections in a more calculated way. Thus, displacement and projection go hand in hand. Displacement is the redirection of an impulse (usually aggression) onto a powerless substitute target. The target can be a person or an object that can serve as a symbolic substitute.

160

Someone who is frustrated by his or her superiors may go home and kick the dog, behave aggressively towards a family member, or get into a bar fight. You will use someone as a scapegoat for your pent-up anger. As such, the aggression may be displaced onto people with little or no connection with what is causing the anger. For example, some people punch cushions when they are angry at friends. A student may snap at his or her roommate when they are upset about an exam grade. Thus, displacement can act as a chain-reaction, with people unwittingly becoming both victims and perpetrators of displacement, as may be seen in the following example.

A man becomes angry with his boss, but he cannot express this for fear of losing his job. A little while later, he yells at his wife because the dinner is cold. The wife then scolds one of the children, possibly disguising this as punishment (rationalization), because of their disobedience. The child then takes it out on the dog, by yelling at him or kicking him. Then, the dog attacks the cat. If we can justify our attack, which is usually done by using the defense mechanism called rationalization, it makes it much easier for us to deal with our displacement, by lessening the guilt we feel over the attack in the first place. If you really want to wake up, you can now use another coping mechanism instead of displacement,

> *Sublimation is similar to displacement, but takes place when we manage to displace our emotions into a constructive rather than destructive activity.*

it is called complete forgiveness. See Chapter 10 – *True Forgiveness* for this tool.

Sublimation

Another coping mechanism of the ego is sublimation. We all have inner impulses of anger and rage, hate and violence, especially when we are living in the ego thought system. However, we have to learn to control them if we are to live in a civilized society. One way we do this is by using the coping mechanism called sublimation, which allows us to act out unacceptable impulses by converting them into more acceptable forms. For example, a person experiencing extreme anger might take up kickboxing as a means of venting frustration. Alternatively, in today's modern world, we seek out classes on anger management in an attempt to control what we are refusing to look at within ourselves.

Sublimation is similar to displacement, but takes place when we manage to displace our emotions into a constructive rather than destructive activity. For example, many great artists and musicians have had unhappy lives, and have used the medium of art and music to express themselves. Sports are another example of putting our emotions (e.g. aggression) into something constructive. The case of Mike Tyson the boxer comes to mind. He was an extremely aggressive teenager, and one day the great boxing manager, Constantine Cus D'Amato, saw that if his rage could be channeled into the boxing ring Tyson could be a world champion, which he later proved to be.

According to Freud, sublimation is the cornerstone of a civilized life. Freud believed that sublimation was a sign of maturity that allowed people to function normally in socially acceptable ways. Again Freud is correct. However, these inner demons never go away; they are always in the subconscious, waiting to pounce. They may cause you great difficulty when they do surface. However, the tool called complete forgiveness will undo all sublimated defense mechanisms and set you free once and for all.

Passive Aggression

Another ego coping mechanism that we have all used and still all use is called passive aggression. Passive-aggressive behavior takes many forms, but can generally be described as a non-verbal aggression that manifests in negative behavior. Passive-aggressive behavior is when you indirectly show expressions of hostility, such as procrastination, sarcasm, stubbornness, sullenness, or deliberate or repeated failure to accomplish requested tasks for which one is responsible. It exists when you are angry with someone, but do not, or cannot, tell them that you are angry. Instead of communicating honestly when you feel upset, annoyed, irritated or disappointed, you may bottle the feelings up and shut off verbally, and make obvious changes in behavior, such as giving angry looks, sulking or being obstructive.

Passive-aggressive behavior is sometimes blatantly obvious. However, it may be concealed, and thus a passive-aggressive individual may not always show that they are angry or resentful.

They might appear to agree, and appear polite, friendly, down-to-earth, kind and well meaning. However, underneath there is much manipulation going on, hence the term "passive-aggressive". Thus, it is a destructive pattern of behavior that can be seen as a form of emotional abuse in relationships, where trust is eroded between people. It is a creation of negative energy which is clear to those involved, and immense hurt and pain may result for all the parties concerned. It happens when negative emotions and feelings build up. We can all be passive-aggressive from time to time, and display some of the behaviors described above.

Frequently, the passive-aggressive person fears competition, and will thus avoid certain situations where someone else would be seen as better than them. There are numerous examples and scenarios that can depict the coping mechanism passive aggression, such as not communicating when there is clearly something problematic to discuss. Another example is when you avoid and ignore the other person when you are so angry that you feel you cannot speak calmly. At other times, you may evade all problems and issues by burying your head in the sand, and procrastinating, or possibly intentionally put off important tasks for less important ones. Sometimes the passive-aggressive person will sulk, and be sullen and resentful in order to get attention or sympathy. The passive-aggressive individual may withhold privileges or expectations, such as sex, cooking, cleaning, emptying the trash, washing the dishes, etc., all to reinforce an already unclear message to the other party that they are angry with them. As it is difficult to let go of this coping mechanism once you habitually use it, many marriages and relationships break down directly as a result of the use of this destructive ego tool. The answer to this ego coping mechanism is also called complete forgiveness.

Altruism

As separated individuals we will go to great lengths to feel good about ourselves for personal gratification, and the coping mechanism termed called altruism is used for this purpose. Altruism is where we deal with internal emotional conflict or external stresses by giving our services to help meet the needs

As it is difficult to let go of this coping mechanism once you habitually use it, many marriages and relationships break down directly as a result of the use of this destructive ego tool.

of others. Unlike the self-sacrifice sometimes characteristic of reaction formation, the individual who employs altruism receives gratification and comfort from the response of others. However, it is important to appreciate that individuals who dedicate themselves to the service of others receive gratification and it makes them feel good about themselves. One should continue with great works by all means, but if you are one of these people who use altruism, you should also employ another tool that will help you to wake up, if that is your choice, and that tool is true empathy. True empathy is joining with a person in truth by empathizing with the truth of who the person is; that is,

165

their eternal identity and perfection in spirit. The ego's empathy is joining in pain and suffering. This is the only joining the ego allows and all it does is breed more pain and suffering.

Restitution

We all have experienced guilt at some stage in our lives, and on that, there is no question. Nevertheless, it is what we do with that guilt that is the most important thing. One way we deal with this guilt is called restitution. Restitution involves relieving the mind of extreme guilt by making amends for a wrongdoing, such as providing payment, or other assistance to those who have been wronged.

Restitution may be clarified by the following two examples:

Let us say that you forget the birthday of someone who is close to you, but at the last minute you suddenly remember their birthday, however, the other party knows that you had forgotten it for some time. They are hurt... and you feel guilty. Your first reaction is restitution. You will think or say, "I will make it up to you". Thus, you are employing the coping mechanism called restitution to deal with the guilt that you are experiencing.

A second example of restitution may be seen in the case of someone who has committed a crime. They may later feel extreme guilt and decide to go to a police station to confess. They are accepting that they have done something wrong, and are willing to make restitution for the harm that they have done in order to feel better within themselves. However, at the end of the day, the guilt that they are experiencing has nothing to do with the wrongdoing that they committed. Let me hasten to explain! You see, guilt is alive and well inside us, and always has been. When we think that we have done something wrong, that guilt within our minds rears its ugly head, and surfaces at the drop of a hat. The ego is just waiting for us to make a mistake, and riddles us with the guilt that is already within us. There is no one on earth who has not experienced guilt at some time in their lives.

Fortunately, there is another way to deal with this guilt. In fact, there is another way to deal with all the ego coping mechanisms that we use daily; the defense mechanisms that simply keep the ego strong, alive and well within us and ensure that we remain asleep. If you wish to wake up, you need to know that there is another way to deal with this guilt that we all carry within us - we can learn and master complete forgiveness. Complete forgiveness is the perfect coping mechanism to master if you want to wake up.

THIRD LAYER - ATTACHMENTS

The final layer that keeps the separated-self separate is called our attachments. Now, when I talk about attachments I am talking about the attachments to our persona, and our shadow. You see, we love to love the people we love, and we love to hate the people we hate. When Jesus said, "give up your possessions and follow me", he meant give up your attachments and follow me. He was not talking about your car, house, money or anything material, he was talking about all the special people in your life. And he certainly was not talking about kicking these people out of your life, but just giving up the way we are

167

seeing them. As long as we keep making some people more special than others, whether it is hate or love, we will pay the price for that. Every time you are in pain and in suffering, it is because you chose to specially love or specially hate someone else. You see, the love we have for the people we think we love is not love, it is special love. Special love is not what true love is because true love has no demands, no expectations, no desires and no needs. On the other hand, special love is wholly conditional love that can turn into hate the moment the conditions are no longer met. Now, ask yourself, do you truly love anyone? If the love you have for anyone is conditional love, then you are fooling yourself into thinking that you love them. The truth is that you love no one but yourself, your separated self, that is. This is the ego's best at work.

Here is a full list of the three layers of the ego's defense system that we all carry with us, which in turn keeps us separated and in pain. These three layers must be reinterpreted and relinquished before we can wake up.

Defenses: rationalizations, denial, judgment, dissociation, suppression, repression, busyness, intellectualization, the ego right mind / false spirituality, resistance.

These defenses must be brought into awareness, recognized, corrected and relinquished.

Coping Mechanisms: displacement, sublimation, altruism, restitution, projection, false empathy, prayer, suffering, time.

The tools that replace our coping mechanisms are Complete Forgiveness and Advanced True Forgiveness.

Attachments: special love, special hate, the body, the persona, the shadow, one's reputation, material attachments, emotional attachments, psychological attachments, victimhood.
The tools that are required to undo our attachments are Self-Empowerment and Advanced True Forgiveness.

The way we undo the ego defense system is by using the following seven very powerful tools, and we will need every single one of them to wake up. They are: awareness, advanced true forgiveness, complete forgiveness, self empowerment, responsibility, acceptance and simple forgiveness. I have explained these seven tools at various points in this book, but for a complete definition go to the glossary section at the end of this book.

SUMMARY

To know thyself, means to know the separated self, not your True Self. This makes sense when you look at it from this perspective: to wake up means to dismantle and dissolve the separated self, every single component, and every single layer that we have just discussed above. When this has been accomplished, you will remember your True Self, and you will know thyself. The concept of know thyself has been misunderstood for centuries. The truth is that you are already enlightened.

All that you have to do to remember your enlightenment is to stop "un-enlightening" yourself. In other words, as long as you keep your attachments in place, you will need coping mechanisms to deal with them. As long as you keep using the ego's coping mechanisms you will require all of the ego's defenses that keep the separated self... well, separate. The key to unlock and dissolve the separated self begins with the relinquishing of your

> *All that you have to do to remember your enlightenment is to stop "un-enlightening" yourself.*
>
>

attachments. Remember, our material attachments are not that important at this stage, it is the attachments to people and our beliefs, be they religious or otherwise, that we must look at and relinquish. An example here could be the relationships with our family members, those we specially love and those we specially hate, both are attachments. Both will bring you pain if not corrected, and detached from. Again it is important to stress that it is only the way we perceive people that we detach from, this is not about physically detaching from anyone or anything.

Next, to dismantle are our coping mechanisms all we do here is simply replace the ego's coping mechanisms with the new coping mechanisms found in *The Course*, such as Complete Forgiveness and Self-Empowerment.

Then, when you have begun dismantling the two outer layers, you will reach the ego's last innermost layer called the defense system. The undoing of the ego's defenses is going to be the greatest challenge to us, because the ego's defenses are foolproof but, fortunately, they are not God proof. We have these tools to deal with the ego's defense system: awareness, Advanced True Forgiveness, responsibility, acceptance and simple forgiveness. We are not asked to do this by ourselves, there are ample tools to do this for us; See Chapter 10 – *True Forgiveness.* As long as we keep using the ego's tools we will remain separate, alone and vulnerable. However, as soon as we begin using these new tools, as discussed in this book, the entire game changes, and you will be well on your way to your awakening.

You will have heard many people talk about enlightenment, and the journey to enlightenment, so what is enlightenment and where do I find it? The most important thing you must realize is that you are already enlightened; it is the separated self that keeps you un-enlightened. As long as you keep aligning yourself with the false sense of who you are, you are un-enlightening yourself. The answer then is simple, stop it, and you will be enlightened. So, what is enlightenment?

CHAPTER 6

~~~

Enlightenment

Enlightenment is a state of mind and is not, as many have alluded to over the decades, an individual experience that is bestowed upon one single person. All one is truly attaining when one attains a state of enlightenment is a shared state of mind. Enlightenment is when you experience yourself as everyone and everything; it is a state of oneness. No single person can claim enlightenment as their own. It is wholly shared, or it is not enlightenment.

Loving the idea of enlightenment, the ego, being a selfish concept of 'me, me, me', will always try and claim enlightenment for itself alone. So you can be sure that the person who makes the claim "I am enlightened" is definitely not enlightened. However, the person who understands what true enlightenment really is will share it as so. This means that those who have attained the enlightened state of mind will know that it is a shared experience of the "one mind" that we all share.

If I or any other person claims to be enlightened, we lose that connection to the shared mind, as there can be no individual ownership of enlightenment. Enlightenment is the recognition that we are all enlightened, and in that enlightenment, we are all One. The one who attains this state of mind has only access to it; they do not own it by themselves. If you claim it for yourself, you lose it. That is why the ego will never be enlightened, as the ego in itself is a selfish desire or wish to be special and unique; someone who is different from everyone else, and more special than anyone else.

So, what exactly is enlightenment? What does it mean to share this state of mind? The answer is "Vision". It is almost impossible to describe what enlightenment is, but its effects can be described. The reflection of enlightenment is seeing or understanding the truth in everyone and everything. This is what Vision is. It has nothing to do with the physical eyes that see; it is seeing with the mind, or, to put it another way, it means understanding. You begin to understand everyone and everything you see in another way. You only see one perspective of people, events and circumstances when you are unconscious or spiritually asleep. However, when you wake up, you will see two versions of everything; one version is looking with the ego, and the other is looking through the enlightened mind.

Enlightenment means freedom from the cycle of birth and death of the physical body. Pain and suffering are inevitable when one is born in ignorance of one's true nature, which is an eternal spirit. When our true nature is revealed to us in the awakened state, suffering is extinguished in that very same instant. You are not here to make yourself perfect, to make yourself holy, or to make yourself into anything. It is the ego that ponders life in that way. You are here to remember who you are. You are here to wake up.

You are not God, but there is nothing inside you that is not of God. Enlightenment is the remembrance of who you truly are, not who you think you are! In that remembrance is the end of everything that is illusionary, which includes all pain, all suffering, all conflict and all sickness. The remembrance of your true nature is also the end of death. When

> *You are not here to make yourself perfect, to make yourself holy, or to make yourself into anything. It is the ego that ponders life in that way. You are here to remember who you are. You are here to Wake Up!*
>
>

you remember you are already enlightened, you will also remember you are eternal life.

A number of separations must take place if you have made the decision to wake up; separations between mind, body and the external world. The mind is attached to the body and the body is attached to the external world. However, the external world and its attachments are kept firmly attached to the body by the mind's needs, desires, ideas and beliefs. The first level of detachment or separation that must take place in order to wake up is between the body and the external world.

Thereafter, only the mind and the body are attached, and these need to separate next. This leaves only a mind; an awakened mind. It is a reluctance to let go of their attachments that keep all seekers of enlightenment asleep; wanting to be enlightened, yet wanting to hold on to attachments is incongruous.

The ego mind is entangled in the illusionary world of form and behavior. It is an uncontrollable and unceasing reservoir of thoughts, emotions and feelings that dictate and rule your life. The ego mind is clouded, unclear, confused and in pain. The result is the same no matter what you choose in the world, and because you are always choosing externally, respite comes and goes, but is never a permanent state. Those who are deep in the unconscious mind are spiritually asleep and unaware of their true self and thus they will seek stimuli outside themselves.

> *It is a reluctance to let go of their attachments that keep all seekers of enlightenment asleep; wanting to be enlightened, yet wanting to hold on to attachments is incongruous.*
>
>

All pleasure, all happiness, all attaining and fulfillment will be sought outside oneself. This is the level of attachments for most people. Demands will be made by them. They will have many expectations and needs. Desires will be sought from everyone and everything. Here they are like ships in the ocean, rudderless, without power and they will be open to all the ills and sickness that this world has to offer. People are powerless because they are expecting other people or things to make them happy. No one and nothing external to you can make you truly happy. Everyone and everything external to you changes. There is nothing external that ever stays the same!

An awakened mind is very powerful simply because it does not rely on external stimuli for anything.

The mind that is asleep is within the ego thought system and as such it is powerless because it seeks for everything in the external world. It is also powerless because its thinking processes are relentlessly ongoing. Thoughts rule its life. There seems to be no control over how one thinks; thoughts produce emotions, and emotions dictate how you live. This could also be called the insane state of mind or the ego mind where insanity rules because there are no sane thoughts to grasp. In other words, every choice you make will ensure more pain and suffering.

> *The mind that is asleep is within the ego thought system and as such it is powerless because it seeks for everything in the external world.*
>
>

As a wise person once said, "The definition of insanity is when you keep doing the same thing over and over again, expecting a different result". Similarly, my definition of suffering is when you keep choosing the same *thoughts* over and over again expecting a different result. *All suffering comes from our thinking.*

The Door into Your Mind

Enlightenment is a process. As you wake up, the mind begins to fill with the light of truth, wisdom and knowledge. However, you will know that this wisdom does not come from you, but through you. Here the mind will be clear and pure. You will still see what everyone else sees, but you will think what no one else thinks. Perceptions will be true. This means that you will see the truth in everything; in every relationship, in every circumstance, and in every event. It is this truth that has set you free and will keep you free. It is also important to remember, on the path to enlightenment, that one path is always as good as any other.

However, if you are constantly changing paths, changing practices and disciplines, you are only fooling yourself. Remember, the path to enlightenment does not change – you change. Enlightenment is like a castle with a thousand doors. Every single door will bring you inside the inner sanctum. There are many obstacles beside each door and each obstacle represents something in your mind that makes you afraid and fearful. The form that this fear takes will change at each door, but the content of the fear is the exact same. There is an old saying that says, "Fear knocks on the door and when faith opens it, there is no one there!" It is only fear that prevents you from opening the door, and you must know that fear is an illusion, but to find out, you must first go through the door.

Constantly changing paths is similar to going to each door and opening it slightly. You then become afraid and you stop and try another door, then another door, and another. All the time, you are really holding on to fear. However, you should know that this fear that you are experiencing will dissolve the second you turn the handle and go through the door. The longer you are on this path without entering through the door, any door, the more pain you will suffer; it is the delay that causes suffering, not the path you are on.

You suffer because you are still outside the castle, and you will try every door, sometimes going back to the same door over and over again. However, the answer lies in being patient and trusting. Pick a path and persevere with the path you are on. Above all else, do not follow someone else's path, instead, choose the path which is true for you.

There are several stages that one will go through to find the correct door for oneself. In the beginning you may not even see the door. In fact, for most, the door will be hidden from plain sight. So you may seek out someone who knows where the door is located. I have a saying in life, "if you want to get to a certain place, find someone who has been there, for it is they who will show you the way". Many say they know the door... but a word or warning: many are also false prophets. Choose wisely, ask many questions, and become satisfied that you have chosen a true teacher and then, with all your heart, follow that path and stick to it.

A true teacher is just a guide, nothing more. True teachers can and never will make choices for you, because that would decrease your power to do so. A true teacher will empower you to use your own power. They will only present a number of choices for you to make, but it is you that must choose. If you are not free to choose wrongly, you will never be free to choose correctly. You will only begin to choose correctly after you have chosen wrongly. Sometimes you may choose wrongly over and over again. That is ok. You will finally make the correct choice when the pain of choosing wrongly becomes too much to bear.

A true teacher can only show you the door. They cannot take you through it, or make you go through it. Only you can open the door and walk through it yourself. A true teacher will guide you on how to remove the obstacles that are in front of the door, but it is you who must remove the obstacles yourself. No one can do this for you; it is your path, your work, your practice, your vigilance and your devotion that will then bring you through the door. The door you choose to go through may not be the same door that others choose. Never let this separate you from anyone. Respect the choices of others, and encourage them, but never tell them that they are at the wrong door. If you do, you can be sure that it is you who is at the wrong door. There is no right or wrong way, there is only now or later. Very few are ready now, and if you are ready, then you will find the right teacher for you.

> *There is a secret place inside you, a door that you can access, and if you can attain it, your world is about to change forever. This place is not a place that is here nor there, this place is but a state of mind.*

There is a secret place inside you, a door that you can access, and if you can attain it, your world is about to change forever.

This place is not a place that is here nor there, this place is but a state of mind.

The Art of Silence

The enlightenment of insights can come like a flash, out of apparently nowhere, but only when the mind becomes still... in total silence. When all thoughts, ideas, concepts and speculations cease, there, like a flash, a knowing of everything comes to you. When the mind is still, an understanding of life, of nature, of death, of knowledge, of insights and enlightenment will rush into your very being itself.

> *The Observer is your Higher Self and is without judgment, while the thinker being the ego, needs judgment, and is, therefore, always in judgment.*
>
>

But such stillness cannot be cultivated because if you cultivate a still mind, it is not a still mind; it is a cultivated still mind. It is still within a concept of stillness. It is an idea of stillness. Remember stillness is beyond all thoughts, concepts and ideas. It is total non-thought, non-conceptual and non-conforming; it just is.

When I am in my center, in the total presence of the Now, I am in this place. When I seek for nothing outside of myself I can remain in my center. However, when I seek for anything from anyone I lose my center and now I am back in judgment, because I have stepped outside of myself. In my center I am the Observer of all life; I am without judgment. The Observer is your

Higher Self and is without judgment, while the thinker being the ego, needs judgment and is, therefore, always in judgment.

All true understanding comes from observing without judgment of any kind. Judgment entails thinking, and thinking entails understanding through ideas and concepts. The thinker believes it will eventually grasp understanding through its own intellect; however, it is precisely that intellect that is the block to experiencing it. Stillness can only be experienced. It cannot be understood by intelligence or intellect. It cannot be written about or documented in a paper, and it cannot be grasped within a concept or idea. Enlightenment can come so quickly, so swiftly, but only to a mind that has accessed the door to stillness and silence. You cannot enter the stillness if you are in judgment, for you must become without judgment to enter this timeless realm within.

If you can become fully present in the here and now, then you can transcend all thoughts. Just sit with your eyes closed in silence, without concentrating on anything, without focusing on time, either past or future. Only then, without any effort or force, can the mind become still. In this stillness, seekers of enlightenment will find what they had long been seeking. It is in this place that you will find all the answers to life – here the meaning of life will be revealed to you.

Here also you will find that which you sought for many lifetimes, for it is here you will find your True Self. You will find an extraordinary change taking place within you, if you can listen with ease, and without strain. In this place, nothing is impossible. A change will arise within you if you do not ask nor seek for anything, or search for anything. It will arrive without demanding it, desiring it, expecting it, or needing it, and in that change you will experience a great beauty within. You will experience a depth of knowledge and insight that you could never have imagined. For it is here within the stillness of your mind that heaven lies.

One of the main conditions for this stillness and silence is space. If you walk into a room full of clutter that has been amassed over many years, it is almost impossible to bring anything new into that room. And if you do, you will not even notice the new, because of all the junk that has been amassed within the room. However, if you begin the process of de-cluttering, you can begin to design and make a new living space that you will enjoy. This is what Jesus meant when he said, *"You cannot put new wine into old wineskins, for the new wine will turn sour"*. It is impossible to accept new truths while we hold on to old truths.

The old must be relinquished before the new can enter. The same process is necessary with the mind. To allow for silence and newness, it must be de-cluttered of all the conditioning, all nonsense and all beliefs that have been amassed over the years. The space you create within the mind is where you will find this silence. If the mind is now empty and without judgment, you have created the space required for insight and knowledge to enter.

Everything that you have ever dreamed of comes within this silence. In this place, every question you have ever dreamed of will be answered. In this silence, you will begin to hear sounds that you have never heard before: the soundless voice. In this place there is no wanting, desiring, needing, expecting or demanding of anything, because here you have everything, because here everything is you.

In this space, there is no concentrating, no exclusion, or no absorbing of any description. You are aware of everything and nothing at the same time. There are no past or future thoughts, just a sense of being, being in the present, here and now. You are naked and empty of all identity. There is no "I" or "you" or "we". There is only a presence of nothingness which then expands into an awareness of everything. In this space, all knowledge and wisdom is accessed by those who enter wholly without identities. There are no names, words, thoughts or symbols, just the experience of pure awareness. There is no resistance, and no forces to be applied. There is just an inner presence that resides in infinite peace.

It is our demands, needs and desires that keep this place from our awareness. It is our constant projections, fears, and beliefs that keep our vibrations so low that we cannot rise to meet the stillness in our minds. You are obviously listening to the voice of the ego if you listen through the screen of your desires because you are listening to your own ego desires. The ego's vibration is dense, heavy and burdensome, and becomes more so as it is fuelled by your ambitions and anxieties.

Awareness is light, a lightness and freedom which is above all physical attributes. Stillness and silence are not easy to attain. But, if you can find this place, you will experience a great beauty and understanding which you will never have experienced before. To come to this place, there must be an inward quietness... a freedom from the strain of acquiring and a relaxed attention of nothingness. Those who choose love can listen, listen to the silence of everything. Fear is one factor that must be overcome to enter this place. Fear exists as long as you hold a false sense of self. Fear is fed by the ego self-image that you hold as your identity.

You are directly in contact with your real and true essence of Being when you listen without ideas, without thoughts, without demands, without names, without concepts, or specifics of any kind.

The more fearful you are, the more powerful the ego self-image becomes. Fear is the dog that guards the door to this stillness and silence within your mind.

You are directly in contact with your real and true essence of Being when you listen without ideas, without thoughts, without demands, without names, without concepts, or specifics of any kind. This is the art of listening... hearing the soundless sound. The ego mind is eternally occupied with getting something or getting rid of something; we are constantly trying to be this or that, to achieve a particular state, to capture some kind of experience and avoid another.

The ego mind is never still, and it is never silent. It constantly listens to the incessant noise of its own struggles and pains, which in turn become your struggle and pains. You are not your ego, but your ego believes it is you. This is the false sense of self that we all carry. It is only the ego that is concerned with the past and the future. The ego is not present in the here and now, and can never be so. However, your true "self" is fully present. This is awareness ... pure awareness.

You really never actually listen to anything because your mind is not free as a result of your thinking that you already know everything. It is impossible to teach anything to someone who believes that they already know it. Thus, listening becomes extraordinarily difficult for that person. That person will struggle and try to force the experience to arrive. This is what keeps the experience in the distance and keeps it far from your awareness. Those who enter this silence have all one thing in common; they have made the decision that they do not know anything. And it is here, in this mind-set, that they will come to know everything. A crowded mind, filled with all kinds of "facts and knowledge", will act as impediments to your entry into this timeless place of nothing and everything at the same time. This place is neither up nor down; it is only here, in the "now".

The Illiterate of the 21st Century

Unlearning is more important than learning. The illiterate of the 21st Century will not be those who cannot read or write, but will be those who choose not to unlearn. A closed mind is limited, and cannot know anything. Open-mindedness is required to attain the limitless. For most of us, learning means the accumulation of knowledge, experience, technology, a new skill, or a new language. It is not this unlearning that I talk about. I talk about our psychological learning, our conditioning, and our beliefs, and it is these that need to be undone. Your cup is over overflowing with darkness, fears, needs, demands, expectations, ambitions, and conquering of all sorts. It is time to empty the cup. Until you do, there will be no space for stillness, for silence, and for light to enter.

The illiterate of the 21st Century will not be those who cannot read or write, but will be those who choose not to unlearn.

The most difficult task of all for you to learn is to just "be" in your inner Being. This is true wisdom, which is possible only when there is no coercion of any kind, no attachments, no influences, no threats, no persuasive arguments, or subtle rewards sought. Wisdom is something that will be experienced by each one of us in our own way, and in our own time. It is not the result of learning anything. You will come to know true wisdom. You will come to know that it does not come from you, but through you. True wisdom only comes when there is Self-knowing. There can be no wisdom without first knowing thyself. This means that the "you" who you think you are must be left behind, and you can only do that in the present, in the here and now. The real you will then come to the fore and you will know all wisdom that there is to know.

Breaking Bad Habits

Living in the past is a bad habit, and you must break that to set yourself free. We relive the past over and over again, first in our minds and then in our lives. The present is never experienced as the present because we drag the past into it. Our future is really our past, it is just that we have not experienced it yet, but we still drag that into the present also. So if you look very carefully at your life and at time itself, you are always primarily living in the past. We think that every day is a new day. This is the illusion of living, because every day is a day that you are reliving the past. This is a bad habit that you must look at and deal with sooner rather than later. You will never be free until you break this bad habit.

Yes, there may be new opportunities arising, new people coming into our lives, new adventures, and new relationships and so on. However, if you look very closely, you may ask, "Is anything really changing?" There is no freedom at all without freedom from the past, because the ego mind is reliving the same scenarios over and over again. We think freedom comes from understanding.

We may say, "if only I could understand things a little better, then life would not be so bad" or "If I could understand my partner, my life would be better", and so on. However, there is nothing really new, nothing fresh and inspiring; it is the same old patterns wrapped up in different paper, repeating themselves over and over again. These are all bad habits, and they are not any different from smoking, drinking or taking drugs.

True freedom comes from a free mind, not a mind full of ideas and concepts. A free mind is a mind void of ideas, thoughts and concepts; it is free from past mistakes and errors and free from future fears and doubts. It is free to live and express love in any way that it feels right to do so. The forming of habits that we relive over and over again leads to conditioning. Good habits and bad habits are really all the same

When you fight a particular habit, you give life to that habit and soon the very fighting becomes a further habit.

as they are the conditioning of an image you have about yourself- an ego self-image.

When we learn that some of our habits are bad for us, such as smoking, we then set about ways to break that habit through resistance or force. Smoking only becomes a problem when you want to stop smoking. It is never a problem as long as you enjoy it. So you say, "I am a smoker, and now I want to be a non-smoker". You think that re-labeling an act will suffice in undoing the act itself. In fact, this process of anti-anything gives longevity to the act itself. Yes, you may become a non-smoker.

However, you will have an inner conflict, possibly for the rest of your life, because you still remain attached to the act by the label you have sanctioned it with. To resist, fight or deny habits such as smoking, only gives energy and continuity to the habit. When you fight a particular habit, you give life to that habit and soon the very fighting becomes a further habit. Now you have developed a habit of fighting habits. Thus, nothing has changed, as you have simply swapped one habit for another habit.

Something interesting then happens; you begin to reflect and think about this quitting process, and you discover that at the very least, the original habit gave you something. It gave you a false sense of pleasure in some way. So you say to yourself, "I was better off smoking in the first place, because it is torture trying to stop". Now you have come up with an ingenious way out! You say to yourself, "Sure I can try again in a few months", while knowing that you have no intention of putting yourself through that torture ever again.

It is important to fully grasp that the mind that has created the problem can never be the mind that solves the problem. All habits are framed in an unconscious mind-set, which is the ego self-image. As long as the mind is breaking down one habit, it is also creating another in that very process. However, when you avoid using force or resistance, you enter a new mind-set that is without judgment.

You now become attentive from moment to moment as an Observer, and when you view the habit, you will see the truth of what is. For example, the urge to smoke will cease when you can observe the feeling that you need a smoke. You will always want a smoke when you refuse to deal with an issue that is in your mind. That is the fuel that fuels the urge to smoke. However, if you do not name that urge or the feeling that you are experiencing, you can look at it more clearly, embrace it, and you will have quite a different relationship to it now. It is the attachment to the feeling that is difficult to give up; not the actual habit itself.

If you do not name and label the habits you have formed, you will have a different experience. But if you name a habit, you now become attached to the name or label, and in so doing, you separate the feeling from yourself. It is words and symbols that separate us from each other. Try not to put a name or label to any emotion you experience because if you do not label it, you will have a quite a different experience.

Once you label something, like a feeling or a habit, you give continuity to the feeling, which in turn gives continuity to the act itself. Look directly at the act, without labels, without judgment, and you will experience a new sensation regarding the act itself. It is important to reiterate that the habit must not be labeled, named or its effects judged as good or bad, or, right or wrong.

Do not judge yourself or others because of the habit, instead, just look at it from a non-judgmental point of view. By doing this regularly you remove the energy from the habit, which is really only a thought. It is the energy that you give your thoughts that gives them power over you, and not the other way around. No habit has power over you, unless you give it the power to do so.

Going Beyond Words

The Course says, "*...words are but symbols of symbols. They are thus twice removed from reality*".[1] Words are the expression of thoughts, and thoughts are the expression of images and symbols; both are outside of reality. I think it is necessary that we should not be trapped by words if we are to understand each other. For example, a word such as "God" may have a particular meaning for you, while for me it may represent a totally different meaning.

So unless both of us take the same meaning from the words being used, there will be confusion regarding what is being said.

It is this judgment that keeps the experience of God out of awareness. In truth, God is beyond all words, thoughts and symbols.

There is an experience behind each word that is written and spoken. You will be able to access that very experience if you can lay all judgment aside while reading or listening. Words, images and symbols will not matter anymore once you have the experience, and there within that experience, there will be no separation whatsoever because the experience will be the same for everyone.

For example, when I use the word "God", you will have your own judgment regarding who or what God is. It is this judgment that keeps the experience of God out of awareness. In truth, God is beyond all words, thoughts and symbols. Once you use a word of any description to describe God, you will lose the experience itself. All thoughts, symbols and words cover up the truth of reality. It is beyond these that you will have the experience itself.

When I use the phrase, "the truth shall set you free", you may think that I mean "free from something", such as free from pain or suffering, free from fear and guilt, free from anger, hate, envy or jealousy. What I truly mean is free from all beliefs associated with the above emotions and feelings. It is only our belief in hate, anger, fear, guilt etc. that gives them their continuity. We use thoughts and words to give longevity and extension to our beliefs in them. The process of recognition is through the use of words, and the moment we recognize the feeling through

World peace begins with you. Seek peace in your mind, and then peace will be seen in a peaceful world.

the word, we give continuity to the belief in something.

All countries, all social structures of society, and all individuals have their very own conditioning as to who God is. It is this individual conditioning, with the use of words and symbols, that keeps us separate from each other, which in turn keeps us separate from God. As long as we, as individuals, remain separate from each other, we will remain in a state of internal conflict that will be projected out into the world, and there, we will be witnesses to the states of our own internal war. We then try and fix and change these projections in the external world.

We must first begin to change our minds about the world, rather than keep trying to change the world. The change we seek must first begin within ourselves, and then you will see that very change projected out into the world. World peace begins with you. Seek peace in your mind, and then peace will be seen in a peaceful world. The biggest error that our educators have failed to learn is that true change begins with the individual, not with the masses. Because we all feel so small and insignificant, we may be inclined to think that it does not really matter if we say or do anything. We always think, "someone else will say or do it". That is the biggest error of all.

If you drop a little stone into a big pond, the ripples of that stone will have an effect on the entire pond itself. Every great change in this world has had its seeds in just one person's ability to look at things differently. There is a way to live in this world, and not be of this world. If you can accept this fact without analyzing it, without bringing all of your past conditioning into it, then you have moved beyond all thoughts, words and symbols.

Once you analyze something in order to understand it, you destroy your capability to experience it. To free the mind from all conditioning, you must see the totality of it without thought. You believe that to see anything, you need words and symbols, and that you need eyes to name it and a mind to understand it. But the truth is that you don't need eyes to see; you need vision.

True vision is the full awareness of seeing, and it is beyond labels, names and thoughts. It is totally without judgment of any kind. To free the mind from all conditioning of symbols and images, you must see the totality of it without thought. To wake up is to be conscious... there in that place you are free. You are free from all conditioning, free from all beliefs, free from all thoughts, free from all images and free from all symbols. Do not try to fight the beliefs, by naming them as right or wrong, good or bad. Accept them as they are. Become the Observer and it is there that you will be free.

Open-Mindedness

An open mind is a mind that is capable of knowing everything there is to know. A man that can say, "I don't know what anything is for", is a wise man indeed, but a man that says, "I know that already", will never be capable of true knowledge and wisdom. There are those who are rich and have accumulated vast amounts of "human knowledge". They think they know everything that there is to know; those are poor indeed. True knowledge comes from experiencing and not from learning in books or within libraries. True knowledge and wisdom cannot be accumulated through study and practice, or given by one to another.

Any attempt to bring this knowledge into words and symbols destroys its purity, its richness, and its uncontaminated cleanliness. When you reach a state of mind that says, "I don't know anything", you have reached the level of humility for knowing everything; not learning everything, but knowing everything. There is no arrogance of self-knowing when you reach this state of mind, and there are few indeed who get to this point. When you can say with all your heart, "I don't know", all conditioning will have ended, all past alliances to beliefs will have been broken, and all past associations of rights and wrongs will have now gone away.

In addition, all memories of sins committed, guilt amassed and fears collected will have evaporated. Here, in this new state of mind, a newness of knowing will come like a gentle soft breeze, and encompass your very being with wisdom and knowledge that is out of this world. This is a mind that has attained full awareness.

Awareness

Awareness just is, it is an awakened state of mind that has a presence on each of the five different levels of consciousness. It is an ever-ready state of consciousness that can only be accessed but can never be learned or disciplined. If you try to learn awareness you are making it into a project of understanding.

Awareness cannot be understood, it can only be experienced.

Awareness cannot be understood, it can only be experienced. Believing awareness can be understood through learning only leads to internal conflict, which becomes a daily struggle and a lengthy battle. Because awareness is outside of the ego self-image that you hold as your identity, the ego will resist all your efforts to attain awareness.

The ego itself will do everything it can to keep you from experiencing something other than itself. All learning is specific learning, but true awareness is non-specific, it is abstract. To try and cultivate awareness through learning is to be specific, which is not compatible with true awareness. Awareness knows. Awareness is a mind that is fully without judgment.

You can only become one with a tree when you look at a tree without judgment, without naming it, or without labeling it. You can become one with birds and animals when you can look at them without judgment that they are birds or animals. In the diagram "States of Awareness", you will see how Awareness opens the door upwards for consciousness to follow. Consciousness needs Awareness to manifest within itself.

You set it apart from yourself as something different. True awareness sees no differences, no division and no separation of anything from

In awareness you will see that the problem you thought was a problem is not the problem. The problem was in your belief that you had a problem.

anything else, or anyone from anyone else. True awareness is a state of mind that encompasses everything as everything. Awareness undoes fragmentation as it unites you in oneness with unity. It is an un-limiting and unlimited seeing of everything as everything. It is the awareness of the totality of your very being at one with everyone and everything. Awareness and problem solving are exactly the same. You silently observe the problem without judgment, without condemnation, without trying to see the cause and without searching for a solution.

Problems only come into being when you cannot find a solution. In awareness you will see that the problem you thought was a problem is not the problem. The problem was in your belief that you had a problem.

It is through awareness that great understanding will come, but only to a mind that is not seeking understanding in the first place. Seeking or searching anything from awareness will inhibit the experience of achieving awareness. Awareness is an act of love; it is an act of looking and seeing everything as love. Love and judgment cannot co-exist; it is one or the other. Where there is judgment, there can never be love. Similarly, where there is love, there can never be judgment.

STATES OF AWARENESS

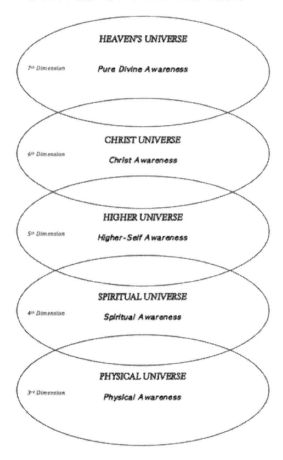

The Pursuit of Happiness

If we are truly honest with ourselves, the one thing we seek most in life is happiness. We know by now that happiness comes from a mind at peace. So we search for this elusive peace of mind to find that everlasting joy in life. We search and search, going from one place to another, from one person to another, from one religious organization to another, from one spiritual teaching to another; all in search of that elusive thing called peace of mind. So, where is it? Does that state of mind really exist in a world filled with conflict, hate and anger? There is a huge difference between inner peace and outer peace. The attainment of outer peace depends on conditions external to you being met in the right way. You have no control over such events, and you are deluding yourself if you believe that you have control.

Yes, rare as it really is, you may find that peace every so often. But you will know by now that external happiness does not last; it is a temporary condition that is fleeting in time. External happiness is a by-product of the many seeming situations coming together at the same time, leaving an instant when you can enjoy that moment of joy.

However, internal happiness is quite another matter. You have real power to achieve internal happiness. Many believe that happiness comes when you get everything that you desire, just the way you desire it. If I can just get the car I want, I will be happy. If I can just get the house, the beautiful woman, the fine clothes... if I can just amass enough money in the bank, I can sit back and enjoy life, and I will be happy. These are the conditions we set for ourselves for the attainment of peace and happiness in our lives. So we set out in life to achieve all of these things, because we believe that the happiness they bring us will give us the peace we strive for.

However, there is a problem with this concept of attaining; when we don't get things just the way we want, we now automatically become unhappy. We associate getting what we want with happiness, and we associate not getting what we want with unhappiness. And because in this world we will never get everything our way all of the time, we will never be happy all of the time, in fact, we will be unhappy most of the time. And if we are unhappy, how can we attain peace of mind?

Unhappiness in the world is not confined to the poor alone, the rich also fall into this same trap of getting and not getting happiness and unhappiness. There is always something missing no matter how much money you have. Is this not true? We seek happiness in many things: in relationships, in our family life, in material things, in spirituality, in religion, in money and in other various places and ways. And, for a while, we feel that we are happy. This is not what happiness is. This happiness from getting what you want is material happiness.

There is a big difference between material happiness and true happiness. We are seeking material happiness when we seek happiness in someone or something external to ourselves. Material happiness will always come to an end because it is an illusion of happiness. And all illusions being nothing in themselves will reveal their nothingness sooner or later. In time you will see through the illusion of happiness you invested in

200

and then you will begin the search once again to seek happiness in some other external thing. This can and will become so frustrating that you will lose peace of mind over and over again, because external happiness simply does not exist. It is always temporary, and will always end!

The problem is not in the seeking of happiness. The problem is "who" is seeking the happiness? Personal identification must be aligned before any further pursuits take place. The "you" who is seeking is really not you. It is an ego self-image that you have identified yourself to be. It is only the ego self that is seeking something greater

> *The ego is a thought of conflict; it is a mind at war with itself.*
>
>

than what it is; it being nothing, it is seeking to become something. And it is really frightening for the ego self to look inside. So it will always set its focus on the external. The ego self relies only on the external gifts of this world for its identity. Its motto is "seek and never find". And it really does not matter if you find it or not, because either way, the ego wins. It wins by your searching and attaining, albeit temporarily, and it also wins when you fail to find it.

Either way, you energize the ego self when you identify with it in your search. It is only when you drop the ego self-image that true peace and true happiness is attained. Peace, joy and love are a contradiction in terms when you associate them with the ego self-image, because it is the ego itself that can never enter a mind that is at peace; a mind with joy and love. The ego is everything that true peace, joy and love is not. It is your ego identification that is the block to peace, joy and love.

True peace and true happiness come only from the absence of conflict. The ego is a thought of conflict; it is a mind at war with itself. When you become the Observer of this conflict, observe it without judgment, without condemnation and without naming it in any way, and the war will end. All conflict will dissolve and dissipate in that space because you have now stepped outside the ego self and you are observing it. You cannot be the ego itself if you are the Observer of the ego. This is why the ego keeps you looking outside yourself for happiness, peace, and that elusive thing called love.

The attainment of happiness in the external is an illusion. Your journey must begin by discerning your Self from your ego self. Happiness is an inside job, and it is never external. Happiness will automatically flow through your very being once you have transcended the ego self-image. You will feel a wave of bliss so intense that you will never believe that it could have been so near all of this time ... it always seemed so far away. In this place, you will experience a peace so divine, a joy so great, and a love so all encompassing, that you will never want to give this up again.

There is only one thing that stands between you and Heaven, it is the belief that you are separate, not only from all those around you in this world, but also from God. There have been many myths and stories about the fall of man, and how it was a disaster for all mankind that Adam ate an apple. I never bought into the religious stories about how man betrayed God, I never believed it, and that is also one of the main reason I left religion so young.

So what is the real truth regarding our fall from grace, and what were the true circumstances? To give you the answer I am going to give you four versions of the separation, and you are free to choose which one you like. However, be careful, there is a real sting in the tail at the very end of this next chapter. Keep an open mind as you go, and you will not fall into the trap of the ego, because the ego is very close-minded when it comes to its belief about itself.

CHAPTER 7

~ ~ ~

The Separation

Not many people know or even care about the topic of "the separation" or the "fall of man". However, this is probably one of the most important concepts for you to try to understand if you wish to make spiritual progress. Everything you think, feel, say and do comes from the concept of man separating from God. There will be two books that I will refer to as we discuss the separation, and in each book there are two versions. One book is The Bible and the other is *A Course in Miracles*. Let us start with the two versions in the Bible first. I want to take a very general approach to each of these versions in religion, so please do not hold me to ransom with this story.

ADAM AND EVE
– First Version of the Separation

According to the Bible, God created Adam as his only Son. He was the first man who was created and he was very special.

He was created 'in the image' of God Himself, and God placed Adam in the beautiful Garden of Eden. In the garden there were beautiful trees with delicious fruit and everything that Adam would need to eat. Right in the middle of the garden there were two trees, the tree of life and the tree of the knowledge of good and evil. God told Adam that he was free to eat from any tree in the garden, but he must not eat from the tree of knowledge of good and evil, for if he did he would surely die.

After some time, God saw that Adam was all alone in the garden with no one for company, so God put Adam into a deep sleep and took one of his ribs and formed it into a woman to be Adam's wife. Adam named her Eve. Also, around this time, God created many animals to live in the garden with Adam and Eve.

Of all the animals God created, the serpent was the most cunning and deceitful. One day, the serpent came to Eve and asked her why would God not allow her to eat fruit from the tree of knowledge? When Eve responded that God had warned her and Adam that if they ate from that tree they would die, the serpent said, "That's a lie!" The serpent then insisted to Eve that if she ate from that tree she wouldn't die, but instead, she would become like God himself. Eve looked at the fruit on the tree of knowledge and saw that it looked fresh and delicious. She thought the fruit would make her wise like the serpent said it would. Eve was convinced. She picked the fruit and ate it, and she then gave some to Adam to eat too.

However, the fruit did not make Adam or Eve very wise, but they did realize for the first time that they were not wearing any clothes! For the first time they felt naked and ashamed and so they covered themselves with fig leaves. Adam and Eve were so ashamed about what they had done that they were afraid to face God, so they hid in the trees. But God knew they had eaten the forbidden fruit.

When God questioned them about what they had done, Adam tried to put the blame on Eve, and Eve tried to put the blame on the serpent, but God was angry with all three of them! And so, the story goes, God punished the serpent by cursing its kind and condemning all serpents to forever crawl on their bellies in the dust and be enemies of mankind. God then turned to Adam and Eve and punished each of them as well. But He didn't stop there, He proceeded to punish all of mankind when He declared that Adam and Eve and all of their descendants would be condemned to a life of pain, suffering and death.

No longer would Adam, Eve and their future children be able to live in the perfect world of the Garden of Eden. Men would have to struggle and sweat for their existence while women would have to bear children in pain and be ruled over by their husbands. Adam and Eve were then thrown out of the beautiful Garden of Eden forever.

The Bible tells us that this story really happened and it also tells us that we are all cursed because of the sins of Adam and Eve. According to this bible story we all live with this original sin from the Garden of Eden. So that means that every ounce of suffering that we have ever experienced originated from this point in history and we are all cursed under this spell of original sin, which was perpetrated by God. So, what does the story in the Bible make of God? If this were true, it would make God a vindictive, wrathful, vengeful, and judgmental God who should be feared. Fortunately, however, this story is simply not true, and like almost everything that organized religion has put forth, it is an illusion of the truth at best and downright lies and deceit at worst. This story was created by old religion to induce fear into an already frightened and condemned people, so that a very select few religious leaders could control the masses and extract great wealth at the same time.

THE PRODIGAL SON
– Second Version of the Separation

The second version of the story of separation that comes from the Bible is the story of the prodigal son. When Jesus related this story, he was telling us another version of the story of the separation. And so it goes that many years ago there was a wealthy man who had two sons. One day, his younger son asked his father for his inheritance. His son had only recently reached adulthood and so the father agreed to his request.

The younger son then left for far off pastures new and green. After a few short years, and after wasting his fortune during a devastating famine, the son found himself so destitute that he had to take a job tending pigs. He was so hungry and broke that he began to eat the same food that he gave to the pigs to eat. He felt great shame at having once had so much and now finding himself with so little.

One day, as he was reminiscing about the good old days, the thought came to him that when he lived at home with his father even his father's servants were better fed and had better living conditions than he currently did. After much consideration, and knowing that his relationship with his father might be permanently severed, he made the decision to return home. He was determined to beg his father for forgiveness and to tell him how repentant he was for not appreciating what he had and for squandering what he had been given.

He hoped that perhaps his father would take pity on him and agree to give him a job as one of his hired servants. He started his journey back home and, to his great surprise and amazement, he noticed that when his father recognized him in the distance he was overcome with joy.

In this story, Jesus clearly exonerates us from the Garden of Eden's story of sin, guilt, fear, punishment, and shame, and also, by the way, exonerates God as a vengeful, wrathful and judgmental supreme Being.

His father ran to meet him with great jubilation and immediately welcomed him back as his son. He then held a great feast to celebrate his return, which included killing a fattened calf, usually reserved for special occasions.

The older son refused to participate stating that in all the time he had worked for the father he never disobeyed him and yet, he did not even receive a goat to celebrate with his friends. The father then reminded the older son that he had always been with him and everything the father had also belonged to him.

But, they should still celebrate the return of the younger son because he was lost and was now found.

The story of the lost son in the bible is a story for all of us and it is meant as a metaphor for our journey back home to God. In this story, Jesus clearly exonerates us from the Garden of Eden's story of sin, guilt, fear, punishment, and shame, and also, by the way, exonerates God as a vengeful, wrathful and judgmental supreme Being. The other important message in this story is that we all have come from heaven, from great wealth, and we can claim our inheritance anytime we choose.

The fear of God is the only thing that stands in our way, and that fear comes from the Bible's story of sin, guilt and fear. In this parable, Jesus is unmistakably telling us that there is nothing to fear and that God is waiting to warmly welcome us home anytime we choose. Jesus related this version in a parable so as to not agitate the Pharisees, the religious leaders of the day. What Jesus was teaching with the parable of the prodigal son would have been deemed blasphemous if the religious leaders became aware of the true meaning within this story that was told two thousand years ago.

There are two other versions of the story of separation that have come into awareness just in more recent years. These versions can be found in *A Course in Miracles*. The stories that Jesus tells us in *A Course in Miracles* are just a little bit more sophisticated and complicated. You see, two thousand years ago, most of mankind was not schooled well enough to understand physics, let alone metaphysics, and no one had ever heard of the concept of the ego. It was not until Freud brought the ego into

210

awareness, over a hundred years ago, that we developed a much deeper understanding of the mind and its inner workings. So let's tell this story again from the point of view of a 21st century intellectual scholar who is a student of *The Course.*

THE TINY MAD IDEA
– Third Version of the Separation

Early on, *The Course* points out that, *"...the Bible says that a deep sleep fell upon Adam, and nowhere is there reference to his waking up".*[1] And that is the biggest clue of all and the purpose of this book: *it is time to wake up! A Course in Miracles* tells us two other stories about how the separation seemed to have occurred.

The story of the tiny mad idea is the first version. In this first version, *The Course* tells us, we were all one with God in Heaven and one day we had a thought that there could be something else other than Heaven. The moment that thought came into our mind, we fell asleep as one and began to dream a dream that was not real. In that dream we heard a voice tell us that we should be the boss, and that God was a tyrant and should stand aside and let us rule Heaven.

That voice we heard was the voice of the ego. So we approached God and requested that we should now rule Heaven and that he should stand aside. And, of course, that request was turned down. Remember this is still in the dream, this really did not happen, but somewhere deep inside us, we believe that it really did.

So, back to the dream, where we believe that we had an argument with God about who should be the boss of Heaven. The voice in our mind, which was the ego's voice, told us that we should be the boss and that we should not accept 'no' as an answer. In the dream we believed that we really did have an argument with God, and so when God would not give us what we wanted, like a spoiled child we said, "stuff you, I am going to create my own world where I will be the boss". And in that same instant we made our first judgment, and the separation seemed to become real for us in our minds.

Remember that what you judge, you reject, and everything you reject is a part of yourself. Once we made a judgment about God and Heaven that meant that we rejected both and in that same instant we also seemed to reject our true Self. We were then propelled seemingly outside the Oneness of Heaven and into separation on the sixth dimension.

Heaven is a state of Oneness, and when you reject any part of it, you reject all of it. That being the case, we are a part of that Oneness, and so when we rejected God we also rejected our true Self that God created. We became the separated self. So, we left the top level, which is the seventh Dimension, and descended into the sixth Dimension. Remember we are all still one with each other at this point. If you look at the diagram "The Separation", you will see that I have called us "*The Separated Self*". Another important point to make here is that every time we drop down a level, we have no memory of the level above that we just came from. So when we arrived on level six, we became totally lost, and, for the first time, we were on our own, and this was not a very nice experience.

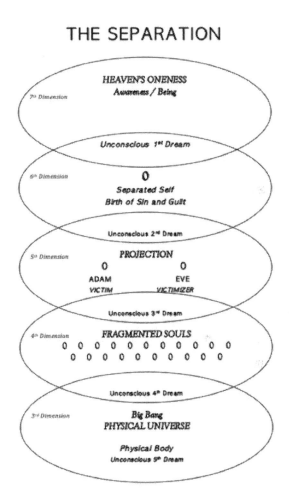

At this point I should make something else very clear here: it is the ego that put that thought in our mind, and it is the ego that wants to be god, but it needs our power to do that. And so the ego's true intention is to deceive us, lead us astray, and use our power for it to become a god in its own right. That is exactly what it achieved - the wrathful, vengeful, fearful and judgmental god that you read about in the Bible is the ego's god. Once we listened to the ego's thought this event came to represent the birthplace of sin, guilt and fear.

The Birth of Sin, Guilt and Fear

To be taken out of the bliss of Heaven and be cast out into the wilderness and abandoned into the darkness of separation was sheer terror for us to experience. At this moment, sin, guilt and fear came into our awareness and it was too much of a horrible experience for us to bear. It was then that we heard the ego in our minds once again. And the ego chastised us for what we seemed to have just done by making us believe something to the effect of, "You should feel ashamed of yourself for what you did to God. All God ever did was love you, and now you have spat in His face and destroyed Heaven. If Heaven is a state of Oneness then you have destroyed Heaven because you are no longer one with God." In that moment, feeling those thoughts of condemnation from the ego was like a bullet to our hearts because those thoughts destroyed us. Also in that moment, by believing the thoughts of the ego, we accepted guilt into our minds and thus we descended further into the dream of separation that we now believed to be real.

214

This is just so typical of how the ego works. The ego will get you to say something cruel to someone and then it will riddle you with guilt for saying what *it* prompted you to say in the first place. For example, the ego might put the thought in your mind to make fun of someone who is less well off than or different from you, then, after a while, the ego will tell you that you are not very nice for making fun of that poor innocent person who has endured a difficult circumstance because they may not fit in as well with others, and thus the guilt will set in.

> *But know that where guilt truly originates from is from the point in time when you listened to the ego for the first time telling you that you were guilty for sinning against God by choosing to separate from Him.*

We all have fallen into this trap, and a few of us on more than one occasion. You may judge people for being too fat, too thin, an intellectual, an idiot, a bully or a wimp, etcetera. But either way, as long as we listen to these thoughts of the ego, you will believe that they are your thoughts and you will go into judgment.

The ego will never let you forget just what a horrible person you are. But know that where the guilt truly originates from is from the point in time when you listened to the ego for the first time telling you that you were guilty for sinning against God by choosing to separate from Him. And today, the ego continues to play the same old trick of sin, guilt and fear.

Going back to the story of the tiny mad idea, as mentioned earlier, once we accepted guilt into our minds, it was at this point that the separation became real for us. We now felt so sinful because we believed that we had betrayed God, just like the ego said, by choosing to walk out of Heaven and separating from Him. Therefore, because of that perceived sin, we also felt enormous guilt. Our true motivation for leaving Heaven was our quest for specialness. Because specialness is relative, when you have Oneness everything is the same and nothing can be more special than the rest. Therefore, herein lies the conundrum, to feel special you have to separate yourself from everyone else, but when you separate you destroy Oneness, and so you cannot have specialness without guilt being attached to it. To extrapolate further, the effect of guilt is fear, and so now we also had tremendous fear to contend with. Every sense of sin, guilt and fear that you have ever experienced in this world has its origins here at this moment in time. These beliefs all stem from the belief that this really happened. Hence, the belief in separation is the true cause of all conflict in our minds.

Listening to those devastating words from the ego saying that the Son of God had destroyed Heaven and abandoned God, the sense of sin, guilt and fear that this caused was too much for the separated self, Adam, to bear. And so the voice in his mind came to his "rescue" once again, the ego's voice that is; the voice of selfish desire. Keep in mind that at this point, this was the only voice that we could hear because he had already chosen to believe that he had separated from God, and so he had rejected God's voice. It is the same for everyone today, and as long we choose to listen to the voice of the ego, we will not hear the voice of God. The ego then tells Adam that he will be put to sleep once again and when he wakes up all his sense of sin, guilt and fear will be gone. So Adam agrees, and goes back to sleep.

The 5th Dimension

Adam now awakens, within the dream, in the fifth Dimension, and has found himself split into two. Just like in the Bible story when God takes a rib from Adam and makes it into Eve, in the story of the tiny mad idea, one becomes two. But in this story it was the ego that made Adam into Adam and Eve, not God. So what has happened is this, Adam is now projecting his sense of sin and guilt onto Eve, which is really just another part of himself. This is the birthplace of projection.

Adam now wakes up and has no sense of sin or guilt because he was able to rid himself of it by using the ego's tool called projection. He feels that now he is innocent of any crime and sees that it is Eve who is the guilty person. That is what projection does, it sees the sin and guilt in someone else, and leaves the perceiver with this sense of being innocent. If you look closely at the Bible's story projection is in there also. When God asks Adam why he ate the apple, he used projection and blamed Eve. When God then asked Eve why she tempted Adam with the apple, Eve also used projection and blamed the serpent. Every time you blame anyone else for anything you are using projection.

At this level of the fifth dimension there is still a problem however, and Adam does not like it because this is still causing him to feel fear. He has gotten rid of the sense of sin and guilt, but the sense of fear is still with him. You see, every time you project guilt onto someone it is an attack, and when you attack anyone it will leave you in a state of fear because you will fear retaliation.

It is the same in this world today, every time you project onto someone and say that they are sinful or guilty of anything, sooner or later, you will end up in a state of fear because you will unconsciously know that you have attacked them and you will fear their retaliation. There are no exceptions to this rule. Alternatively, if you never projected

> *Every time you project guilt onto someone it is an attack, and when you attack anyone it will leave you in a state of fear because you will fear retaliation.*

your guilt onto anyone, you would never ever feel afraid of anything, and I mean anything! You would be in a state of complete fearlessness, which is also the state of bliss. And now Adam was in a horrible state of fear because of this seeming attack/projection onto Eve. So Adam turns to the ego once more to fix the problem.

The 4ᵗʰ Dimension

The problem in the fifth dimension was that there was only Adam and Eve. So each could only project onto each other, and then, after a while, this would not work because both would have gotten fed up and would say to each other, let's go home and say sorry to God.

But the ego also has a very clever and cunning plan, and that is to get Adam, and now Eve, as far away as possible from Heaven and God. So now the ego puts both, Adam and Eve, back to sleep once more. And the fall of man continues as Adam and Eve wake up in the fourth dimension. The difference between the fourth dimension and the fifth dimension is that now there are more than the two of them. Each has fragmented

> *Another way of thinking of this would be to see this as the birthplace of the persona and the shadow, or the emergence of the concept of the Yin and the Yang.*
>
>

into billions and billions of seemingly different souls and entities. This is the birth of the Spiritual Universe or the fourth dimension.

To recap the story so far, the first split was when we seemed to leave the seventh dimension where we were in Oneness with God and entered into the sixth dimension where we took on a new identity called the separated self. In this place we were still in a state of unity with each other where we were all One, but wholly unconscious. Then the second split occurred within us as we entered the fifth dimension and divided into two parts. One part of us was sinful and guilty and the other was peaceful and innocent. Another way of thinking of this would be to see this as the birthplace of the persona and the shadow, or the emergence of the concept of the Yin and the Yang. This is the true meaning of the Yin and Yang. The Yang is the white part, the perceived innocent part of us, but within its center you will notice the dark spot, that is our hidden guilt.

And the Yin is the dark part, and again at its center, you will notice a white spot, that is the innocence in other people that we want to hide when we project our guilt and darkness onto them. Both of these parts of ourselves are illusionary because we have made them up and they do not exist in reality.

We all want to be the Yang because we want to perceive ourselves as innocent, and that means that inside us is our hidden darkness. However, for us to be the Yang someone else must be the Yin and, therefore, we project our darkness onto others, and hide their innocence because we want it. We believe that to have innocence we must take it at another's expense. That is why everyone is so invested in seeing other people do guilty things, say guilty things and be guilty. Because if they are guilty, that means that we must be innocent. Our perceived innocence is an illusion, and our perceived guilt is also an illusion. Each of us has these two parts within us, and we also see these two parts in everyone else. These are the two rooms that we all carry with us. In one we have the persona that is everything we love in other people, and we secretly love in ourselves. And in the other we have the shadow that is everything we hate in other people, and that we also secretly hate in ourselves.

The 3ʳᵈ Dimension

Now we fall asleep for the last time, and in its crowning glory, the ego creates the physical universe. The ego now creates the physical world using the power of our One Mind to do so. The ego tells us that it will create a new world and that world will be just like Heaven. The ego falsely tells us that in this new "heaven" we will now be our own gods. The ego, using our own power to create, creates the big bang eruption out of nothing, and hey presto, the physical universe is created. So, then after billions of years, we emerge in a body and we will now call this body our home, and with this body we will create other bodies just like our own. In this illusion, we become self-creators, just like God, and we now begin to create ourselves over and over again, just like God.

However, the ego has another clever plan for itself. The ego knows that once we are born into the body we will have no memory of ourselves as spiritual beings, and that we will also have no memory of the agreement we had with the ego itself - in fact, we will have no memory of who we are or what we are. The agreement was that we would be gods in this brave new world, however, that is not to be the case because once we are born into our bodies the ego will now run the show in our minds for the rest of our lives.

The ego's voice in our minds now tells us the thoughts we think are out thoughts and that they belong to us. Hence, the ego crowns itself as god in our minds. The ego then invents itself in religion, writes the Bible and sets itself up as this new god who made heaven and earth. The god in the Bible is the ego god, who is judgmental, vengeful, hateful and who will strike you down for your bad deeds. However, the god in the Bible has nothing to do with the real God. So, now you have two Gods and two worlds. You have the god in the Bible that rules the world of separation and you also have the God of Heaven and the state of Oneness. Only one of these is real. It is your decision to choose one. One will bring you death, while the other will bring you eternal life. You are free to choose, but you are never free from the consequences of your choice.

If the third version of the story of separation of the tiny mad idea appeals to you, you can believe this version of events found in *The Course*. However, given that the origin of this version of the separation is rooted in guilt, where the Son of God made the mistake of wanting to know what else there was besides

> *You are free to choose, but you are never free from the consequences of your choice.*
>
>

Heaven and then challenges God and destroys Oneness by appearing to separate from God and its higher Self, then you will be seeing a lot of guilt around you. *The Course* very clearly tells us that this did not happen because it occurred only in a dream, that it could never occur in reality.

So far, we have looked at three versions of the story of separation, but there is another version of the separation in *The Course* that can help take you to another level of understanding and get you to the truth of what all life is really about in this physical experience. The fourth, and, for me, the truest version is as follows...

THE MEANING OF LIFE
– Fourth Version of the Separation

What if there was another version that lets us know that we really did not do anything wrong? What if there was no apple in the garden? What if there was no face off with God? And what if there was no fall from grace or from Heaven? What if we did not really seek specialness? And what if we did not really fall asleep?

What if the tiny mad idea occurred inside the dream? In fact, what if we were

Heaven cannot be found until you first become lost.

never awake to fall asleep? These are the questions one should be asking, because the answers to these questions will bring you the answers to the meaning of life: Who are we? Why are we here? How did we get here? Where are we going? How will we get there? All of these questions will be answered here.

Your higher Self cannot be found neither by searching for it, nor by understanding it. If it could be found, any ego could find it. Instead, you must lose your separated self first by becoming completely empty inside. Heaven cannot be found until you first become lost. In other words, "you" must become lost first, and then your higher Self will find you. This is how we wake up to the true reality of life!

You see, we have always been in Heaven, but we were just never aware of it. Our condition in God is akin to a fish living in water. The fish does not know it is in the water. There is no separation between the fish and the water and they live in a state of oneness. It is only when this union is broken that all hell breaks lose for the fish. It has been the same for us. We can choose, if we desire, to be the same as the fish; we can very easily attain a state of oneness with everyone and everything in this world, right here, right now.

It is just a state of mind, and when you are in this state of mind, even in this world, you will experience nothing but bliss. However, just like all hell breaks loose for the fish when it separates from the water, the same goes for us every time we seek outside ourselves. The moment we believe any thought that is not love, we smash our Oneness and all hell breaks loose. When the union of our Oneness with God seemed to break, our lives were propelled into a seeming hell. However this was not a mistake that we need to feel guilty about; instead, this was a very necessary occurrence, as you will shortly discover.

A fitting analogy for our seeming separation from God can be described as follows: An unborn child developing in its mother's womb does not know its inner or outer worlds. It does not know its creator - in this case, its creators being its physical mother and father - and it does not even know that it is a baby itself. The unborn child lives in a state of non-duality as it considers itself one with the mother in bliss.

Now, the only way that the child is going to grow and get to know itself and everything else in its life is to be born. To achieve this it must separate from its mother and experience itself outside of the womb. Once it separates, which is quite a harrowing time for the baby, it then learns who its mother and father are, it learns about itself, the world and everything else. The child did nothing wrong, there was no sin in the separation at birth, nor guilt after it does separate. The child goes to school to learn its lessons and all it needs to know.

This is very similar to what is happening to us in this physical experience in that we have done nothing wrong; there was no big sin perpetrated neither in the garden nor in Heaven, or even with God. In this fourth version of the separation, the silly story of the tiny mad idea of sin, guilt and fear in the third version above, was totally made up by us once we were already asleep in the first dream to convince ourselves that we were separate. We are simply being born and when we begin to wake up spiritually, it will be us literally being born into the state of Awareness from the state of Being. This is the meaning of life, this is why we are here, and where we are going is towards Awareness in Heaven. We are all moving into the state of Pure Awareness, just the same as that of our Creator.

So why did we have to separate to wake up? Let us look at it this way first: if we had not believed that we were separate and did wake up in Heaven, we would encounter some serious problems. These problems – too many to mention here –are highlighted and addressed in the concept of the tiny mad idea itself when we had the ridiculous idea that we somehow confronted, betrayed, or even disobeyed God.

Also, throughout the entire *Course* we are reminded of these problems; they are at the deepest level within the structures of *The Course* itself. If we were to wake up in Heaven, confusion would reign within us as to who God is. We are not God, but there is nothing within inside us that is not of God. If we had woken up in Heaven without knowing who we really were we would have made the mistake of thinking that we were God, and thus challenged God for the throne as the tiny mad idea suggests.

Additionally, if Heaven is a state of Oneness, we could never have known who we were when apart from God, because, well, it is a state of Oneness. Even though God is the Creator and we are the Created, there is nothing else that is different between us. In Heaven there is no consciousness

The meaning of life is transformation, not the story of sin, guilt and fear! Being is transcending itself in this transformation into Pure Awareness.

because, in a state of Oneness, consciousness is not required since there is nothing that is separate from anything else to be conscious off. So in Reality, we exist in a state of Being, which is a part of God who is Pure Awareness. This Pure Awareness has always existed, and in its extension, it created the state of Being, namely us. Being and Awareness are both states of Mind within the One Mind of God. Being is not aware of Awareness, although Awareness is fully aware of Being. This is what is going to change.

Being is moving into Awareness. Being is you not being aware of anything, although, you are in a state of bliss, just like a baby in a mother's womb, and this is how we have all existed to date. I say, "to date", because we are all just about to wake up from our life of pain and suffering and remember our state of bliss. Within that state of bliss we will then wake up into the higher state of Pure Awareness, which is Home!

The meaning of life is transformation, not the story of sin, guilt and fear! Being is transcending itself in this transformation into Pure Awareness. Now you know that whichever story you choose will take you down its own path to help you to wake up; you are free to choose one of the four stories

Homo sapiens evolved because of the introduction of the split mind that gave them the ability to differentiate between right and wrong, and good and evil.

of separation described herein to identify with, but you will not be free from the consequences of your choice!

The Age of Perfect Man

This is a monumental time in the evolution of mankind. The last big shift that occurred for mankind on his spiritual evolution occurred just over forty thousand years ago when Homo sapiens first appeared. There are seven stages of human spiritual evolution and Neanderthal man was the fifth stage, while Homo sapiens is the sixth stage today. What signaled the shift from the fifth stage to the sixth was that Homo sapiens evolved because of the introduction of the split mind that gave them the ability to differentiate between right and wrong, and good and evil. In *The Course* it says that God endowed his children with consciousness, which means that the two rooms of right and wrong and good and evil were introduced in our minds.

As I have already discuss, but will reiterate here, this event happened on earth around forty thousand yeas ago with the extinction of Neanderthal man and the emergence of Homo sapiens – Us. Neanderthal man only had one room in his mind. He was totally unconscious, which meant that in his mind he had absolutely no imagination. He could think but he could not reflect on what he thought about. This is because he did not know right from wrong, or good from bad. Neanderthal man had the same awareness as that of an animal, say a dog or a horse.

Today's modern man is moving into the seventh and final stage of spiritual evolution, which is referred to as the perfect age of man, the spiritual age. In 2048 we move out of the age of Jesus – Pisces – and into the Age of Aquarius – the age of light and truth. Mankind is waking up. As no mass awakening has occurred yet, the pieces are being put in place for this momentous event. Although it will begin in 2048, this event really kicks off at the end of this century 2100.

My point is that you have a choice: you are here to wake up and return home to the state of Heaven which is Oneness, or you can continue to return to this world over and over again to a life of fear and separation for as long as your heart desires. This is the only true free will we have, while all else is an illusion of free will. The only choice we have is to choose God and Oneness or the ego and separation. The former will bring you eternal bliss, while the latter will bring you only fear.

Know Thyself

Throughout *The Course* we are asked many times the question: "What am I?" In other words, we are told: "Know thyself". It is imperative that we come to know ourselves while we are in physical form because in Heaven we are in a state of Oneness where there is absolutely no way that we can do that. As mentioned earlier, if we had proceeded to wake up in Heaven first, we would have mistakenly believed that we were in fact God because there is no separation between God and us to know the difference.

As we have been created in the image of God (Spirit), and, as we are repeatedly told in *The Course*, there is absolutely nothing inside of us that is not of God, we would have actually believed that we were God, a problem that is referred to in *The Course* as the authority problem. To address this problem before waking up in Heaven, we have to come to know ourselves first. The authority problem is just as rife in this world today as it was thousands of years ago. However, the authority problem is not with God, but rather, it is us that has a very serious authority problem with each other.

As long as we continue to see each other as separate, and as long as we continue to judge each other as to who is right or wrong, and who is good or evil, we will always be in conflict with each other. This means that as long as we allow each other to starve to death we have an authority problem. In fact, as long as we continue to kill each other over land, oil, religious beliefs, and many other differences, we will have an authority problem. However, if your journey is to wake up in this lifetime, you are asked, as an individual, to solve this problem here. If you cannot, you will continue to return to physical form until you do.

Dreams Within Dreams

To come to know ourselves, we would have to lose ourselves, and the only way we could really do that would be in a series of dreams within dreams. Hence, the concept of the tiny mad idea came about. If there is nothing outside of Heaven, and nothing else exists, we would have to dream an entire story of a world of separation and a story to go with it. We needed to not only dream it, but it was imperative that we would believe it. There was only one way that we were going to believe such a story, and that is through pain. Pain will make you believe any story in your mind, and it is this pain that convinces us that this story of separation is truly real. In addition, there would be another problem if we woke up in Heaven first...

Sooner or later, as *The Course* tells us, we would have had this thought: Is there something else other than Heaven? If that is the case and we did not experience everything that Heaven is not first, then it would have been too late. Once we wake up, that is it. It is Heaven for eternity and there is nothing you can do about it. Therefore, we needed to address this problem as well. In the dream we will experience everything that Heaven is not until the day comes when we want to experience nothing else but Heaven.

If Heaven represents a state of unconditional love, then the love in this world would be conditional. If Heaven represents perfect Oneness, then in this world there would be separation. If Heaven represents the state of eternal bliss, then this world would be eternal fear. Therefore, it is not until even a single hair on your head wants nothing else other than Heaven that you will be ready to wake up.

> *If Heaven represents the state of eternal bliss, then this world would be eternal fear. Therefore, it is not until even a single hair on your head wants nothing else other than Heaven that you will be ready to wake up.*
>
>

Many will find life so difficult being separate, so fearful that they will think that they are ready to wake up, when in fact, they are just wanting to run away from the pain and suffering that being separate engenders. Therefore, a device would be required to make sure that no one wakes up before they are ready to. This device is the ego. The ego relentlessly tests each individual with every desire or idol that someone could ever become attached to. The name of the game for the ego is attachments, and the more attachments you have, the more the ego is in charge of your life. Undo attachments, and you begin to weaken the ego.

If Heaven is a state of shared Oneness, then the ego will be a thought system of selfish separation. No one will wake up until their heart makes the decision, not their intellect. The ego thought system itself will also be pre-programmed to wake up, and you, in a body, will be programmed by the ego in the ego thought system.

At some point in your evolution, you will have a calling to wake up, and the device known as the ego will be your mentor and teacher. It will test you over and over again until you want nothing else other than perfect peace, perfect happiness, and the perfect bliss that is rightly yours, for eternity. At first you will see the ego as a monster or the devil that is trying to destroy you, and therefore you may respond by attacking the ego to try to destroy it.

However, that is the last thing that you should do because what you resist you make stronger. Instead, you are asked to reinterpret the ego as a device that will help you and not hinder you. It is helping you by constantly showing you that every time you seek outside yourself you will experience pain because what is outside does not exist and pain tells you that what you are experiencing is simply not true. Like the ego, everything must be reinterpreted including pain. If you choose you can see pain not as a punishment, but rather as a safety device that tells you that you are outside of your center.

In other words, you are focusing either on the past or the future and you are simply not present. Pain and all that is of the ego must be reinterpreted through the emotion of love rather than fear, and as we are reminded in *The Course*, *"...you have but two emotions, love and fear."*[2] If you see the ego as a device that helps you rather than hinders you, you will have reinterpreted the ego from a thought system that terrorizes you, punishes you and enslaves you into one that is now your

232

teacher and mentor and that will help you and prepare you for your divine awakening.

The Three Objectives

Of the many choices we had to wake up, we chose the way of the ego. The ego is a device that we will use as a means to make us believe that we are separate from God, Heaven and our true Self so that we can eventually come to know ourselves. To "know thyself" would be one of our three primary objectives in our transformation from Being into Awareness. The following are the three objectives:

1 – Know Thyself

How would you come to know thyself? You would lose the identity of the true Self, and make a false self. Why? So that you will have a more profound knowing that you are not God after your experience as a separated self. In other words, you will be greatly humbled by your experience as a slave that lives in a body, within the ego thought system, that gets sick often and then eventually dies. This is how you are going to undo the authority problem you would have had if you did not know yourself before waking up in Heaven.

2 – Experience What Heaven Is Not

Our second objective for being in the physical world is to experience everything that Heaven is not. Why? Because God knows that nothing else exists, and we do not! The physical world enables us to experience everything that Heaven is not so that a more profound knowing of Heaven will arise within us thereby providing us with a greater knowing and appreciation of what Heaven is when we wake up. Heaven is a state of unconditional love, while in the physical world there is no love that is without ambivalence, which means that there is no love that does not contain hate. Only one of these loves is

No one will wake up until they transcend the ego by reinterpretation. Those who wish to attack and fight themselves with the ego are in for the long haul.

real and only one of these loves can fulfill us because it is what we truly are.

When we search outside of ourselves for love in the world we choose the ego and as long as this we do this we are denying the most unbelievable treasure, which is a state of pure bliss and unconditional love within us. Life is a choice, love is a choice, and Heaven is a choice. How do you choose Heaven? You simply say "no" to the pain that is conditional love because it will hurt you sooner or later. When we learn this and we understand that there is nothing else that we want in this world, we begin to empty our cup and the process of severing our attachments has begun so that we can achieve our goal of attaining complete emptiness. In other words, you are ready to wake up.

3 – Wake Up

Our third objective is to reach the point in the dream of separation where in our hearts we genuinely want nothing else other than Heaven; now we are ready to wake up. To make sure that you want nothing else the ego will be the device that tests those who think that they are ready to wake up. No one will wake up until they transcend the ego by reinterpretation. Those who wish to attack and fight themselves with the ego are in for the long haul. The ego will resist all attempts at waking up, until the student is ready, which means that as long as you remain attached to anything external to you, even your own body and its image, you will remain unconscious and asleep. This must be seen as a good thing rather than a bad thing, because the experience will be much too terrifying if one is not properly prepared for it. The ego will ensure that if you have any doubts about waking up, it will bring them into your awareness.

SUMMARY

In a contract that we have forgotten, we agreed to wake up and become co-creators with God. While we have always existed in a state of Being, we are now being born into Awareness. In other words, we are about to wake up for the first time in our existence. And so to ensure that this happens we first need to accomplish three objectives: To learn who we truly are, to learn what Heaven is not and to choose Heaven above all else. The way we will do this is by experiencing what it would be like if we could experience the impossible: to separate from God. Since it would be impossible for this to happen in Reality we need to experience this in a state that would be akin to having a series of dreams where we can experience the impossible as if it were real. And so our awakening process begins.

The seeming separation takes place under the laws of cause and effect. Once the first dream is initiated, everything else follows automatically. Once we go into the dream to experience the separation we incorporate into the dream the device called the ego. The ego is essentially a thought system that exemplifies the opposite of Heaven as it is based on sin, guilt and fear and its sole purpose is to take us as far away from Heaven as is possible by relentlessly making us believe that we are separate from God and our true higher Self. With the ego's help we then create our story to explain to ourselves why we would have possibly left our state of bliss so that we can cope with our new experience. Now, consider that the more guilty, fearful and painful the story is, the more guilty, fearful and painful the experience will be, which will make it seem more real and more unlike Heaven. And it has turned out that way exactly.

As mentioned, the first objective was to truly know ourselves and the way to truly know ourselves is to first lose ourselves by creating a false self that would become the manifestation of the ego's thought system of sin, guilt and fear. The pain and suffering that this false self would suffer would be our motivation to eventually find another way. Then, once we discover that this self is not who we are, we set about to dissolve this false self, and as we do, our true higher Self emerges characterized by a constant state of peace and unbreakable joy that encompasses our awareness in every moment. Similarly, on

236

the second objective, there was only one way we could experience everything that Heaven is not, which is to experience it in a dream since in Reality there is nothing else other than Heaven. To ensure that we will be satisfied with and value Heaven the dream affords us the illusion of pain and suffering in a way that feels so real that once we decide that we have had enough we can be sure that we will never question our choice for Heaven *ever*. The third and final objective was to wake up only once we genuinely want nothing else other than Heaven. To wake up it is necessary to consistently and irrevocably choose against the ego no matter how appealing and enticing its worldly treasures and attachments may appear. The ego is instrumental in this third objective by testing us until we become resolute in our decision for Heaven, which will ensure eternal peace.

In the Dream of Separation

The ego would create the story of sin, guilt and fear, and provide us with the tools to remain as a separated self, which is a choice that has remained unconscious to date. The dream route that we chose will seem to bring us all out of Heaven as one, then we will fragment and project ourselves into a world of separation. We will need a story to go with the separation, and the more painful the story, the more believable the dream will be for us. Hence, the Bible stepped forth with the first story, of Adam and Eve and the sin in the Garden of Eden.

This story worked, because for two thousand years, most of the western world fell for it, hook, line and sinker. This story completely dis-empowered millions of millions of people in the world to this day. However, it is time for the story to be retold. It did its job of convincing us that we have separated from God, and the guilt and fear that followed that story made it all very believable for all of us. However, in version two of the separation, the story of the prodigal son, most people are not aware that in this story Jesus is in fact talking about the separation. But knowing this, if one wishes to remain loyal to the Bible and its teachings then they can reinterpret the Adam and Eve story with the story of the prodigal son. This will help eliminate guilt within the lives of those who may be waiting in fear to be judged by a vengeful and wrathful God. What is the difference between the two versions? Immense guilt.

Similarly, it is the same scenario with those who are students of *A Course in Miracles*. What is the difference between versions three and four? Immense guilt is also the difference. In the third version the story of the tiny mad idea tells you that you have to rectify an enormous wrong that you seem to have made when you had thought that you could be better if you separated from God. Your only way to return home, if you choose this version, is by dedicating your life to finding and undoing the guilt that you have projected onto every person, every relationship, every circumstance and even onto yourself. In other words, if you are attached to the third version, you are attached to guilt and only by undoing the guilt you will return home.

This can be done, but however, in this state of mind, your life will be immersed in guilt because you will see guilt in everything and this is an unnecessarily painful approach to living in this world. The fourth version of the story offers a different approach. In the fourth version, there is no guilt, because the story tells us that the seeming separation is not due to a mistake you made but rather it was meant to be this way. It is a story that is good for you. It is good for you in many ways. You are literally witnessing your own birth as you wake up and this is really going to be an unbelievable experience. In this version you will simply be detaching from everything that you are attached to right now.

You will be spending a life attaining complete emptiness. It is really just as simple as this: everything that you react to, as good or

> *You are literally witnessing your own birth as you wake up and this is really going to be an unbelievable experience.*

bad, right or wrong, you are attached to. Once you identify this and take responsibility for *all* of your reactions then it is a simple case of undoing your attachments by reinterpreting good and bad, right and wrong into just the one concept of what is true and what is false.

None of the four versions of the separation are right or wrong nor good nor bad. Whichever version you identify with, that is the one that will be most helpful in your waking up process. However, there is still one more sting in the tail, as it is found in *The Course*. In lesson 189 of the workbook you are asked to do the following:

"Simply do this: Be still, and lay aside all thoughts of what you are and what God is; all concepts you have learned about the world; all images you hold about yourself. Empty your

mind of everything it thinks is either true or false, or good or bad, of every thought it judges worthy, and all the ideas of which it is ashamed. Hold onto nothing. Do not bring with you one thought the past has taught, nor one belief you ever learned before from anything. Forget this world, forget this course, and come with wholly empty hands unto your God."[3]

Every single concept, idea, and thought you ever had must be reinterpreted into the concept of either what is true or what is false, until not one is left. Then, the last concept that you will ever hold in your mind for relinquishment will be the concept of what is true and what is false. It will not be needed from then on because there will be nothing that is untrue or illusionary in your Awareness when you wake up in Heaven.

It is only when your mind attains complete emptiness that everything will be revealed to you. Every question that you have will be answered, but then again, you will have no questions because you will be everything and know everything. When you can attain this state of Mind the rewards are literally out of this world. Everything is a state of Mind, both Heaven and hell are not places that are here nor there, rather, both are a state of Mind that dwells within you. I assure you, know the Mind and you will know Heaven.

Heaven is a choice, as suffering is a choice. If you are suffering right now, it is always because you have chosen to suffer right now. If you disagree with this, then your suffering will continue. Why? Because you are playing the victim by thinking this suffering was created by someone or something else. If your thinking is not going to change, then your suffering is not going to change. So what is the root cause of all suffering in this world? In content it is the belief in separation and in form it is the belief that we are separate from each other. Your own everyday suffering begins with your refusal to take responsibility of *everything* in your life. You are creating your own suffering and you are doing this in several ways. But ultimately, if you want to put an end to it you must recognize and take responsibility for everything that you are experiencing. If you do not take responsibility and recognize the truth of your suffering, then the ego will jump up and down for joy, because the ego just loves and adores those who refuse to take one hundred percent responsibility for everything in their lives. You see, if you do not take responsibility you will continue to believe in the illusion that you are the victim and, therefore, there is nothing you can do about it.

CHAPTER 8

~~~

The Root Cause of All Suffering

If we are rigorously honest with ourselves, we will realize that we can be deeply miserable within, even though we may have obtained all of our worldly wants and needs: money, romantic relationships, cars, beautiful houses, jewelry, prestige, etc. Being miserable, we strive for happiness, and go blindly in search of this elusive happiness in various ways, via religion, spirituality, material comforts or by social means. But do we really understand why we feel the way we do? Why is it that we feel so miserable? Are we happy when we are not suffering? The answer has to be: "Yes, I am!" However, we are only happy that we are not suffering. Being happy that we are not suffering is not what true happiness is, despite the fact that we frequently appear to settle for this travesty of so called "happiness". Therefore, suffering always returns with a bang.

Much of the time we believe we suffer because things are not as we want them to be. For example, I would not be suffering if you just loved me the way I want, or if I won the lottery and

243

were able to buy everything I wanted, or if only I had this or I had that. You cannot buy happiness, you cannot own it, and you cannot get it. You can only uncover true happiness from within.

One day we all must realize that all suffering is self-created. That all suffering comes from our choosing to look out into the world, with demands, expectations, needs and desires. The cause of all of our personal suffering comes from seeking outside ourselves on a daily basis. When Jesus said, "lead us not into temptation", that is what he meant – *let us not seek outside ourselves.* Seeking outside ourselves is the very temptation that Jesus is referring to. Every time we seek outside ourselves we will suffer, period. I will suffer if my demands, expectations, needs and desires are not met, or I will make you suffer; it really does not matter to the ego who suffers, as long as someone does.

You may be suffering grief over the death of a loved one. You may be seeking answers and explanations over the circumstances of their death. You may be suffering because you expect justice, and you are demanding immediate punishment to be served. You want this pain to end, and believe that the answers you are seeking and the actions you expect will bring an end to your pain. Yes, they will bring relief from this suffering. However, if you ask someone who has gone through this process if it led to an end of suffering, their answer will usually be "no".

There is a good reason why you may get respite from suffering, but never get an end to it. One part of your mind wants answers and this requires that you keep reliving the experience in the hopes of finding the answers. All the while another part of your mind wants relief from that very suffering that you keep playing over in your mind. This form of suffering will never come to an end as long as your mind is split between both of these wants. Here is another spiritual insight: The mind that is searching for the answers to suffering, is the same mind that is creating the suffering.

Have you ever asked yourself, "Is your suffering any different from the rest of the world's suffering?" If you were asked if the sufferings of men and women who were wealthy and had much material attachments were any different to the sufferings of those who were hungry and down and out, you may argue that the sufferings of these very different groups is completely different. The affluent people would receive little sympathy while the people who are starving and desolate would likely get much

The root cause of all suffering comes from seeking outside ourselves on a daily basis.

more sympathy. You may argue that individuals living in a war torn country suffer more than others who live in a peaceful environment. You may argue that the sufferings of those men and women living in poor countries are very different to your suffering. And the truth is that yes, the form of their suffering may be different, as we all experience suffering in many different ways.

However, the content, or the root cause of all suffering is the same for everyone. You may disagree with this view. The reason for this disagreement is that you may fail to see all of humanity as one. We are one in spirit, but we are seemingly many different bodies in physical form. Just because we look like we are separate from each other, and we feel separate from each other, it really does not mean that we are separate from each other. The true nature of every human being is spirit - that is why we are one.

The Course says, *"Minds are joined, bodies are not"*.[1] We all have the same mind, but we all appear to live in different bodies. There is no order of magnitude in suffering, suffering is suffering regardless of what you believe the cause is. The root cause of all suffering is the belief is separation, both in form and content.

The root cause of *all* suffering will never be understood until we look at the true cause of any suffering. As long as we, as individuals, continue to see ourselves as special, unique and separate from each other, our suffering will continue. If you think about it you will see that it really does make sense.

Heaven is a state of bliss, because it is a state of Oneness. This world is a state of chaos, because it is a state of separation. We suffer as individuals, but suffering will begin to end the very moment we begin to know everyone as part of ourselves. Nevertheless, we don't want to look at others and see them as we see ourselves. The ego mind-set will not allow this as it goes against everything the ego stands for. The ego revels in individuality, in uniqueness and in specialness. The ego will never allow humanity to think or live as one.

You may feel that this concept rings true, but wonder how you can deal with your own suffering as an individual. The answer is that oneness begins with our self. It starts out with you as an individual and grows into the oneness with everyone and everything just by your willingness to consider that no one is separate from you for any reason and without exception. To end your own personal hell you must first come to the understanding that all of your suffering is self-created and no one else is responsible for it. Secondly, you must understand that your suffering is the result of your desire to be special, unique and an individual. You are choosing to continue a life of pain and suffering if you cannot arrive at this point and accept that suffering is self-created. This acceptance is your choice, but at least now you will know the reason for your continued suffering even if you choose to blame others. Next, you must realize at some point that no one else

> *The mind that caused the suffering will be the same mind that is now trying to escape from it, and how can the same mind that caused the problem have the answer to it?*
>
>

can end your suffering. It is you, yourself, who must deal with it as it is an "inside job".

You must next come to the understanding that you cannot escape your own personal suffering. This is because the mind that caused the suffering will be the same mind that is now trying to escape from it, and how can the same mind that caused the problem have the answer to it? It can't. This mind is the mind of the ego that will delude you into thinking that it has the answer, while knowing that it is deceiving you into more suffering. It has a good reason for doing so, as the more you struggle to escape suffering the more you feed and intensify the ego itself.

Insanity prevails as you are resisting suffering by forcing certain thoughts out of awareness. The ego just loves these two energies: resistance and force. When these two energies are applied at the same level of consciousness, the result is a deeper unconscious mind-set. When consciousness is split the result is unconsciousness. The separated mind is at war with itself and the result is suffering.

The separated mind is at war with itself and the result is suffering.

Thus, the root cause of all suffering is a mind at war with itself. Moreover, this internal conflict, or war, will be projected outwards and thus cause a war in the external world. It is for this reason that world peace cannot be attained. To achieve world peace, peace must first be realized internally and that peace may then be projected outwards. You must become the peace you seek. As an individual, you can do this all by yourself. The power to choose between looking outside ourselves to meet our needs and looking within is the only real choice. And choosing to look within is real power and is the only true power that we have as individuals.

Now, as individuals, we must not try to escape our own personal suffering. Instead, we must look at it from a different perspective. Suffering will dissolve and dissipate into the nothingness from where it came if you can stand back and become the Observer and look at it without judgment, without seeking anything in return, without naming it, or without labeling it as good or bad.

It does not matter in what form the suffering is manifested; violence, starvation, sickness, homelessness, impending death, not getting things your own way, it really could be just about anything. Suffering will be part of our human existence here as long as we continue

*What I do to you, I do to myself
...what I think of you, I think of
myself...what I say to you, I say
to myself...how I feel about you,
I feel about myself.*

to see everyone else as separate from ourselves and from each other, and continue to strive to dominate each other, compete with each other, own and possess each other. Within the concept of separation, there will always be conflict. This is the true root cause of all suffering.

When you become one with nature, you will see the flower and the tree at one with yourself. You will not want to own it or to possess it. When you see a beautiful flower, you will not pick it because you will know that it will then die. People pick beautiful flowers in order to own them and possess them. They would never kill them if they truly believed that they were at one with themselves. This concept also applies to people. If you truly believed that you were at one with everyone on this planet, you would never again harm another human being as you would know that you are harming yourself.

Knowing that we are connected with everything, our motto in living our life would be: what I do to you, I do to myself ...what I think of you, I think of myself ... what I say to you, I say to myself ... how I feel about you, I feel about myself. If we can come to know that within a relationship, our partner is one with us, we could never hurt or harm that person ever again. It is only when we believe that they are separate from us that we want to own and possess them and therein lies the root cause of all pain in relationships.

You cease to see suffering as anything other than a part of yourself when, as the Observer, you become one with the form of suffering you are experiencing. In reality, the form of the suffering does not matter, the answer is always the same; take responsibility for *all* the suffering you experience. You will stand in the light of truth if you can absorb it inside you, own it, embrace it, love it, without desiring to blame some else for it, and without needing someone else to suffer because of it. Suffering never comes from any given situation, suffering always comes because of your thoughts about the situation.

Pain is the great awakener but most people will go to great lengths to avoid it. A good friend of mine lost her husband a few years ago, and the grief she experienced was so tremendously overwhelming that she began to wake up. But within a few months, she found another person to share her life with, and she fell back into a deep sleep, back into the same old routines and habits. Yes, pain is the great awakener. In order to avoid pain, most people will return to dreaming by finding another attachment, another person, and go back to sleep. We all have done this many times. We get a wakeup call and we swear that things are going to change. However, we soon forget the pain when we replace it with some material object such as a golden trinket, another career, or another person. If you reflect on your life you will now recognize that you have had many wake up calls and when the pain became too much to bear you searched until you found someone or something else to hide the pain once more.

Another friend lost his home in the recession, his marriage then fell apart and, to top it all off, his family disowned him for being such a failure. In one fell swoop, his happy dream fell apart. However, he began to wake up. He began to inquire into the nature of life. He looked closely at this world and what it all meant. He really was on his way, until one day, he met another woman and began his dream all over again. He found a job, started saving for a new home and very soon he was fast asleep once more. He soon found himself back on the hamster wheel of life; some days feeling depressed, some days feeling angry. Most days he was a walking zombie. He began to drink heavily to cope with the pressures of life once more. His life was one of going through the same emotions every day. Then his new relationship fell apart. Again, because of his excessive drinking, he lost his job, and returned to me looking for the answers to life.

Life gives us many opportunities to wake up. It kicks us in the teeth over and over again, but we never seem to learn until we are beaten into the ground. Then, we will finally start to wake up and begin to ask, what is this all about? It is only when one begins to question what life is, question what we see and feel, and question what we think, that we will finally wake up and arrive at this one thought that changes everything: "There has to be another way". There is another way, it is called True Forgiveness. True forgiveness brings an end to all suffering once and for all. It begins with taking complete responsibility for everything. When you take full and complete responsibility, suffering will being to end.

Taking Responsibility – The End of Suffering

You are where you are because of who you are and the choices you have made up until now. Everything that exists in your life exists because of you: your thinking, your behavior, your words and your actions. You are responsible for your actions – all of them.

You are responsible for your thoughts and behavior, whether deliberate or unintentional. When you make excuses or try to blame other people or external factors for the way you feel, or for the life you have led, you are failing to take responsibility. And when you fail to take full responsibility for everything in your life, and I mean *everything*, you are now accepting and playing the role of the victim. You cannot be a victim unless you choose to be one. Everything in life comes down to choice, and if you believe that you do not have a choice in all matters, or even some matters, you are really saying, "I am a victim of this person, or of that circumstance". In shouldering responsibility you are giving yourself the power to shape the outcome of everything in your life. No one has the power to hurt you, unless you give them the power to do so. You give people power over you because you want something from them. If you did not want anything from anyone, you would be able to stand in your true nature and not allow anyone or anything control your emotions. You can believe that you are a victim and if you do so, you will seek and find people to victimize you. Alternatively, you can believe that everything in your life is your responsibility, and that you are completely responsible for all your successes and failures, your happiness and unhappiness. In taking the latter conviction, you escape from hell. All of this is wholly dependent on you and you alone. When you first come to this realization, it can seem like a huge responsibility. It seems much easier to

Once you accept total responsibility for everything that happens to you in life, you will soon discover that this also enables you to find solutions to life's difficulties far more quickly.

simply just blame other people for how miserable your life really is. However, when you do that, you disempower yourself because that means that you will play the victim.

The less responsibility you take, the less control you have. Alternatively, the more personal responsibility you take, the more in control you will become, and you will become more successful as you gain more control of your life. Therefore, taking responsibility for everything in your life equals success. It will also make you feel good about yourself, in addition to ridding yourself of all the negative personality traits such as anger, fear, resentment, hostility and doubt. Once you accept total responsibility for everything that happens to you in life, you will soon discover that this also enables you to find solutions to life's difficulties far more quickly.

A negative person who refuses to take responsibility will always try to apportion blame for the way they feel or the way they behave. What they are really saying is, "it's not my fault because if it were not for this person or that person, if it were not for this event or that event, I would be happy, successful, and rich". That person will go through life never changing, and their so called "luck" will also never change because they are accepting and playing the role of the victim that does not allow them to be happy, successful or wealthy.

You cannot blame the other person if you are in an unhappy relationship. You may wonder why not. The truth is that no one forced you into this relationship, and you can walk away from it at any time you please. But you will not. Why? Because by your unwillingness to take responsibility for *everything* in your life you are playing a role that calls for you to be victimized, and believe me, I know this role very well. Or you might possibly walk out of the relationship, but if you are still unwilling to take responsibility for everything that happened in that relationship you will then carry this lesson into your next relationship. You will repeat the same lessons as in the previous relationship, if you do not take full responsibility. This is because you are playing a role that calls out for another relationship where you will be victimized. You cannot play the role of the victim if you do not have someone to victimize you and you cannot stop being a victim until you empower yourself with the understanding that it is you yourself who is creating your own experience as a victim.

The victim will always seek out people who will abuse them or situations that will victimize them. You can never play this role again if you accept total responsibility for your life. In accepting responsibility, you are accepting a willingness to develop yourself and grow into an independent powerful human being that relies on no one and nothing external to you to be happy. Many of us become trapped in a state of inertia, often because we are too afraid to try anything new in case people question us or decide to mock our ideas or plans. You must start making different choices if you want a different life.

Taking responsibility is not easy, it is not easy to admit past mistakes. It always seems much easier to blame and point the finger at someone else. However, if you do that, there will be grave consequences for you, because you will play the role of the victim which means that you will suffer. Taking responsibility can be very painful. Your inability to accept responsibility for your actions and behaviors is always a result of insecurity. This is because by taking responsibility when things go wrong, you may feel that you are admitting to being weak and powerless, and thus lose the respect of others. However, the opposite is the true, taking responsibility earns you respect and trust because when you admit responsibility you are being honest with yourself and your honesty will enable others to respect and trust you. There is great power in admitting that you are wrong, because you will no longer have to fear the consequences of your mistakes, instead you are now in a position to make things right every time and move forward in life. The ego tells you just the opposite, that you are a failure. But here is the twist, when you are wrong and do not admit responsibility, the ego will never let you forget it. It will remind you time and time again that you are weak and vulnerable, and also that you are a liar. This is the price you will pay for not taking responsibility. Accepting responsibility is a measure of your self-worth, and is a true sign of strength and courage that we all have within us. Having this ability can empower you to grow in ways that will bring you great rewards and accomplishments in life.

> *Suffering is not of God, it is a man-made experience which we all choose of our own accord.*
>
>

The one thing we must accept and take responsibility for is for the pain and suffering that we all have or are experiencing. Otherwise, that pain will make you suffer your entire life. The choice is yours, but you are not free from the consequences of your choice. You can end suffering once and for all, or you can continue to suffer. After all you do have free will. Suffering is not of God, it is a man-made experience which we all choose of our own accord. Up until this point, you may have not been aware that the choices you have been making are what brought you your suffering. However, it is your choices from here on that matter. What you do about your awareness of how and why you are suffering is now up to you.

So how do we undo the suffering once we have taken responsibility for everything in our lives? We do this by the practice and process of taking full and complete responsibility through using the tool called True Torgiveness? See Chapter 10 – *True Forgiveness.*

CHAPTER 9

~~~

The Illusion of Death

In this chapter I share many of the metaphysical experiences I have experienced that relate to what happens to us after we leave the body. This chapter contains important information for many people, especially those who are about to pass over. I share these experiences with the hope that they will bring comfort to not only those who are about to make the transition but also to their loved ones who they leave behind.

The Illusion of Death

Throughout my life I always knew that I was not a body but I never knew who I truly was until I woke up. The point here is this: you are not your body, your body is just a vehicle that you use for transportation and communication and that is it. *A Course in Miracles* tells us that that the body is wholly neutral; it does not see anything, for it is the mind that interprets everything one sees. The body does not feel anything. All pain that you have ever experienced or will ever experience has always been in your mind and always will be in your mind until you deal with it. As we just discussed in the previous chapter, all pain comes from the belief that we are separate from each other and that we are separate from God. This belief in separation is the root cause of all suffering.

Suffice it is to say, the more we go into what *A Course in Miracles* tells us, the more this world begins to fall apart. I transcended my body more times than I have had flights on airplanes, and I have been to a good number of places. In each out-of-body experience I could see, hear, feel, smell, and even taste. So, if I was experiencing all of this without my body, then what *The Course* says in Lesson 17 of the Workbook about the body being neutral and that our experiences are created by our thoughts is true. I knew this from my own experience before I came to *The Course*, so it was another tick in the box for me, it confirmed that this book is spot on. In fact this book validated every single out of body experience I ever had. It was not until I woke up that I found out that nearly everyone in the spiritual community was desperately trying to attain out-of-body experiences. To my surprise, what I was frantically trying to stop prior to my awakening, many other people were trying to experience. Not only was I trying to stop them, I had very deliberately kept them secret all my life because of what my Dad said to me when I told him about it.

Early on, when the experiences first began, I was so frightened that I went to my Dad to see if maybe he could make sense of it. Instead of providing some comfort or suggesting something I might do to make them stop, like I had hoped, he said, "We may have to take you to see a shrink if those experiences continue." Near the farm where I grew up there was a mental hospital. From time to time patients would escape and run into the woods next to our property. Security personnel would then come to look for the mental patients, and to me, it seemed as if they were hunting them down.

I, therefore, had a very clear image of what it could be like to become a mental patient and that was definitely something I was sure I did not want to experience. A few weeks after I had told my Dad about my out-of-body experiences he asked me if this was still going on. Although the experiences had continued, I immediately told him, "nope, all that has stopped". The thought of possibly becoming a mental patient terrified me so much that I never told another soul again, thinking that, like my Dad, everyone would think I was mad.

Today I use these experiences to access information about which I receive many visions. I would like to share with you just some of these visions here. The diagram "States of Consciousness" below outlines the entire separation, from top to bottom. There are five universes, from Heaven downwards to the physical universe. Each Universe is a state of consciousness.

As you can see from the diagram "States of Consciousness", there are five levels of ascension. The place you will be passing over to first is not Heaven, because in the Divine, Heaven is at the very top. Right after the human experience you will go to a place in the lower heavens called the Spiritual Universe. You have been there many times, and in each occasion you have chosen to come back here once again for another human experience. You are not a human being. You are a spiritual Being enjoying or hating your chosen human experience.

The beliefs that you now have about what will happen to you once you transcend the body will influence how you experience the transition. If you are a spiritual person, your experience of the Spiritual Universe will be a mystical one in which you will enter in a stream of light. If you are Catholic, your experience may be one akin to reaching the Pearly Gates where Peter is checking names as you enter. If you are a child, your entry into the Spiritual Universe may be a magical experience where, for example, all your favorite toys will come to life and play with you.

However, if you think you are going to hell, then that will also be your experience. If you think you deserve to be in limbo, than that also will be your experience. It is what you believe in that creates your experience. So, be careful what you choose to believe in, because that will be your experience, and if you believe that you should be punished, then you will believe that you are being punished. All of these experiences, including limbo, will be very short lived. These experiences are only your entry into the Spiritual Universe, and once they are over you will find yourself experiencing your life review. You will have some serious questions to answer and some big decisions to make. Depending on the decisions you make after your life review you will then design and create the script for your next human experience.

STATES OF CONSCIOUSNESS

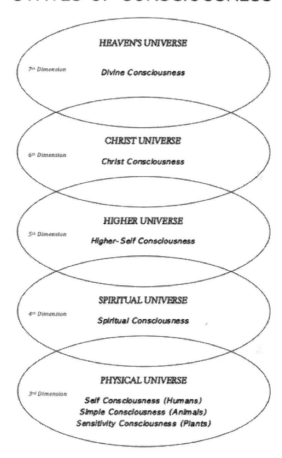

Before I woke up, I never felt more alive than I did in my near-death experiences, even when the finality of it terrified me. I know now with certainty that death is not the end of anything, but the beginning of everything. Death is a seamless transformation that will occur and you will not even know it has happened right away. In a few cases it might even take you quite a while to figure that you have died, but you will. There is nothing to fear.

Revelations

As we discussed earlier, revelation as described in *The Course*, is direct communication from God to you, or in my case from God to me. For the past seven years I have been receiving, on a regular basis, many revelations that have come from God to me for the purpose of sharing this information with the world. You may ask, why would God be speaking me? And of course, this was a question a woman once asked me. She said, "God must have been scraping the bottom of the barrel to choose you". I agreed with her, and I told her that I felt the same way. So I asked God, why me? This is the answer that I received, *"When you can let go of every grievance you ever have held against anyone and specially yourself, when you can let go of every attachment to every person you hold or will ever hold, when you can let go of all attachments to the world of illusions, and when you can let go of every thought, belief, and concept that you have ever held, then you will hear my voice, and only then, you and I become one"*. This is revelation.

"All are called, but few choose to answer"[1]*,* is a famous line out of *The Course.* All are called means that it does not matter who you are, or what you think you have done, you can awaken by your own choice. It is inevitable that everyone will awaken sooner or later. In that, there is no choice.

The only choice you truly have is this- how and when will I choose to wake up. That is your true free will, all else is an illusion of free will. From my own experience, it is not about what you believe, it is about what you want to believe. You can believe in illusions but there is another way; you can believe in the Truth as only the Truth will set you free. I heard the call and I answered. This led to my experience of revelation. It is inevitable that at some point, when each person is ready, they too will answer and will also experience the Love of God that is experienced through revelation.

Additionally, over the last seven years, I have also been asked a great number of thoughtful questions in regards to our human experience and our relationship with the Divine. I often found the answers to these questions that came through me, deeply insightful and healing. One question in particular I would like to discuss is, *"What happens when we die?"*

When we lay our physical body aside in death and return to the Spiritual Universe, we all will have to answer these three questions:

1. How much wealth did you accumulate?

2. How did you accumulate it?

3. How much wealth did you bring with you?

Just for a moment, pause, still your mind, and look deep within to see if you know the answers to all three questions before we go any further. How would you answer these three questions if you were asked right now?

We will come back to these questions later.

Physical Death Is a State of Mind

The Aramaic word for "death" translates as, "not here, present elsewhere". And "elsewhere" is where I would find my mind from time to time, since I woke up. My body would be here, but my mind was now fully awake, and often it would take me to far off places that lay deep within the consciousness of the universe and beyond. Physical death, I have come to understand, is a transition between two states of mind, not two worlds of existence. It is neither here, nor there, but a state of mind where time and space is distorted, but not completely diminished, or eliminated. It all has to do with the person's personal beliefs and state of mind at the time of transition. You will still carry the illusion of a body with you as you transcend to the spiritual universe.

All the drama that has been accumulated at the level of the brain will disintegrate along with the death of the brain. The only thing that remains at physical death is the mind of the individual, with its essence as Spirit, which is eternal, immortal and indestructible. There are no external forces to cause decay of Spirit. There is none to speak of, because there is no "external presence." Transition from physical consciousness back to spiritual consciousness can be difficult, because the more

266

materialistic the individual is, the greater the difficulty of transition.

For a few, it can be an extremely frustrating situation because they never did anything about their spirituality during their time on earth. The physical death of a person is not the loss of life, but a loss of physical consciousness. Physical consciousness is where you believe that you are a physical being that was born and will die. The five physical senses reinforce your physical identity, and indeed, the reality of the physical world we experience. The body cannot sustain life without the consciousness of the individual that is in the mind.

> *Physical consciousness is encompassed by dense thoughts of separation, with its consequent effects of guilt and fear. It is these thoughts that must be undone to break the cycle of reincarnation.*
>
>

Therefore, without a body, human consciousness would not be possible, as the body itself enables the soul to consciously experience physical consciousness with its five bodily senses. When a person experiences physical death, a loss of physical consciousness will be experienced and verbal communication will be eliminated. You simply step outside your physical body. However, consciousness will still be experienced through the non-physical senses, in other words, through the mind. Spiritual beings cannot communicate physically with humans because of the different vibration of each level of consciousness.

The vibration of Spiritual consciousness is much higher than physical consciousness. Physical consciousness is encompassed by dense thoughts of separation, with its consequent effects of guilt and fear. It is these thoughts that must be undone to break the cycle of reincarnation.

If you think of a great weight that weighs you down, and keeps bringing you down, then that is what these heavy thoughts do, they keep bringing you back here into this physical world, into a physical body lifetime after lifetime. It is the belief in separation that must be overcome, not the separation itself. Because in truth, there has been no separation from Reality or from God, it is only our belief in the separation that must be undone.

It is this belief that compels the Soul to return to the physical universe in order to continue its growth, learn from it, experience separation, and make a choice. That choice will always be between oneness and separation, God or the ego. Truth or illusions. Love or fear. However, we don't have to wait until we transcend to the Spiritual Universe to choose, these are the choices we make every day. We are always choosing between heaven or hell by the thoughts we choose. Like the swing of a pendulum, an individual will continue the cycle through life, death, and rebirth, until it awakens and remembers its true identity.

In my first "experience" on the 29 of September 2008, I had what is often called today a "spiritual awakening", which means that I woke up to the consciousness of my true inner spiritual nature, and everyone else's too. When we leave our bodies aside at death in this life, we all return to that level of consciousness for a short time. There, in the Spiritual Universe, we will review our life that has just passed, and begin to write a new script for another new life here on Earth.

Shortly after you lay the body aside you will begin to remember your spiritual identity and begin adapting your spiritual body. Your consciousness now also will be spiritual. In most cases you will have the urge to try and use your old senses, like trying to talk, or trying to touch people and so on, but this will quickly pass. The transition you will undertake will bring you from physical consciousness to spiritual consciousness.

There are physical laws here in the physical universe, as there are spiritual laws in the Spiritual Universe. So, what are the spiritual laws that are a much higher way of living? For one, we will have a knowing, not a belief, that we are all one. In this world, we believe that we are separate from each other. We all think that what I think of you means nothing to me, or you. In the Spiritual Universe, what I think of you, I think of myself. What I do to you, I do to myself. And what I say to you, I say to myself. In the Spiritual Universe, we receive by giving; what I give to you, I give to myself.

In this physical world, if I have something, it means that you do not have it. If I want something, I have to take it from you, now I have it and you do not. Nothing is wholly shared here, in spirit everything is shared equally. In spirit, if I want something I must give it first. The spiritual universe's thinking and thought processes are the total reversal of the thinking and thought processes of this world. "As above so below" means, that to live a better life and live life at the higher level of consciousness, we must adopt and live the spiritual laws of the "above", of the Spiritual Universe, on this level, the physical universe which is "below".

Spiritual consciousness is much higher than physical consciousness, because physical consciousness is encompassed by a strong belief in the limited physical universe and our limited physical bodies as our natural home and identity, while spiritual consciousness is without limits. It is the mind that does the thinking, not the brain which is just an organ of the physical body. The brain only does what the mind instructs it to do.

Likewise, the body does not feel, it is only at the mind level that all thoughts and feelings exist.

> *The brain only does what the mind instructs it to do.*
> *Likewise, the body does not feel, it is only at the mind level that all thoughts and feelings exist.*
>
>

Spiritual beings cannot communicate physically with humans because of the different vibration of each consciousness. When an individual returns to Spirit, they will become deprived of verbal communication, because they no longer possess lungs, a voice box, tongue and lips to manipulate a language.

The only alternative means of communication available to them is that of the mind. Oral communication by human voice is always preceded by thought form, followed by the forming of sounds and words. Spirit is unable to hear sound, because they do not have physical ears. What they see, is the forming of thoughts before oral communication takes place, and they are able to "see" without eyes and be "aware" of that preceding thought form. This process is known as "telepathic communication". If you can think of a musician playing a song on a piano striking different notes to make a melody, he first must think of which notes makes what sounds. The musician then proceeds to strike the piano on a certain key to make a certain sound. Well, the music is in his mind, and the piano is his sound box. So, he now can make the piano play the song in his mind. He first thinks of what to play, and then takes action to make that into sound.

Well, that is the same with our minds, we first think of what to say, and then our mind directs our voice to speak exactly that. In the Spiritual Universe, we hear the thought only, and that is how we communicate with each other, mind to mind, because we are all one mind in Spirit. We hear each other's thoughts in the Spiritual Universe as clear as we hear each other's voices in this world. It is only here, in the physical universe where we believe we are separate from each other. This is the reason why we are all here, to correct this mis-belief.

When self-consciousness is separated from the body, as in "death," the individual will experience a rapid change in perception as the individual's mind races rapidly through a tunnel of light toward the brightly lit ocean of Spirit. This bright light, when entered, brings warmth and comfort to the departed. The departed soul will find itself engulfed and cradled in a non-separated state of peace, love and ecstasy. Soon after, the tunnel of light, which is the stream of consciousness that carries the individual's awareness from one reality to another, becomes withdrawn and retracts itself from the physical universe.

An individual who feels that they must suffer hellfire for their wrongs in life in order to be atoned, will actually suffer and experience that event, because that is their belief. All suffering of hellfire experienced by the individual is occurring only in the imagination of his or her mind. The same rule applies to the

When you experience physical death, you will not believe that you are dead.

religious person who believes that they must pass through the pearly gates to enter heaven. All are nothing more than the experience of personal and religious beliefs of the eternal individual before they awaken from their physical sleep. All "beliefs" are replaced with Truth, Knowledge and Wisdom when a person enters the Spiritual Universe, but only for a brief moment. The soul of that individual will then once again return to the physical world to experience another lifetime, with more lessons to learn.

When you experience physical death, you will not believe that you are dead. This is why the wake and funeral concepts are so important. They will prove to you that you are physically dead. This is your opportunity to say goodbye to all of your loved ones, and even though they will not experience you, you will experience them. Then, after a brief period you will be met by someone you have already agreed to meet who is on the other side in the Spiritual Universe. They will appear to you shortly after all proceedings have ended, and they will accompany you on your return. You both will enter a portal of light, and this portal is how you will get to the Spiritual Universe.

An interesting fact is that portals are all around us, and have been for centuries. Many have been witness to them, without realizing exactly what they are. If you look into the sky, and if you are lucky enough you might see one, they are the spirals that have been seen for thousands of years in the skies above many countries. They are one of the oldest symbols known to mankind. If you look closely you will see that there are two types. One spiral goes in a clockwise rotation, which is an entry into the physical dimension. The other goes in a counter clockwise rotation, which is the portal to the Spiritual Universe. If you suddenly see a UFO and then it is gone, that is where it went; these ships use the spirals, but they are not permitted to do so. Anytime this occurs, it is always because of an error.

At the start of this chapter I asked three questions that you will be asked upon your arrival in the Spiritual Universe. The answers you give will determine your next choice in the cycle of life and death known as Samsara.

The first question was, how much wealth did you accumulate? Here, the question is not in reference to material wealth, but Spiritual wealth. Spiritual wealth is what you do for others, not for yourself. If you have spent a life in service to others, you have gained enormous Spiritual wealth. What we do for others we do for ourselves. If you have amassed great material wealth for yourself, you will have no wealth above. If you have amassed great material wealth, and shared it for the

273

better of humanity, helping those who have little or nothing, you have now amassed great spiritual wealth within also. If you live in the top 1% this time around, and you do not share your wealth with those who have none, you will live your next life in the bottom 1%. Everything must be balanced.

The second question was, how did you accumulate your wealth? If you have amassed great wealth at the expense of others, you have not spiritually advanced in any way. In fact, your next physical life experience will be one of poverty and lack. You will design your next life experience to undo your selfish choices of greed and self-interest to one of giving and sharing. If on the other hand you have accumulated great spiritual wealth from giving and sharing, which is a life devoted to helping others, you have amassed great spiritual wealth within.

The greatest spiritual wealth one can accumulate is through the process of forgiveness. There is no greater gift that you can bestow on another person than the gift of true forgiveness. This type of forgiveness is also described below in Chapter 10 – *True Forgiveness*. Please go to this chapter to learn and master this art.

The third question was, how much wealth did you bring with you? If you have led a life seeking material wealth, then you have brought nothing with you. There is no material wealth in the Spiritual Universe, or anywhere else in the heavens above. If, on the other hand, you led a life of devotion to helping others, you have grown spiritually within, and you will bring that wealth with you.

Finally, if you have led a life of true forgiveness, which means that there is no one you hold a prisoner to your guilt, and you have detached completely from the material world and its attachments, you will not return here and will remain in the Spiritual Universe, to ascend to the Higher universe and then

All judgments are self-judgments, which means that if you judge other people harshly in this life, you will judge yourself even more harshly at your life review.

beyond. Forgiveness is the key to Heaven, it is your choice, and your choice alone. After this process has occurred, you will be taken to a very special place for your life review. Here you will get the chance to look back on your life and see the lessons that you learned, and the lessons that you missed, or failed to learn. This process is very important, because it is on the basis of your life review that your next physical incarnation will take place. All judgments are self-judgments, which means that if you judge other people harshly in this life, you will judge yourself even more harshly at your life review.

Life reviews can be very harrowing experiences for most people, especially if you have neglected the lessons you were presented with and ignored your life script. In other words, if you choose to hate, rather than to love, if you choose self-interest over shared interests, you will feel that pain at your life review. If you have hurt someone, you will feel their hurt as your own, because we are all one. Every ounce of pain that you cause to another you will experience as your own at this review, unless that hurt has been forgiven in yourself.

This is so crucial to understand; *ALL forgiveness is self-forgiveness*, which undoes all pain in your life, and therefore undoes all pain in your mind. When you hurt another, and you refuse to rectify that hurt, or ignore it, you will feel that hurt at your life review. There is no escaping this process, and now guilt will arise once more in your mind and you will set out to write another new life that will make amends for these errors.

Life here is always on the up, we are all waking up, albeit slowly or rapidly, either is good. So, it all depends on whether you really wish to return to Heaven and God, or you choose this world once more. You are choosing heaven or hell at every moment, in every day. What you choose here, you will choose in the Spiritual Universe. If you choose to love unconditionally, which forgiveness does, you will return Home. If you choose a life of indulging in the material world, a life of selfishness, then you will be back here once more. The choice is always yours. Choose wisely my friends, you will not regret your choice for Heaven, I can assure you of that.

A life review can also take place here and now, by you, yourself. You can clean your mind every day and every night, if you so choose. Each night you can honestly look back on your day and see what you have done for others, rather than what you have done for yourself. You can look back at all the people who you may have hurt, or who have seemingly hurt you. You can use forgiveness to do this, and then, when you return to the Spiritual Universe, your life review will be an amazing experience to behold. You will be free to remain and enjoy the splendor of total love and bliss for eternity. If you can live a life of shared interests, which is done by you using forgiveness every day, you will have amassed great spiritual wealth within.

It is impossible for you to forgive someone else; all forgiveness is self-forgiveness. The most precious gift that you can give to others is to take responsibility for everything that you feel, all of your emotions and everything that happens to you in your life and then forgive yourself. By doing this you will live a life where you will not project your anger and guilt onto others knowing that you are the cause of all that you experience. And by forgiving yourself, you will remove your own guilt, thereby enabling love, which is your true nature, to come through you and be shared with others.

When your life review is completed you will now be met with three Awakened Spirits who will help you design and write another life, they will help you to choose a family, a country, a gender and a personality to aid you on your journey back here once more. You will write your next script.

The Script

The Purpose of Incarnation

Is there such as thing as reincarnation? The answer depends on which level and who's perspective you are looking from. If you look at diagram "The Cycle of Life and Death" below, you will see the life cycle that we are all experiencing lifetime after lifetime. From the physical world's perspective, yes, reincarnation is true. However, if you look at this from the Christ Universe on the 6th Dimension, you will now know that we experience all life times together, in one lifetime. This is the illusion of time, and perspectives.

So, what is the answer, is reincarnation true or not? It is true at the 3rd and 4th Dimension levels as long as we believe that we are separate from each other. However, reincarnation is an impossible concept at the 6th and 7th Dimension levels where all lives are experienced in Oneness.

When an incarnation takes place and you enter into a physical body, you will have amnesia and totally forget your Divinity and identity as a spiritual being. Before your incarnation takes place you will be fully aware of this. *The Course* describes this state as the "veil of forgetfulness". As a spiritual being, there is a part of you that has been suppressed and denied that needs to be brought into awareness, and this can only take place in our physical, emotional and psychological close relationships.

When we incarnate, we leave a place that has no contrast, where there is no right or wrong and there is no good or evil; it is a realm of peace, love and happiness. We then incarnate into a world that seems to be the exact opposite, a world of sin, guilt and fear. We cannot experience projection in the Spiritual Universe, for we can only project onto a seeming separate entity that we deem guilty and sinful. In spirit we cannot project, because we do not perceive separation, we do not perceive someone else as guilty, nor do we perceive victimization and attacks.

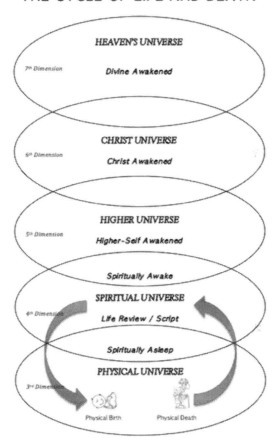

THE CYCLE OF LIFE AND DEATH

We can and only will project onto someone we perceive as guilty, sinful or someone who we believe has attacked us. Our conditioning as a human being experiencing a physical body is only temporary to each incarnation. Our human personality resides in a classroom, and every day we have a set of lessons to learn from. We can either choose to learn these lessons or resist them, the choice is always ours to make, and this is where our free will really is. However, remember this also, all lessons will be repeated until learned!

The lives we lead sometimes seem to be a life of meaningless pain and suffering. All of our most difficult experiences are, in truth, experiences rich in hidden spiritual growth, spiritual understanding, and of self-knowing. We write the script of everything in our lives ourselves before we are born. All of our circumstances, relationships, and events are carefully planned by us to achieve our objectives which we ourselves set out to experience. You may have experienced challenges such as illness, accidents and near-deaths, being out-of-body, addiction, alcoholism, victimization, persecution, and isolation. All of these you carefully wrote, planned, and scripted to aid an awakening. We have the choice to use each experience to learn self-knowledge, compassion, understanding, and empathy for all those who surround us in our relationships. Or we can choose to ignore the lessons and suffer, and it is this ignoring, that leads to further suffering.

If you look carefully at your life, you will see the same lessons being repeated over and over again. This should tell you something really important, you are not learning the lesson that is being presented. Each lesson will be repeated until it is learned. We cannot learn these lessons in spirit, because in the Spiritual Universe there is only love, peace, and happiness in abundance. Only in the physical world can lessons of pain, suffering, victimization, persecution, and death be experienced and learned. No one can truly die, it is only the vehicle we call the body that dies.

> *Only in the physical world can lessons of pain, suffering, victimization, persecution, and death be experienced and learned.*

Each of us have chosen our parents, our brothers and sisters, where and when we are born. We have chosen our religion, our schools, and our lovers very carefully to fulfill what we need to learn and experience at this time. We also have spent many past lives with many of the people that are in our lives this time around. It is our task to remember who we truly are; to remember that we are spiritual beings, experiencing a physical life, not human beings experiencing a spiritual life.

In our script is the life that we all have planned, and you may think, why have we planned this particular life in this way, what are the lessons we have to learn, and why? When you can remember this you will have broken through the veil to your higher consciousness. This is called an awakening; this is the true purpose of why we are here. This is the true purpose of all of our experiences here, to remember who we truly are, and return home to the higher realms of heaven and the state of Oneness.

Your waking up is just the first step in the process for that return. Many do wake up and then return to sleep because they are not truly willing to let go of their attachments in the physical world. All grievances must be forgiven, all material idols of fame, specialness, wealth, power, and greed must be seen as just that, idols. Your belief in sin, guilt and fear must be relinquished fully. Death then, will be brought to truth, and seen as an idle wish for those who seek separation. Death is an illusion, seek death and you will seem to die, seek life and you will never die, for those who remember their immortality can never die.

All experiences of suffering brought to us by our seeming persecutors and victimizers are in fact gifts. Our life has been scripted in such a way that can enable us to re-discover our true identity, which is a Divine Spirit of God. We are all part of the unified Oneness of Heaven, it is just that we are dreaming that we have separated, thus we seem to have lost the memory of our true identity. All of our lessons here are designed to regain this memory, to regain our birthright of who we truly are.

In many cases in which a person is asleep or unconscious in the dream, there are many wake-up calls that have been scripted before birth. All of these wake-up calls coincide with lessons to be learned, no experience is wasted. First there may be a small crisis in your life, and if this does not awaken you, then there is a bigger crisis, and so on until you begin to wake up. All pain and suffering is by choice, and choosing to be separate from God is motivated by a selfish desire to feel special and different from others. God does not punish anyone, nor will He ever.

All suffering is what mankind makes for itself, it is self-created, not God-created. Free will is an illusion, as there is no free will in Heaven, for everything is perfect Oneness. The only true free will that we have is in this world; we can choose between Oneness and separation, Love and fear, God and the ego, Truth and illusions. All other choices are illusions of free will. In perfect Oneness there is nothing to choose from, for all is One. But, we are free to dream whatever we wish, and it is our desire to see ourselves separate from others that is the true cause of all suffering.

Accidents of all kinds appear to be random affairs that just seem to happen. They seem to be very unfortunate events where the universe is seen to be conspiring against us. This could not be further from the truth. Some accidents seem to be minor events and others appear to be life-threatening, but all in all these are carefully planned by us before birth, to aid in the growth of our self awareness that will result in our awakening. An accident is never an accident; it is a pre-arranged moment in time that was written by us and us alone before we were born. This must seem insane to some people, you may ask, why would some people choose a life of pain and suffering?

However, in each experience there are two outlooks to take on all events that occur on this physical plane. You as an individual can wallow in self-pity, and say why me?! Or you can use this as a way to raise your consciousness and spiritual growth by looking at the positive side in every experience and using that energy to look again at the choices you have made and the life you have lived. In every situation, there are negative and positive outcomes. Train your mind to look only at the positive outcomes and your life will improve in an instant.

Always ask yourself around any difficult situations: How can I move forward with this? How can I help others who are going through or have gone through this? What can I do now to be of service to my fellow man? All of our scripts are designed to be of service to each other, to unite with each other, and to love each other unconditionally. In the higher states of Heaven, we only have true unconditional love for each other, which is why it is called Heaven.

In Heaven there is no pain, no suffering, no conflict, and no judgment of each other. There is simply no separation of any kind from anyone or anything. It is only the belief that we are separate from each other, and God, that causes conflict to arise. If you knew that you were truly the same as everyone else, you could never be in conflict with anyone ever again. When you wake up you will know, unequivocally, that to hurt someone else is the same as hurting yourself and this is the key for us to love one another. This understanding of Oneness is central to our awakening which is the door to eternal bliss in our lives. When you wake up, you will know this, not believe it, but know it! It is this knowing that we must all learn to experience before any of us can return home. This is why you are here, this is why we all are here, to remember we are one family in Spirit, experiencing different physical lives from each other, but being still One. To reach a higher level of consciousness we must overcome anger, depression, and the 'why me?' attitude. All are lessons that must be accomplished.

Accepting What Is

Our final lesson is acceptance of what is. It is a beautiful process, turning despair, isolation, persecution and victimization into love, compassion and understanding. The life we planned is to provide us with the many opportunities to express ourselves through compassion, empathy, forgiveness, understanding and love. Addictions and victimizations cannot be experienced in the non-physical world.

The secret to waking up is knowing this: I am doing this to myself.

Only in the physical world can you experience all of these unloving emotions and behaviors. Only in the physical world do we have the opportunities to experience spiritual growth, negative emotion, and disability. This is where all of our lessons will be learned. When we experience tough challenges in our lives, our first instinct or reaction is to always blame someone or something else for our misfortune. We have never come to the one true realization that it is us doing this to ourselves. The secret to waking up is knowing this: I am doing this to myself. The world is not to blame, our parents are not to blame, our teachers are not to blame, our spouses and partners are not to blame. Until we learn to take full responsibility for everything in our lives, it will keep getting tougher and more painful.

I will explain to you why this is so, and you may reject it, or you may agree with it, that is up to you. Either way, at some stage, in either this lifetime or the next, you will come to this very conclusion yourself. When we incarnate from the spiritual realm and into a body in this physical world, it does not mean that you have travelled from one place to another. It means that you have changed perception, not places. All perceptions are different states of consciousness, and if your perception is still enshrined in the idea that you are a body, then that will be your level of consciousness, and you will be under the laws of physics.

If, on the other hand, you are willing to change your perception into believing that you are a spiritual being, then your consciousness will be metaphysical, which is higher than physical consciousness. An awakening is a change of perception. When you wake up you will have a different level of consciousness, and a higher state of mind. Therefore, the higher you experience consciousness, the freer you will be from all pain and suffering. You may find the concept of pre-scripting your life hard to fathom, and particularly the choice to have painful challenges astonishing.

The more traumatic our challenges may be, the more we grow into spiritual awareness, the more spiritual awareness we have, the greater chance we will awaken. This is the choice that is available to all of us, and we may accept the challenge and grow, or pass up the challenge and learn it later. But one thing is for sure, we will all learn life's lessons, the easy way, or the hard way. That choice is always up to us.

Learning Through Opposites

We learn only through opposites. We chose to experience the exact opposite type of life to that of the lesson we are seeking to learn because you can only learn an appreciation of what you have, by not having it. It is only when you will seek and try to understand and appreciate what is missing in your life, which is always love, that you will appreciate it more when you discover it for yourself. Life's challenges are powerful means for questioning the meaning of life- for example, why would someone choose to be part of a highly dysfunctional family?

As I stated before, everything in this physical world is the opposite of the spiritual world. As *The Course* says, "...all perception still is upside down..."[2] meaning that everything here is the opposite of the truth. So, someone who chooses to be part of a highly dysfunctional family where there is no love and compassion will go in search of them, and either come to appreciate love and compassion more deeply or, choose to be bitter and angry with their lot and blame their parents and family. It is the absence of love that best teaches its true value and meaning. A lack of love in your outer world will eventually turn you inwards in search of love.

This world was made to be unloving; it was made that way so you would blame the world and the people in it for not loving you the way that you want. All love here is love/hate, I will love you if you love me, and when you stop loving me the way I want, I will hate you. You will eventually learn this, one way or another, and the sooner you learn it, the less painful your search will be. The more you turn inwards and away from your outer world, the more self-knowing you will become. All life's challenges will teach you that to know yourself, you have to turn inwards and discover your true Self.

The people in our lives that give us the greatest challenges are in fact mirrors of ourselves which reflect back to us what we need to heal. These challenges then, are really gifts, and when you can recognize them as gifts your healing has begun. The body itself is the vessel that we use to

> *The people in our lives that give us the greatest challenges are in fact mirrors of ourselves which reflect back to us what we need to heal.*
>
>

bring this awareness to us. Healing will be completed when you can see through the challenge, when you can see through the person who is reflecting back the challenge to you, when you can see the light in the other person, then that light becomes a reflection of your light, and you will come to know the other person as yourself.

When you cease to think of yourself as limited to your own body, or as a limited personality, you will recognize that you are part of the whole, that you are in fact the complete whole that needs no completion from another body. To wake up is to use life's challenges and lessons to heal our minds, and to give us a comprehension and understanding of spiritual growth that will lead us to a greater knowing of who we truly are, which is eternal and immortal beings of light created by Awareness.

Self-Knowing is Self-Loving

The temporary loss of identity and its subsequent rediscovery will give you a much more profound self-knowing and self-appreciation of life and love. *Know thyself,* no matter what the lesson is, and you will grow spiritually taller. There are never any exceptions to this rule, and everyone is growing spiritually all of the time. No matter how painful the lesson, you will learn from it, and it is pain that is our greatest motivation to seek for another way. To express and extend love when your true nature is forgotten and suppressed is your one fundamental lesson in life. You are love, and through self-knowing you will become aware of self-love. All self-knowing becomes self-loving. It is only through self-loving that we can extend and express true love, because you can only extend what you believe you are. If you believe that you are separate, guilty and fearful, that is what you will project. If you come to a state of self-knowing, of self-love, then that is what you will extend.

This is your only one and true task here in the physical world, to know thyself. This is achieved through forgiveness and the un-doing of the self that we have made. The lack of love in your life is the great motivator in our search for love. It is always what you lack in life that you will go in search for, it could be love, compassion, unity or empathy, or it could be fame, glory and wealth. Your real choice is whether you search within yourself or outside of yourself. The choice is yours, one will bring you Heaven, the other will bring you hell.

Time exists here only for learning. Lessons can be learned in less painful ways, but if they are not, then lessons will become greater in their challenge. All lessons can be learned sooner rather than later, but they also can be delayed indefinitely. To delay learning is also painful, so that is what time is for; we can chose when we are ready to learn our lessons. This is the true use of time. When a lesson keeps coming up over and over again, we will eventually get the picture, just like in the film "Groundhog Day" with Bill Murray. In this movie, Bill Murray's character has the experience that the same day keeps recurring over and over again, until he learns his lessons. It is the same for us, the golden rule of life is, *lessons will be repeated until learned*!

The Akashic Records

As previously stated, I had a second awakening in my second "experience". I woke up to what is known as a Higher Self-Awakening, which is a higher level of consciousness than Spiritual Consciousness. In this level of consciousness, you have access to all the knowledge and information that is contained in what is known as the Akashic Records.

The psychic Edgar Cayce was world-renowned for accessing the Akashic Records on behalf of those many individuals for whom he gave remarkable individual personal readings. The Akashic Records are said to hold all the records of both human and spiritual knowledge, including all human experiences. Every thought, every deed and every action ever taken by anyone is held on record in this great Hall of Records.

The Akashic Records are metaphorically described as the "Library", and are also sometimes likened by those familiar with them to a "universal computer" or "The Mind of God". The Akashic Records were often referred to by Edgar Cayce in his writings. He stated that *"...each person is held to account after life and 'confronted' with their personal Akashic Record, showing what they have or have not done in life, in a karmic sense".[3]*

These records are free from, and independent of, all religions and faiths. Who are you? Why are you here? What is your soul's purpose? It is said that the answer to all these questions are to be found in this great Hall of Records.

> *The Akashic Records can be accessed by a quiet mind, and how you achieve that stillness is up to you.*
>
>

It is well documented that Edgar Cayce himself produced several hundred psychic readings from the Akashic Records for many people throughout his life. He claimed that they would one day be accessed and opened, and as a result, all humanity would move into a new era of knowledge and enlightenment, through the information that is recorded there. Such states of consciousness, it is said, can be induced today at certain stages of sleep and meditation.

Not only mystics but ordinary people can, and do, perceive the content of Akashic Records. Yogis also believe that these records can be perceived in certain psychic states. It is asserted that to gain access to the Akashic Records, every individual human can become a psychic medium, via various techniques and spiritual disciplines such as yoga meditation, silent meditation, or formless prayer.

The Akashic Records can be accessed by a quiet mind, and how you achieve that stillness is up to you. In my night-time trance-like states, when my mind became very still and silent, I was able to transcend my physical reality and become a witness to the conscious states necessary to access the Akashic Records. My awakening had opened a portal from my physical consciousness, through my spiritual consciousness, and into my higher consciousness. It was in this way that I was now able to access all information from the Akashic Records.

After those extraordinary experiences of late 2008, which I have previously described, I entered an entirely new way of living. At night, when my mind settled down, I became accustomed to entering into a silent state within myself. When all thoughts and mental content were eliminated, my consciousness was elevated to an internal, heightened state of awareness of seeing, thinking, and being. My experiences as I have already said, generally defied physical description, and can at best be only hinted at.

During these experiences, I came to a new clarity of knowledge, insight, awareness, revelation, and illumination beyond the grasp of my thinking mind, and beyond any intellect I have ever known. Here in this place, I was witness to "the voice within". The very first time I heard this voice, it was crystal clear and pristine in clarity. It was distinct from any other voice I had ever heard. It was, however, a soundless voice and although I heard it as a voice, it did not sound like a voice as I knew it. It was in the purest thought form imaginable. It was not until much later that I found out how I was able to hear in this way. In this physical world, we rely on our physical senses to communicate. We use our ears to listen and our voices to relay audible words for discernment.

But what I was not then aware of was that all words we speak come first from thoughts, and then into sound. Everything that you have ever said has firstly come from a thought, before it is transformed into audible words, so we can hear these thoughts telepathically. And because of my spiritual awakenings, I became conscious of telepathy, and was able to communicate from mind to mind with Spirit.

As the nights went by, the communication became stronger and stronger, and much information was revealed to me, simply because I asked. And of course, I asked everything I could think of to ask, and everything was answered. The Akashic Records are also, in truth, a state of mind. It is not a place, or is there a special someone who gives out information. But it became very clear after some time that once this information came into my mind, it stayed there.

So no matter how long I waited to write it all down, it was always there in my mind to be accessed. Each night, I would enter first into that silent state of mind, and then into a further state of consciousness that would open up a portal into these higher realms of knowledge.

There is only one way that one can transcend the ego, and that is through detachment, or self-forgiveness. This world has not yet fully understood what true forgiveness truly is, because the religions of this world have used forgiveness to keep the entire populace feeling sinful, guilty and fearful. True forgiveness as described in *A Course in Miracles,* and in Chapter 10 – *True Forgiveness* in this book, truly means self-forgiveness; it is never about forgiving another person, or forgiving what another person does. To forgive oneself, one must always take full responsibility in every situation that one has conflict in. This is not an easy thing to do, and that is why true forgiveness is just so damn difficult to apply. Why? Because it is the ego that you are detaching from, and that is what true forgiveness is. It is complete detachment.

CHAPTER 10

~~~

True Forgiveness

The Illusion of Choice

True forgiveness undoes the role of the victim that we have all played and continue to play. Through practicing true forgiveness you will end all suffering that you will encounter from now on. True forgiveness will bring you peace, joy and love. It is only through the practice of true forgiveness that you will attain freedom. But first let us take a look at the forgiveness that religion has preached, because this is not what true forgiveness is. If we do not understand what false forgiveness is, we will never understand what true forgiveness is.

You may believe that you have gone through life making important choices. The fact is you have never had a choice in anything. Eckhart Tolle writes in his book, *The Power of Now*, *"Choice implies consciousness. Without it you have no choice. Choice begins the moment you dis-identify from the 'mind' and its conditioned patterns, the moment you become present. Until you reach that point you are unconscious spiritually speaking".*[1]

And I agree totally with what Eckhart says, but if you say to the average person on the street, who is unconscious and asleep, that they have no choice in life, you may get a very different answer. So why is it that people still believe that they have a choice in everyday life when it is very clear that they cannot avoid suffering and therefore do not? I want to take what Eckhart Tolle says and take it a bit deeper. The fact is that while unconscious you have no choice, but you do have "the illusion of choice".

The ego knows that you will not long remain in any mind-set if you feel like a prisoner. You will automatically try to break out. No one likes to be a prisoner under any circumstances. Their first thoughts are always, "How do I get out of here?". So the ego devised the most devious and cunning system which has ever been created, that would give you the belief that you did have a choice. This system I call "The Ego Right Mind".

During my studies of *The Course* in my first year, one thing stuck out like a sore thumb more than anything else - it was the ego right mind. Now I want to take you through the ego right mind, explain how it works and show you what its purpose is. Because, remember, everything has a purpose, and if you can understand the purpose, you can understand how to correct it.

THE EGO RIGHT MIND

What is the ego right mind?

What I refer to as the ego right mind is the ego mind-set that wants to be good, holy and even wants to wake up and be enlightened, but which still sees and believes in the separation. The way it may manifest can vary greatly. For example, a spiritual teacher, or guru, who is teaching from the ego's right mind, will take great pride in being wise, benevolent, humble and holier than everyone else. Or a student of *The Course* will take great pride in believing that they have the truth while everyone else is wrong. The ego right mind is very judgmental, righteous, and religious. It is a mind that is filled with specialness in every way, and those in that mind, will project that specialness out by surrounding themselves with people who are "special" and like-minded, and will also surround themselves with followers who look up to them and confirm their specialness.

At some point or another, every student of *The Course*, and in fact, almost every religious and spiritual seeking person on this planet falls into the trap of the ego right mind. It is so subtle that you can become stuck there for years, even lifetime after lifetime, without ever knowing why you are not progressing. The purpose of the ego right mind is to fool you into believing that you are in fact, in your true right mind and you will not know that you are still a prisoner of the ego thought system. Once in the ego right mind, it is a struggle to get out, and the only way out is through awareness. And once you become aware you can begin the process of waking up by using true forgiveness.

So let's look at what false forgiveness is, or "forgiveness-to-destroy" as it is described in *A Course in Miracles*. Forgiveness to destroy takes many different forms, all designed to fool and trap you into believing that you are doing God's will through forgiveness. If you are going to forgive - which the ego really does not wish you to do - then the ego's defense is to fool you into false forgiveness. The ego very cleverly conceals the true purpose of false forgiveness, which is to keep you different, separate and unequal with everyone else. There are four major ways the ego uses false forgiveness to fool you, which all end in the same result, more pain, more suffering, more fear and more guilt. Let's go through each one and uncover the ego's scheme.

Forgiveness that Separates

The first and most common type of false forgiveness is forgiveness that separates us from one another and it can be found in the religions of this world. This is where you as a 'good Christian' and a 'much better person', forgive the guilty sinners of this world. This form of forgiveness gives you, as an ego, the feelings of being godly, gracious, and innocent, by forgiving someone who is guilty and sinful. Immediately you can see how you and the person you are forgiving have become different and separate. This is not uniting with another; this is reinforcing separation by seeing differences. By using this form of forgiveness you are condemning yourself, because how you see someone else is how you see yourself. You cannot see sin and guilt in someone else and escape sin and guilt in yourself. Once you see sin in anyone, you make it real for both of you.

Forgiveness that Condemns

The second type of false forgiveness, not unlike the first, is also a trap. This form takes the shape that you as the forgiver are not better than the person you are forgiving, believing both of you to be guilty and sinful. Now you must believe that you both deserve the wrath and retribution of God because you both have sinned. You may have joined yourself with this other person, but in fact, you just separated both of you from God. Now God has to be seen as a judgmental and vengeful God who must punish the wicked and evil for their sins. Can you condemn yourself and still remember God?

Forgiveness with Hate

The third type of false forgiveness takes the form of a martyr as you sacrifice yourself at the hands of another. You sit in silence with a gentle smile, all the while inside you fume with anger at how this other person has hurt you. You do not show the bitter pain you feel because you feel that it is God's will that you should suffer in silence, but in your mind you hate the person with utter contempt. However, because you are so godly you will grin and bear it, after all, you think to yourself, it is God's will. So with saintliness you bear the anger and hurt that another gives. You do not show the bitter pain you feel. This is cruelty at its best – turned on yourself. You are condemning yourself once again as a victim of another person and of this world. This is passive aggressive.

Forgiveness with Blackmail

The fourth type of false forgiveness takes the form of bargaining and compromise. I will forgive you if you do not do that again, or, I will forgive you if you do this, or I will forgive you if you do that. What we are doing is we are putting a price on forgiveness to have our needs met. In other words, blackmail. You enslave another person because in their slavery is your release. Do this to anyone and it is you that is enslaving yourself. True forgiveness gives, as God gives, with no recompense. You can only truly give as God gives, all else is a mockery and illusionary giving. Steal someone else's innocence and you condemn yourself to death. See innocence in everyone, and you are claiming your own innocence.

We have all at some time practiced at least two, three or maybe all four types of false forgiveness described above. And if your state of mind is not in a perpetual state of peace and happiness at this very moment, then the reason now is very clear. These types of forgiveness simply do NOT work because they are specifically designed not to work. This is the ego right mind at work, very cleverly deceiving you into thinking that you have forgiven your brother through one of the various types of false forgiveness when instead all you have done is create more distance between you and others by asserting that the guilt that you have projected onto them is real thereby causing you to experience more pain, suffering and hell.

The True Right Mind

The true right mind is the objective for every student of *The Course* and in fact every spiritual seeker. That is what true forgiveness does - it takes you from the ego right mind, into the true right mind. The true right mind is a higher state of consciousness, because it is on level 2. Getting there is the easy part, the hard part is staying there, because it is your attachments to the ego that will keep bringing you back down once again. The true right mind is a mind that is at peace, but this peace does not depend on anything external. It is a mind that is based on equality, the equality of everyone, no exceptions.

No matter what your race, your creed or your beliefs, you will see yourself at one with everyone. Being connected to spirit, the true mind is creative. Being inspired is being in spirit - that is where the word inspired comes from. When you have successfully transcended your ego mind to your true right mind, both will dissolve and disappear. What will emerge then will be the one mind, the mind of enlightenment.

So, true forgiveness is vital for your transcendence from the ego mind to your right-minded higher Self mind and then on to enlightenment. It is also vital for you to sort out in your mind which type of forgiveness you are using, true forgiveness or false forgiveness, because one will keep you stuck, and the other being true, will set you free.

So, what is true forgiveness as described in *A Course in Miracles*? Well, there are three types of forgiveness in *The Course*. Each has its own purpose in helping you to wake up to the peace, joy and love of heaven on earth. Let us take a look at each one.

Advanced True Forgiveness (ATF)

"No gift of Heaven has been more misunderstood than has forgiveness".[2]

A Course in Miracles says, "The therapist sees in the patient all that he has not forgiven in himself, and is thus given another chance to look at it, open it to re-evaluation and forgive it."[3]

Healing and unconditional love are the same, because both only exist in the absence of judgment. Heaven only exists in a state of mind where judgment is absent.

This is probably the most important line in *A Course in Miracles*. The sin that you see in another person is the very same sin that you have not forgiven in yourself, and now you have another chance to forgive yourself. You will always see in another a reflection of how you see yourself. There are no exceptions to this rule. This is how we truly forgive ourselves. We can only forgive ourselves by forgiving ourselves for how we react to other people.

However, when you forgive yourself, it is important that you are careful to apply true forgiveness as taught in *A Course in Miracles* and that you don't make the mistake of applying false forgiveness, which is forgiveness to destroy as explained earlier.

There is a big difference here.

It is in only when you look upon another without judgment that true healing occurs. Healing and unconditional love are the same, because both only exist in the absence of judgment. Heaven only exists in a state of mind where judgment is absent. This is why it is called heaven, it is a place encompassed with total unconditional love. So let's go through each step and begin the practice of waking up, for it is only through forgiveness that you will wake up, and it will happen gently and slowly at your own pace.

When should we apply ATF, and when is it not required? It is important to understand what true forgiveness does before we go any further. True forgiveness takes us into the true right mind and detaches us from the ego thought system. True forgiveness detaches us from the past, from all past errors. True forgiveness undoes those heavy dark thoughts of fear and guilt, and will one day bring them to an end entirely. On that day you will be completely right-minded, and fear and guilt will be distant memories of an old life that is fading fast. So, when do I need to use ATF, and when do I not? The answer is in the call for love.

THE FIVE STEPS OF ATF

Step 1 - The Call for Love or The Extension of Love

The extension of love is when a person is extending love to you and you graciously accept it by returning it. Remember we receive by giving, and what you give you receive. What this means is this, if you meet someone and they smile at you, or hold a door open for you, this is called the extension of love. That person is sending you love, and the most polite and mannerly thing to do, is say thank you and smile back. That is you sending love back. And then, if you get the chance, you will do the same for someone else, smile or hold a door open, or whatever. These little acts of kindness are better for you then going to the gym, or for a spa. It is the love we give to others that we give to ourselves. You see, we are all either extending love or calling for love, all of the time, and it is important to know which is which.

When someone is angry with you, they are calling out for love. When someone is rude, arrogant, abusive, insulting or hateful, they are still calling out for love. It is our job to answer that call, with love. So how do we do that? First we must discover whose call for love is it? If someone is angry with you, shouting at you, and you do not react to that person, then that person is calling for love.

If you have not reacted, there is a strong possibility that you are already in your right mind, and if you are, anything you say or do will be correct. However, you must be very careful, because if you have denied your reaction, you may be hiding your own guilt deep within. Be very careful here, because the ego does not want you to practice true forgiveness, and if you do begin this practice, the ego will retreat and you will begin not reacting. Do not deny your reactions, if you do, you will be covering up your guilt and hate within. If you are not in denial and do not react, you may already be right-minded and will not need to do ATF.

However, let's say you do react and you react negatively to someone with say fear, anger, sadness, shame, etc. You are calling out for love, because it was you who reacted to the situation, and now you must forgive that reaction in yourself. This person has just showed you something that you have not forgiven in yourself.

Step 2 - Take Responsibility

What is it that you see in this person? What aspect of the ego do you see that this person is showing you? Recognize this aspect and identify it because this person is showing you what you have not yet forgiven in yourself.

By holding this in your mind you are recognizing that the problem is not outside of you, it is not in this other person, but rather the problem is in you. It is always an aspect of your own mind that needs correction. Never ever think that it is the

Only your ego will try and see another ego, and only your ego will try and correct another ego.

other person that needs to be corrected. Only your ego will try and see another ego, and only your ego will try and correct another ego. But remember there is only one ego and it always belongs to the perceiver - you!

Remember, to recognize the aspect you have projected before you move to step 3.

Step 3 - Undo and Remove Judgment

For clarity, let us use the example that the aspect you see in this other person is that this person is victimizing you. You simply cannot look on another person (body) and forgive them, they must be removed from the picture by you recognizing that the problem lies within you and not in them because it was you who just reacted. Remember this other person is just the mirror reflecting back to you how you see yourself. You must own the projection that you see in them. The ego's judgment says that you have attacked me and now I am justified in defending myself against that attack. The ego's judgment must be removed for ATF to be applied. We remove the ego's judgment and replace it with right-minded judgment.

So far, in the first step you have recognized this person is calling for love. In the second step you have acknowledged that the problem is not in this other person, the problem is in you. And now, in the third step, you remove your judgment on this person and what is left is the ego aspect you have projected out. Next, to undo this projection and experience the healing, which is the miracle, you must go to step four.

Step 4 – Undo Projection by Owning and Releasing

In the fourth step, now that the person is removed and you are left only with the aspect that you have projected, you are asked to undo the projection. To do this you now simply say and mean it in your heart: "This is a part of my own unhealed mind; this is the projection of my error and it belongs to me". Then, because you are now claiming it as your own you have the power to undo it and release it. Remember, only when you claim it as your own will you have all the power to let it go. Every time you do this, you wake up just a little bit more.

Step 5 - Release and Heal

The last step in ATF is releasing and healing. True forgiveness is impossible without your Higher Power, because the fifth step belongs to it. Step five is to simply hand over the part of your mind that you had denied. This step is very important; our projections must be recognized as ours and handed over to our higher power in order for the healing to occur.

Doing the five steps in ATF is what living *A Course in Miracles* really means: practicing forgiveness every day.

Summary -The 5 steps of ATF

Step 1: Firstly, ask yourself, is this a call for love or an extension of love?

Step 2: Acknowledge that what you see in this person is what you have not forgiven in yourself. This step recognizes that this person is wholly innocent.

Step 3: Remove this person from the scene of the crime. This step is undoing judgment.

Step 4: Bring back your projection into your own mind and own it. This step is undoing projection.

Step 5: Release and heal your mind. This step is you detaching from the ego.

Complete Forgiveness

Next we will move to Complete Forgiveness. Like ATF, Complete Forgiveness is one of the most powerful tools in *A Course in Miracles*. While ATF deals with our projections and shows us that what we see in another is what we have not forgiven in ourselves, Complete Forgiveness deals with our emotional problems and issues that have not yet been projected but that are causing a negative emotional reaction within our mind and in our lives. In other words, ATF is a reactive tool that brings back our projections, while Complete Forgiveness is a proactive tool that deals with our emotions before they are projected out onto other people, places or circumstances. Both are very important tools to use regularly depending on the situation.

Pain Is Inevitable, Suffering Is Optional

One of the most important passages you will read in *A Course in Miracles* is this, "*Nothing external to your mind can hurt or injure you in any way. There is no cause beyond yourself that can reach down and bring oppression. No one but yourself affects you. There is nothing in the world that has the power to make you ill or sad, or weak or frail.*"[4] There is absolutely nothing and no one external to you that can hurt you or cause you any pain whatsoever. You will never suffer again if you can truly understand the depth of what this is saying to you. When we are in pain, our first reaction is to look for someone else to blame. This may be your partner, your parents, your friends, your boss, your community, your government, some other countries' government or just about anyone. These reactions are all "rationalizations". And just what is a rationalization?

There is a line in *A Course in Miracles* that says *"I am never upset for the reason I think."*5 That sentence depicts what a rationalization is. It is a lie we tell ourselves over and over again which we believe to be true. You are rationalizing your pain every time you blame someone or something external to yourself for the pain you are experiencing. Furthermore, you keep that which you rationalize. That means that every time you rationalize your pain, you keep it, and in keeping it, you suffer. We think that we know why we are in pain, and we then blame this person or that situation for causing us that specific pain.

Perhaps you have just ended a relationship and you are hurting. You may be blaming your ex-partner for that hurt. This person has possibly betrayed you with someone else and you are devastated. Your first reaction is to think that this person has hurt you very much, and the reason you are in pain is because of him/her. This is what most people think after coming out of a close relationship. If you think this, you will believe this, and if you believe this, you will suffer. Remember, the pain has always been inside you. It is impossible for someone else to hurt you, as nothing external to you can hurt you in any way. All the pain has always been inside. It has been covered up deep within, and then someone comes along and lifts that cover off, and we blame them for hurting us.

However, there is another view, and if you can begin to understand the enormity of what I am conveying and accept it, then you can become free of all suffering forever. Jesus said "the truth will set you free".

The following explains what he meant. Every bit of pain that you have ever experienced or ever will experience in the future comes from your belief that you are a separate human being. Those who have reached the awakened

Oneness and bliss go hand in hand, as suffering and separation also go together.

or enlightened stage in their journey have one thing in common: they all know that they are one with everyone and therefore one with God. You cannot be one with God and not be one with each other. God is oneness and we, as His children, are one and equal with everyone else here. Heaven is a state of bliss. Why? It is because heaven is a state of oneness. Oneness and bliss go hand in hand, as suffering and separation also go together. You are free to believe this or not, but you are not free from the consequences of your choice.

In understanding the premise of Oneness, if you think back over your life and recall all those people who you believed that you had hurt in some way or another, you will see that it was not possible for you to hurt any of them. Why? Because all pain was already within them from the very moment they were born. And consider this also. Think of all the people that you believe hurt you. You begin to see that it was impossible for them to hurt you as all the pain that you ever endured was always inside you. This concept will free your mind of all pain, and in doing so, it will be your escape from hell. If you can accept this new concept and allow it to germinate and grow inside you, it will forever change your life, and the life of all those around you. This is your escape from the hell that you live in.

You will always suffer unless you can bring the pain you are experiencing to the truth. All suffering comes from our unwillingness to look at things another way. As stated previously, all pain is within, and always has been within. So, where does it come from? All pain within comes from our belief system,

> *All pain is in the mind. It comes from our belief that we are separate from our Creator and each other.*

and unless you are willing to look at this and relinquish your old outdated beliefs, you will always experience more and more suffering.

So what exactly is suffering? Without fail, you are suffering if you are not experiencing "bliss" every single second of your life, every moment of every day. Rationalizing the pain or even mild discomfort you experience is what keeps you asleep, and also keeps the pain in your mind, which leads to more suffering in your life. However, if you are on the journey towards waking up, there is another way to look at this, in fact, there is another way to deal with this. And when you discover what that is and apply the concepts it will increase the joy and bliss in your life like you have never experienced before and it will set you on your path to waking up. Let's explore that now.

All pain is in the mind. It comes from our belief that we are separate from our Creator and each other. The Bible tells us that we sinned against God, and because of that sin we feel guilty and now that guilt leads us into a state of fear, the fear of punishment. So, every ounce of suffering that we have ever experienced has come from our belief that we are separate from God and each other. Therefore, when we undo our belief in separation, we undo all our suffering as well. All suffering is in the mind, because all beliefs are in the mind. We must go to the cause of suffering, our beliefs, and undo them there. The effects of suffering are felt in the body, but the cause of all suffering is in the mind. And once you undo the cause you also undo the effect. This is the law of cause and effect. If there is no cause, there cannot be an effect. This law cannot be broken.

Now, you could disagree with the Bible's teaching and say that you do not believe in the Adam and Eve story of sin and guilt. But that would be a case of denial. Let me explain. All fear that you experience in this world comes from your belief in the separation, it comes from guilt, whether you believe the Bible story or not. You will continue to suffer if you continue to rationalize that someone else in your life is causing your fear and pain. However, if you are in any way willing to just try this method of undoing the fear and pain you are experiencing, you will see that this really does work. This method has worked for countless people since they began using it.

UNDOING EMOTIONAL TRAUMA
Undoing Grief

Some people may be in tremendous pain as a result of having lost a loved one. Certain individuals can spend their entire life in this state of pain. This is suffering and it need not be. There is another way to look at and deal with this state of mind. All grief that you have, or will experience, comes from the loss of God in your awareness. This is the truth of all loss, whether it is the loss of a relationship, the loss of a job, or the loss of a loved one. All grief due to any seeming loss comes from the belief in the separation, period.

Now, instead of rationalizing the pain you feel by believing that it comes from the loss of a person, a place, or an event, bring that pain to the truth. Because it is the truth that will set you free. Simply repeat the following words in your mind and then you will come to know them to be true in your heart: "This pain I feel comes from my belief in separation". Continue to repeat these words every time you feel that pain. I guarantee you that you will find true peace of mind within a few days to a week. There is powerful energy in thoughts. The most painful events of your life have always come from one single thought that you believed to be true. All thoughts produce emotions, and emotions produce behavior. Thus, you release your pain by not rationalizing your thoughts. This will end your suffering and grief.

Undoing Fear

Fear is a very powerful emotion and to live a life of fear is to live a life of suffering. It is important to remember that what you fear you empower, and the more you empower fear the stronger it becomes within you. Hence, the more powerful fear is, the more you will suffer. The problem is that when we rationalize our fears, they become strong within our minds. You may be fearful of things such as flying, spiders, rats, heights, certain people or certain situations – these are all rationalizations. You will keep that particular fear strong within you as long as you keep rationalizing. This is suffering, but this suffering is avoidable. In order to eliminate fear once and for all simply repeat the following the next time you experience fear in any given situation: "This fear I feel comes from my belief in separation". Keep repeating these words every time you feel that fear. You need not believe what you are saying, but that will not matter. What matters is that you are now not rationalizing the problem. You are bringing the problem to the truth, and the truth will set you free!

Undoing Guilt

The undoing of all guilt is done by following the exact same procedure. All guilt that you have or will experience has come from your belief in separation. You could feel guilty after having done something or said something. Possibly you feel guilty because you did not do or say something. The form of the guilt is not important. Rather, it is the content of guilt that is important and the content of all guilt comes from the belief in separation.

You need not believe the words that I am saying as the words are not important. It is your thoughts that are important. So, every time you experience any guilt in any situation simply repeat the following in your mind: "This guilt I feel comes from my belief in separation". Keep repeating this process every time you experience any form of guilt or shame. You will be set free from guilt. It is the truth that will set you free.

Everything in your mind and in this world is built upon cause and effect. Every thought that you have ever experienced has an effect on your emotional state, which filters into your daily life. The thought of guilt produces thoughts of shame, which produce the emotional experience of fear. All guilt calls for punishment, which is the true source of all fear. Thus the true source of fear comes from the guilt that is within our minds; fear does not ever stem from what we think we have done or not done, but from guilt.

When Jesus was being tortured, torn and crucified, he experienced no pain whatsoever, but he uttered the words, *"Father, forgive them for they do not know what they do"*. Nowhere in the Bible does it say that he cried out in pain at the crucifixion. Why? Because Jesus did not believe in separation. He knew he was one with God, and therefore was one with and equal to all of us. All pain is in the mind. Jesus had no belief in separation and therefore had no pain in his mind. All pain in the body comes from the pain in our minds, which comes from our belief in separation. Undo the belief in separation, and you undo all pain in your life, and when you undo the pain in your mind, which is your belief in separation, that is the end of suffering. The truth will set you free.

Simple Forgiveness

Simple forgiveness is really the simplest form of forgiveness that there is. It deals only with our judgments. When you have awakened and begin to live life truly for the very first time, you will automatically use simple forgiveness to remain awake.

Simple forgiveness has three steps:

Step 1: Recognize that you have judged this person, place or circumstance.

Step 2: Correct that judgment by bringing it back inside and taking responsibility in recognizing that you are seeking nothing from this person, place or event. When you have no investment whether they like you or not, you will be without judgment.

Step 3: Hand over your judgment to the higher power. You simply hand over all judgments that you have made. This process will keep you connected to source and also keep you awake.

You can see how important it is to not only learn and master this form of detachment, but to apply it. If you would now like to take it one step further, and practice another form of detachment, then the next chapter is also very important. Self-empowerment is so important not only to every spiritual seeker, but to every individual in this world. If you are not self empowered, you are self-crucified.

So what is self empowerment?

CHAPTER 11

~~~

Self Empowerment

The first thing that is important to come to understand is that you cannot make other people love you, or even like you. You do not have power over any external thing, and you will never be self empowered as long as you feel that you do. I now have a golden rule on how I live my life, and it is this: what other people think or even what they say about me is none of my business.

There is genuine power in this rule, because in truth, I have no power over how others perceive me. In this world, people are going to believe what they choose to believe, and there is nothing that I can do about that. In accepting this, I don't even attempt to think about what you or anyone else thinks of me. To do so would be a waste of time and effort on my part. Furthermore, I have real power over how I feel at all times because of my new way of thinking. In any situation, I give no other person or no external thing any power over me. Thus, I am fully self empowered.

In this world, self empowerment means having power over others. People may feel powerful because of their wealth, their possessions or circle of influence, however, this is not the self empowerment I speak off. The power I am referring to relies on no one and nothing external to you. True self-empowerment is not in the power of having, it is in the power of Being.

No one has the power to hurt you unless you give them the power to do so. And why are we inclined to give others power? We give our power away in the belief that we need to be liked or loved by certain people. However, if you really think about it, this logic is irrational as you have no control over how other people think much less over what other people think or even what they say about you. Now is the time to stop disempowering yourself, right now! For example when someone spreads rumors, this can be very hurtful for a lot of people. How much would it hurt you if you learned that someone had been spreading vicious rumors about you? Likely, it would hurt quite a bit. Would you do anything about it?

You may seek revenge on that person. But would revenge really change anything? Yes, you may gain some satisfaction from seeking revenge, but under the laws of projection, vengeful acts come back to hurt you. On the other hand, on hearing the malicious rumors, it is possible that you may wallow in self-pity and feel sad and gloomy for weeks? The point is that these responses would be unnecessary if, in the first place, you did not care about what others thought or said about you. There is true power in self-empowerment which is the power to make real choices and real decisions.

You are either empowering your true Self, or your false ego-self all of the time. There is never a time where you are doing neither. You empower your ego-self every time you feel guilty, afraid, judgmental, or jealous. You empower your ego-self every time you feel angry, sad, irritated, annoyed or depressed. As long as you continue to empower your ego-

> *You are either empowering your true Self, or your false ego-self all of the time. There is never a time where you are doing neither.*

self, you will remain spiritually asleep and in pain and fear. However, as soon as you being to disempower your ego-self, you begin to empower your true Self. This is the only true choice you have, it is the choice between your false self and your true Self.

Self empowerment has five stages; self awareness, detachment, discernment, forgiveness and action. To be self empowered is to question the perceiver of the experience. You are not who you think you are. If you do not begin to question who it is that is afraid? Who is angry? Who is feeling guilty? Who is feeling fearful? And if you do not question all of these feelings, emotions and reactions to external stimulus, you will never wake up! It is only your false self that can feel like this, while your true Self can never feel any of these emotions.

So, the first step in self empowerment is self awareness. It is the power to question the perceiver. Let us say that you are having an argument with your girlfriend, and you have become angry. And in that moment you are both fighting and arguing with each other. But later, when things calmed down, you look back on the entire situation using these five steps. Well, in this first step you now question who was it that was angry? Who was the self that reacted with anger? This step is so important because it stops the ego right on its tracks. This first step will calm down any situation in an instant if you can remember to use it. This is the difference between being awake and asleep.

When you are asleep you lose awareness of your true Self, and you will get lost in the dramas of this world with your false self. When you lose self awareness you will disempower yourself, then you will get caught up in the events and behaviors of the external world, in the activities going on in your body, or in other bodies. Should you do so, you become mindless and leave yourself in a state of mindlessness. The hardest lesson you will probably ever learn is self awareness. To be self-aware is to be mindful, and to be mindful is to be self empowered. You are on the first rung of the ladder to self-empowerment when you learn to be mindful, and to be self-aware. You become self empowered when you stop holding others responsible for your pain, and take full responsibility for everything you feel.

The second stage to self-empowerment is detachment. The power to detach is the ability to step back from whatever the current situation is. You must learn to detach in any situation in which you feel angry, threatened, depressed or anxious. Other people may seek to draw you into their web or you may become drawn in by a variety of reactions to external situations: through feelings, emotions, and confusion – your potential reactions are countless. The power to detach is therefore fundamental for self-empowerment. It is crucial to understand that you are an actor playing a role, a player in the game. You are lost as soon as you merge into that role and forget that you are the actor.

If you begin to believe the role you are playing, you will get lost in the game and become caught up in the identity of the role. You will then fight or die for this self that you believe is you. Every time you are in an argument with someone, you are fighting for your

When you can detach emotionally from any situation, you detach from the ego. You disempower the ego itself.

enemy, the ego, and you will one day die for your enemy, the ego. This is how the ego continues, you will sacrifice your life for it, and you will never know that you are doing it. This is the greatest con trick in the world.

When you can detach emotionally from any situation, you detach from the ego. You disempower the ego itself. If you do not detach you will end up fighting a battle for the ego, and it is only the ego who wins those battles. On the other hand, by remaining detached you will remain self empowered because self-empowerment holds your awareness in your true Self. It keeps you awake which leads to inner peace. Inner peace begins the moment you choose not to allow another person or circumstances to control your emotions. Awareness of being the actor playing a role, will keep you free from judgment and condemnation. You can only make real choices when you are in a state of full self awareness of your true self and detached from any emotions.

To be right-minded is a quantum leap from being wrong-minded. Quantum leaps in creative thinking are born from being in the right mind; a still and silent inner world that becomes the receptacle for the genius you truly are. A genius sees what everyone else sees, but thinks what no one else thinks. The way to build this inner power is through mindfulness; simply learning to be quieter by speaking less, thinking less and growing a discipline within the self. Thinking on level 1, is not creative; it is the regurgitation of what you already know. By being self-aware and detached, you will begin to make real choices through discernment.

The third stage is discernment, and this is the power of using true choice. It is the choice of what is true over what is false, rather than what is right over wrong, or good over bad. You cannot discern if you are emotionally involved in any situation. This is why the second stage is so important, you must detach to discern clearly. If you do not detach, you will be making decisions based on emotional involvement, and then, you will always be wrong.

Remember this all begins with self awareness. By being self-aware you have the power to detach from any situation and discern accurately. Discernment is the power of clarity; seeing with different eyes, and hearing with different ears. It is about trusting your highest Self even in the face of contrasting opinions. It is the power to listen to what is known deep within you. This power delivers a capacity to look beyond past, present and future implications of different options and possibilities. To discern correctly is to be without judgment in choosing. If you react and make a choice based on any situation being right or wrong, good or bad, or guilty or innocent, you are discerning wrongly.

There is no right or wrong, there is no good or bad, nor guilty or innocent. There is only what is true and what is false. This is true discernment. The power to discern is like a window that allows you to step out of the limited aspects of the two rooms you have of past and future, and, as an Observer and decision maker, see the reality of any situation here and now.

The real power of discernment is to first see what is false, and then choose against it.

We have all made future plans that were dependent on our past. Our futures then became simply different versions of the past, thus leaving us with no real choice. Self awareness brings you right into the present moment, and it is here that your true power lies, in the here and now.

The real power of discernment is to first see what is false, and then choose against it. It is the power to choose truth, and to stand alone in that truth no matter what. It is intrinsically connected to self-empowerment, and takes much or all of its strength from that power. The power of discernment flows more easily if your self awareness has been exercised well. Even if a person knows the best course of action, they are bereft of the

323

power to choose if they don't have the power to follow that knowing.

One who uses this power is making the following declaration: "I trust myself and I am clear that my actions are right. I am prepared to stand by my choices and to allow and be accountable for the consequences of my choice. I will stand alone if necessary. I believe I am acting correctly". Sometimes, when you are the only one who can see truth, it requires extraordinary inner knowing to make a stand, to act decisively and to move forward. Whenever something – a situation, a person, an event – is awkward or out of kilter, the self empowered have the power to accept 'what is' rather than to expect or try to change anyone or anything. The self empowered have the power to know that the future is in many ways already written and that it is up to them to have the courage to stay on the path in order to see it unfolding.

To summarize up to this point, in the first step we become self-aware. We question the perceiver. Then, we detach emotionally from the situation. You cannot make good decisions based on emotional reactions. In the third step then, we discern what is the best course of action for all concerned. You must take the best course of action for your highest Self. We make that decision based on what is true and what is false. The fourth step now is forgiveness, and the only true forgiveness is self-forgiveness.

Self empowerment really comes from being right-minded. The ego self is a wrong-minded thought system, while the true Self is a right-minded thought system. And it is forgiveness that take us from that wrong-minded aspect of ourselves, our false self, into our right-minded true Self. Simply put, forgiveness takes you into the right mind. The right mind is a thought system that is based on love, peace and joy. It is compassion, caring, sharing and oneness.

The wrong mind of the ego is based on self-interests, fear, guilt, hate and anger. This is what you are truly discerning: Which mind do I want to experience the world in? This is the only true choice you have in this world, to be wrong-minded, or right-minded. And if you use forgiveness every day, you will one day end up fully right-minded. There you will be fully self empowered. Remember, you cannot forgive another person, or what another person does. You can only forgive yourself.

Forgiveness is vital to your inner wellbeing. All health matters that will arise within you will stem from decisions you have made not to forgive. In any situation where you have reacted to another person, place or event, you must apply forgiveness. The world is a mirror that only reflects back to you how you see yourself. If you get lost in the role of the actor, you will think that there is good and evil, right and wrong, heaven and hell, all around you. If you lose self awareness, and merge into this role, you will disempower yourself all over again.

Through forgiveness, self-empowerment will give you the ability to be at peace with the state of all things, to sense that there is a plan, and that you are a humble instrument privileged enough to play a part in this unfolding. It is the understanding that what is "in the way", is the way. What is in the way are the obstacles to progress and spiritual advancement. It is these obstacles that must be looked at and overcome.

The obstacles that emerge are only telling you that you are still thinking in the same way you have thought before. It is a pattern of thinking that labels the situation as a problem; the problem only exists in choice. Each so-called obstacle calls for you to pay attention, and to access the un-programmed inner world, the new filter, in order for you to see more clearly. Forgiveness will remove all obstacles in your path and enable vision to emerge. See Chapter 10 – *True Forgiveness*.

The fifth and final stage now is action; remember, sometimes the best course of action is to take no action at all. But if you need to take action, after having followed the above four steps, your mind will be clear and pristine, and you will be sure and correct in all decisions that you make at this point. Most of all, because you have applied true forgiveness, you will be right-minded. And being right-minded, you will not make any wrong decisions. If someone needs to be brought to justice, then that will be the best course of action to take. If you need to ring the police, you will ring the police knowing that this is the best and most loving action you can take to save this other person from future harm to both themselves and others. If you need to walk out of a relationship, then walk away, knowing that this is the right action for you to take. Being spiritual and applying true forgiveness does not mean that you let yourself be treated like a punching bag for others to abuse you. You must value yourself above everything else in this world. You are not here to suffer, you are here to wake up to the incredible spiritual being that you are.

The world is the way the world is. Allow it to be, and then seek to perceive it differently. Otherwise, you become caught in the play, in the game, in your reaction, and once again you have forgotten you are the actor and you have once again become lost and disempowered. Remember, the more disempowered you are, the more empowered the ego is. If the vision of a beautiful future is powerful enough within you, you will attract all that is required to manifest that future. You are the instrument, but not the knower of all things. A seed of contentment will surely grow worthwhile fruit since what is inside you contributes to what manifests in your outer world.

The people closest to you, those in your personal relationships, will test you the most, similar to how a child tests its parents.

People react when they feel the discomfort of change, projecting and blaming those they believe are responsible for their own discomfort. This is not always rational, but when people feel threatened, they resort to survival tactics. Self-empowerment is the power to handle whatever anyone doles out. It is the power to see beyond the behavior, recognizing the motivation which drives the behavior and then dealing with it.

The people closest to you, those in your personal relationships, will test you the most, similar to how a child tests its parents. You will win their trust if you pass the "test"- by being without judgment- and instead, answering their deeper need, which is always a call for love. Through the power of forgiveness, self-empowerment will lead you to be free from vices such as: ego, jealousy, envy, attachment, anger, and greed. You have attained self-empowerment when your self-worth is not based on position, reputation, status or externals of any kind. Having attained self-empowerment, you have a knowing of the true power of your higher self. You have let go of all external stimuli that are destructive, useless and wasteful.

Self-empowerment is the power that allows you to let go of all negative emotions, and to hold nothing from past errors in your heart, or anything that lies in your desires for a perfect future in your mind. Letting go requires courage, forgiveness, trust and purity. It means your life starts anew from this point onwards.

Self-empowerment is the strength to say "no" to negativity, and "yes" to peace. Self-empowerment requires you to let go of all the confines of your false identity. You will have greater understanding and compassion for yourself and for others when you let go of the expectations you have of yourself, and those that you believe other people have of you. In letting go of expectations, you become free to make decisions that are incisive and imbued with the power of truth, rather than with what is false.

Self-empowerment will hold a vision of a new world for you, and a new way of living and working. It will compel you to let go of your age-old attachments to the ways of this world. You will let go of the ego's attraction to your limited identity. You will go beyond the opinions of others, and of behaviors destructive to yourself and to others. And, most importantly, self-empowerment will help you let go of "what I think I know", and "who I think I am", and empower you to gain the ability to choose a new life and a better way of living.

The main attributes of self-empowerment are peace and happiness, and the end of fear. Nothing will be too formidable to handle. The self empowered are equipped with all the powers needed to face whatever comes: fears or other overwhelming emotions, lack of self-worth, attacks or denigration by others, and situations that seem impossible and insurmountable. The self empowered do not, in any way, accommodate untruth or illusion, whether within their own character or in external situations. Because self-empowerment's underlying drive is love, it is the instrument of truth.

Thus, the person who is self empowered will deal with all that seems to be blocking the way forward through love, no matter what level of fear is involved. Nothing is allowed to hide; nothing dark or unsaid is enabled. Self-empowerment is the power that will bring you into the light. It is not aggressive, but rather, it is an assertive and powerful sense of who you are. You are light.

Everything External Changes

All external things have always changed, and always will change. However, you can only be happy and at peace when things are constant, and thus what you need is a constant. Only within you will you find everything you have been seeking; no ups, no downs, just a constant state of peace and happiness. Sounds boring, right? Remember, excitement and thrills are not happiness, they are both drugs that will have downsides. You will suffer hangovers from these highs that will be quite the opposite from happiness: they will be hell.

Sometimes it may be a painful hell and other times a dull hell, but hell nonetheless. Take a look at the things you have worked so hard to attain all your life. You were convinced that you were going to be happy when you attained them. How long did the happiness last? The truth is that you got tired and bored of them after a while and then you started over and moved on to the next attachment.

For example, maybe your partner did not bring you the happiness that you thought he/she would. So then you started looking for a new partner. Alternatively, you may have sought other things to bring you happiness; a new car, a new job, etc. Before you know it, you will have spent your entire life looking for external things that you thought would bring you that happiness that you craved so much, but it never came.

In truth, it is only you who can bring you the happiness that you seek. In order to do that, you must start looking in the correct place, which is always internally. Imagine a life that has no anger, no hate, no anxiety, no fear, no guilt and no attack. That is happiness. That is peace. Is that something that you would consider? If it is, then know it is inside of you. Seek it and you will find it for it is deep within your mind.

Attachments

Our lives are is like the tracing of a heart monitor. It has its ups and downs. However, it is the flat line on the monitor that ironically illustrates what it is to be alive, what real life is all about. This is the constant that you are looking for. Let me clarify this point for you. The flat line appears when all life goes out of the patient and they are then presumed to be dead. Your life, living as a false self, is the line that goes up and down pointing to the highs and lows of life.

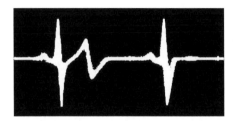

The Heart Monitor

For every high there is a low, and this continues throughout your entire life. It is your attachments that bring these highs and lows – moments of sheer joy and moments of severe loss of peace. You experience joy when your attachment gives you what you want, whereas, it is depression and anger when your attachment doesn't give you what you want. However, the flat line represents the constant, a constant state of awareness, a constant peace, a constant state of happiness and a pure constant love.

A flat line represents your true reality, without rushes of excitement, without severe depressions, but rather, just a constant state of being. To live the flat line is to live every day in bliss. It is not boring, but the ego will make you believe that it is.

Happiness is not about getting what you want; it is about loving what you have at any given moment.

Why? It is because there is no ego in that state of mind. It is a state of mind which you have now gained access to; it is the enlightened mind.

Enlightenment is a constant state of pure being; you are awake and fully aware at all times. On the other hand, when you are asleep, you are like a candle in the wind, with outside forces controlling how you will behave, how you feel, and how you exist. That is not living. That is being a prisoner to the external, with its consequent suffering. The constant changes are why life is so tiresome and why people are weary and fed up.

In reality, the only change you need is to slow down and become a constant being. The personality that you think you are needs many attachments to exist. You are always feeding this personality with attachments, and that is what is so demanding. What is making you so tired and weary is constantly feeding and serving a personality that is not who you are. That is slavery.

Freedom from this slavery does not lie externally, but rather it lies internally. Freedom comes from making different choices, and choosing different thoughts. Examine the demands of your attachments. Become aware of them, and choose to drop those that are valueless and keep those that have value. Attachments that demand your loss of peace through anger or depression should be the first to go. Happiness is not about getting what you want; it is about loving what you have at any given moment.

Attachments that need to be looked at and dropped are those that contain the following: demands, expectations, needs and desires. Drop them because they have no true value

You are not here to change the world, the world is here to change you!

and they will eventually hurt you. Attachments that demand your happiness will take your happiness away from you. Drop them before they drop you. Have preferences rather than attachments that have power over how you feel. Don't let your peace and happiness depend on any one of them. You are becoming right-minded when you can achieve this. If you are unhappy or angry, you have attached yourself to something that you are trying to change.

Acceptance is the key to happiness, and acceptance is the key to life. The biggest error you will ever make is to try to change the world, or to try to change another person. Accept that it is not your right to do so. Instead, recognize that when you change, everything and everybody else will change.

You are not here to change the world, the world is here to change you. You will never change anything in your life by trying to change the external. You are still going to be you, even if you change partners, change countries or change jobs. You might change these things and be happy for about a week or so. But you will always end up where you are now. Changing anything external will not change who you are. However, your whole world will change if you can change your mind, if you can change your thought system.

There is only one way to drop your attachments, and that is through awareness and understanding. Similarly, there is only one way to be right-minded, and that is to drop your wrong-minded thought system. The wrong mind has been programmed for attachments, needs, judgments, desires, hates, loves, fear, guilt and death. These are all false beliefs, false fantasies and false idols. Dropping your wrong-minded thought system requires change.

However, do not change your behavior if you have not changed your mind. Changing your behavior without changing your mind will not change who you are, and therefore will not change anything. In fact, to do so would be worse, because then you would be in conflict with your needs and desires and your right-minded attributes would be conflicting with your wrong-minded mind-set.

Another way to say this would be to say: Do not try to be good, and above all do not try to put on a show of holiness for others to pay you homage. You will naturally be good and act accordingly when you become right-minded. Life will then naturally flow from your right-minded thinking, and it will be peaceful, happy and loving. Peace and happiness is the natural state of being right-minded, and being right-minded you will automatically be happy for no reason whatsoever. Imagine how liberated you will be! Imagine how free you will feel when you no longer need to depend on any person or anything ever again for your happiness. That is living; that is a life.

How wonderful life would have been if you had been told at home or at school that seeking out all kinds of attachments would bring you nothing but pain? How free you would have been from all the pressure of attaining all these non-essential attachments? How glorious would your life have been? How loving and carefree the world would be without the stress involved in the attainment of attachments?

Do not educate your children to be rich and famous. Rather, educate them to be happy so that when they grow up, they will know the value of life, not the price of riches and fame. Attachments such as riches and fame destroy your capacity to be free. Attachments also destroy your ability to love because it is the attachment itself that you love. Further, it is the image of the attachment that you love the most, and whether it is a person or a thing, it will end up destroying you. Love is not an attachment. Love just is. Love does not come in the image of a person or a thing, because love is clarity of life, clarity of living — it is you.

Undoing Attachments

The attachments that we must undo are fundamentally, only thoughts. Every person in your life represents just a thought. It could be the thought betrayal, the thought of guilt, the thoughts of special love, or special hate. We are attached to our false identity, to our beliefs, ideas and concepts. We could be attached to the thought that you are a victim, and this means that you will remain attached to the thought of the victimizer, for life. All these are the attachments that we must detach from.

So, how do you detach from your attachments? The answer pertains to value. How much do you value peace? How much do you value true happiness? And how much do you want to live every second of your life in bliss? Look at each and every one of your attachments and the value that you have put on them. You would not be attached to them if you did not value them. How much do you want to keep them? Ask yourself what these attachments have brought to your life and you will see that they did not bring you the peace and happiness that you were seeking. Thus, having assessed the value of your attachments, ask yourself what value you place on true peace, love and happiness? That will begin the process of detachment.

For example, think of that time when you were heartbroken over a relationship that ended, and you thought that you would never get over it. You did. As time passed, you let it go, and then you got into another relationship, another attachment. And you didn't learn, you got hurt all over again. Simply doing the same thing over and over again, expecting a different result is the very definition of insanity! Attachments will destroy your capacity to love because all you will be concerned with is the need to be loved. And this need to be loved will conceal the love that you already have. You are saying that you don't have love if you are searching for love. Everyone has love within. Search for it within yourself. Find it, and you will never need to search for external love again. You don't need to be loved– you are already loved and always will be. You just need to connect to the love within.

You don't need excitement to be happy, you need peace to be happy. Excitement will bring a downside, and you don't need any downsides in your life. You have had enough of those! You don't need people to be happy either, instead, you need to find yourself to be happy. You don't need to keep making yourself attractive to feel loved. Because you are a spiritual being you are love, not a body. If you are not happy at this moment in your life, then look truly at your life, value what is valuable and detach from what is valueless. It is that simple. Write down everything that has brought you pain, suffering and a loss of peace. Write down your attachments such as those you seem to hate that are surrounded by fear and guilt. Now look at them. Look deep into them. Do you really need these in your life? You don't! Start to detach these from your life, one by one, and I guarantee that you will be a different person before long. You will be free. You will be liberated from all external emotional attachments, and this means that nothing or no one will ever take your peace away again.

Remember, I am talking about how much you are attached to seeing people a certain way, and to seeing the world the way you see it. I am talking about a change in perception. A new way of seeing people and a new way of interpreting the world and what happens in it. I am not talking about giving up relationships, possessions, money or anything material. I am talking about our special relationships, our attachments to certain people in our lives and our attachments to how we think things should be in life. I am also talking about our thoughts, we are attached to so many thoughts, it is these thoughts that we have to let go. And these thoughts that we have are all invested in the people closest to us, which are our close special relationships.

Unlearning

When you begin to wake up you will be more peaceful, happier and you will be more loved and loving. Waking up means undoing and unlearning everything that you have ever learned. I learned everything under the sun at school; everything about every country, every planet, every substance and every mathematics problem. No one taught me about life. No one taught me how to think, instead, I was told what to think.

We spend all of our time and energy trying to change the world and trying to change other people; our spouse, our boss, our friends and our enemies – always trying to change the external. In our relationships, we are always trying to get the other person to change. We believe that if they would just change, we would be happy. And we go through life always trying to change what doesn't suit us. If we continue on this path, always changing the external, we will always be changing everything because it will never be right. But really, the only thing we have to change is our mind. When we do that, everything else will automatically change with it. Change can only happen through awareness and understanding, not by conflict. The more we fight to change something, the more resistance we will encounter.

Make peace with yourself; find the middle way, the balance. When Buddha accessed the enlightened mind, he did so by finding the middle way, the balance of life. By gaining

338

understanding through awareness, and by looking at the true value of what we have and who we truly are, we will find that middle way. We fight to keep what we value and the more we value it, the more we will fight to keep it. Alternatively, the less we value something, the easier we will find it to let it go. Whether you are aware of it or not, peace, joy and love have true value for you. These three qualities are what life is, what living is, and what enlightenment is. This is your true nature.

The above process of looking at my attachments worked for me. I began dropping all of my attachments by looking at the cost involved. I could then see how meaningless my attachments had become, and how they regularly cost me my peace of mind. I no longer valued what they offered me. At best, they were superficial, and at worst, they were insane. It was an easy decision to drop my investment in needless pursuits of seeking external belongings. I now began to see the truth in everything I was witness to. I also began to see what was not real; what was illusion. Somewhere in between truth and illusion, I began to live my new life. Oh, what a strange world we live in. The internal search is where you begin because there is a place inside of you where nothing is impossible. Looking back on my life from the perspective of being awakened, I was able to see the material, physical and psychological attachments of this world that made me the person I thought I was. If my state of peace was to continue unabated, I had to seriously look and undo the many attachments that I carried with me; attachments we all carry with us.

Letting Go

Letting go is the secret to attaining happiness. To get something new, you must let go of something old. Letting go is the hardest thing of all to do, but if you can manage to let go of the following mind-sets and attitudes, you will achieve true happiness.

Let go of comparisons, because you are comparing yourself with self. Let go of competition, because if you win, you will surely lose. There can be no winners in life; either we all win or we all lose. Let go of judgments. When you judge another, remember, your judgment defines you, not the person you judge. Let go of anger, as all anger comes from not getting what you want, just the way you want it.

All fear comes from denying who you truly are: you are spirit, not a body.

Let go of regrets as you have not done anything wrong, and so, there is nothing to regret. All regrets are lessons that you have just missed out on and these lessons will come around again. Let go of worrying because all worrying comes from the ego, and the ego wants you to worry. That is how the ego gets its energy from you. Worrying shows a severe lack of trust. Trust more and worry less. Let go of blame. Blaming is a projection of our own mistakes onto others because it is easier for us to blame someone else, than to blame ourselves. Let go of guilt as there is nothing to be guilty about. All guilt comes from not knowing who you truly are. Let go of fear. All fear comes from denying who you truly are: you are spirit, not a body. You are immortal, eternal and forever loved. Just for today, let go of who you are not.

Being kind with your words towards yourself and others creates confidence within you and those to whom you speak. Being kind in your thoughts creates profoundness with those you think of. Being kind in giving creates love within both yourself and the receiver. Make peace with your past, because it is screwing up your present and will be repeated in the future. Don't let the sadness of your past or the fear of your future ruin the happiness of your present; the here and now. From this moment onwards, let your motto in life be, "What others think of me is none of my business". Don't compare your life with that of others, for you have no idea what their journey is all about. And most importantly, always remember that no one is in charge of your happiness, except you.

You will be happy every single day of your life if you can accept that you are happy with what you have at any given moment, and rejoice in that fact. Happiness comes from acceptance of what is. The whole universe will be yours when you come to know that there is nothing lacking within you. This shift will not happen outside of you, but will occur within. As I have previously stated, my philosophy is as follows: "It is not my business what people say about me, or think of me. I expect nothing and accept everything just as it is". This philosophy really does make my life so much easier to live. Freedom comes instantly when I accept things just as they are.

You will always lose your peace of mind when you entertain the illusion of problems in your life. Every problem that you have ever experienced has only been experienced in your mind. And when you bring peace to your mind, you can solve the problem. By choosing peace in a non-peaceful environment, all non-peace will dissipate.

You will lose your peace of mind when you disagree with anyone on any matter. There is a line in *The Course* that says, *"I could see peace instead of this."*[1] I use this line more than any other line out of *The Course*. During a disagreement with someone or in any given situation, should I hear the ego's little voice say "I am right", I choose happiness by allowing the thought, *I can choose peace instead of this.* And I am always at peace because of this choice. Not feeling peaceful is always the result of errors in our thinking. If you look back over your life, the most painful experiences you have ever endured were only thoughts.

It is your insistence that external things must change that takes your peace away. To be at peace within your mind is to not seek to change anyone or anything. To find true peace we must let go of the way we see things and people in the world. It is the way we perceive that we must let go, because it always involves seeing guilt in someone else. If this perception continues, you will never be happy. It is said that acceptance is the key to happiness. This may be true, but the key to true happiness is peace. Thus, before you reach happiness there must be peace. So, that means that acceptance is the key to peace, and peace will bring forth your happiness.

This all sounds good, but, in the real world, how can you reach states of peace when all things around you are chaotic?

How can you attain peace when you are with difficult people such as an irate boss, or when you are under financial pressure with bills to pay, or other fear-provoking situations? In these moments of extreme anxiety, you can train your mind to choose peace by remembering the line from *The Course*, *"I could see peace instead of this."*[1] If you do not believe me, try it! It really does work, and will continue to work as long as you want it to work.

It is at the precise moments of chaotic interactions with people and with the world that you can go to that quiet serene place within your mind, and choose the peace of God rather than the chaos of the ego. In cultivating awareness, the most important lessons can be learned when you are in disagreement with someone else. There you are, right smack in the midst of confrontation with someone who is argumentative, irrational, and is insisting that they are right, and demanding that you agree with their righteousness. In the midst of this chaos, in that moment, you may be at peace if you can have enough awareness to remember and repeat, "I can choose peace instead of this". Let the other person be right. You have the peace and nothing else matters. The other person will also be happy because being right is what they demanded of you for your peace of mind. What you give is what you will receive. So, by giving peace, you received peace and now both of you have peace. This really does work as long as you can let go of your attempts to be right all of the time.

Raising Your Vibration

The people who give us the most trouble or problems in our lives are our greatest teachers. We would never have the opportunity to learn if it were not for these people in our lives. It is only through learning that we reach the higher vibrations. The people who push our buttons are the teachers who will show us what we have not yet mastered.

> *How and what we think will determine what frequency we are vibrating at.*
>
>

What we see in them is a reflection of what we have denied and suppressed within ourselves. All that we have suppressed will surface as we interact with our "teachers" and then we will see what needs to be overcome, and know what to let go of; be it fear, guilt, judgment, or being victimized. These are all lower vibrations.

We want to raise our vibration to a higher frequency where we will be able to experience the higher vibration frequencies of peace, happiness and love. Vibrations are within thoughts, and thoughts are within vibrations. How and what we think will determine what frequency we are vibrating at. What holds us in the lower vibrations are our judgments, our sense of fear, the guilt we carry, the anxiety we feel, the depression we are experiencing, and a sense of being victimized. These are all just thoughts, and thoughts can be changed. Remember this line, "I can choose peace instead of this". This line will raise our vibration, and I guarantee that any anger or annoyance will dissipate very quickly.

There are a few simple ways that you can raise your vibrations and emotions on a daily basis. Here are some examples: Be defenseless with someone whom you used to fear. Be tolerant with someone who you used to be intolerable with. Be gentle with someone whom you used to be harsh with. Be positive with someone whom you used to attack, and resolve any and all old issues that keep coming up. Make peace with someone whom you used to be at war with. Finally, love someone whom you used to hate. All of these new ways in thinking will raise our vibration. Examples of how we lower our vibrations on a daily basis include: impatience, disappointment, worry, doubt, blame, anger, hatred, jealousy, guilt, fear, anxiety, grief, pessimism, frustration, insecurity and irritation. These all lead to your descending into depression, loneliness and unhappiness. You must finally realize that all pain that you experience is self-created and it will keep you immobilized and angry. You must realize at a deeper level that, "I am doing this to myself". For me, when I finally realized this, I woke up.

All pain is suppressed guilt, and it will lead to illness if it is not dealt with. Rather than blaming someone else for your pain, accept it as your own. Say to yourself, "I chose this pain and now I can choose otherwise. I can choose peace instead of this". Then, watch your pain dissipate. Believe me, it will. Now you are learning... now you are healing...now you are waking up to your true power to choose. This holds true for all non-peaceful relationships, and holds true in all circumstances. All pain in your life comes from your belief that you have been a victim in some way.

The biggest obstacle to our peace of mind is the ego. We can only experience God in a peaceful mind, and so, to ensure that never happens, the ego's goal is always for us to keep losing our peace. Our journey towards knowing peace is our journey towards knowing and remembering God, but the ego does not want us to know God. To know God means the end of the ego, so it is literally a life and death situation for the ego.

Therefore, the ego has a huge investment in keeping you in a state of non-peace. From the ego's point of view, it is necessary that you are always focused on attaining something external. It does not matter to the ego what that something is, as long as it is external. Examples of attaining something external may be seen in the following: "I would be happy if I could only be with this person", "I would be happy if only I had enough money", "I would be happy if I could only get that job", etc. There are many more examples! These examples depict the idea that your happiness depends on getting something external. The problem is that you may fail to get something that you want and therefore you will lose your peace. Alternatively, you might attain something you want and it will make you happy for a while. However, you eventually realize that the thing that you attained was not what you thought it would be, and so you lose peace once more.

Keep in mind that your loss of peace was always the ego's motive and so the ego is very eager to have you continue believing that you need to search for things outside of yourself to be happy. The last thing the ego wants is for you to start searching within because that is where peace is; that is where

God is. God can never be found externally; not in a "holy building", not in a "holy person", not in a "spiritual place" or in a "special book". God only exists within you; within your mind. The ego knows that...and now, you do also!

One simple tool that may be used in order to avoid losing your peace is that you stop blaming others or stop blaming circumstances for your lack of peace. No one, and I mean no one, has the power to take your peace away, unless you give them permission to do so. For example, if someone says something to you that takes your peace away, then you must have believed that you could be attacked in the first instance.

Being in the wrong mind, you believe that you can be attacked, as the ego is fighting for survival. It is the personality you believe you are that can be attacked, because it is false, as is the ego. If you are right-minded, you have no need for defenses. You will know that you cannot be attacked. You will have no need to be right, and you will choose peace instead. It is only the ego that needs to be right and only because it is false. The ego is a fraudulent thought system, emanating from a fraudulent thought.

The ego will clutter your mind with all kinds of thoughts such as: how terrible you are, how terrible other people are, how terrible the world is, how uncaring and unloving you are, how uncaring other people are, or how unloving and uncaring the world is. All of these are expressions of the ego's wrong-minded thought system. All of these thoughts are designed to take your peace away, and for you to be a victim of yourself, of other people, and of the world. The ego just loves victims who believe that there are guilty people out there who committed these wrongs. On every occasion that you listen to and believe in these thoughts, you are strengthening the ego's wrong-minded goal to keep you in a state of distress. Just for one day, observe how many times you buy into this way of thinking and ask yourself honestly, "How does that make me feel?" There is however another way to live in this world. There is another set of thoughts to choose from and there is another mind to choose.

The ego just loves victims who believe that there are really guilty people out there who committed these wrongs.

You will become a peacemaker when you become right-minded. Remember, to have peace, you must give peace. Each and every day you are provided with countless opportunities to be a peacemaker. You cannot give away what you do not have. If you are not at peace within yourself, you do not have peace to give away and you are unable, therefore, to become a peacemaker. Being a peacemaker is not about judging who is right and who is wrong, or who is innocent and who is guilty.

The true peacemaker will see both parties the same, neither being right nor wrong. The peacemaker will see both parties as innocent. In order to be a true peacemaker, it is vital that you are non-judgmental. In all situations, you will express love to everyone involved, because you are coming from the right mind and you are a messenger from God. You will not need to worry about what to say or what to do, because whatever you say or do will be loving towards everyone. It cannot be otherwise coming from your right-minded, non-judgmental mind-set. Take heart, everyone is on the road of spiritual advancement, whether they know it or not.

Letting the Past Go

Everyone goes through events that will be experienced as happy or painful. However, because in the external world nothing ever stays the same, even the happy experiences can bring us a sense of loss and pain when they come to an end. The past cannot be changed or edited, it can only be accepted and released as lessons learned or unlearned. All attachments to the past must be let go.

The most difficult attachments that you may resist dropping are your past experiences of pain and suffering. People cling to the attachments of pain, trauma and loss. These negative experiences will leave you stuck in the past, bringing that emotional pain and suffering into the present, and leaving you fearful of the future.

This clinging to past negative emotional attachments will leave you in a state of depression, which leads to severe sadness and unhappiness. The root of all depression comes from loss. You believe that you are depressed because you have lost your attachment, which may be a person, a place or a thing. In reality, the reason you are depressed is because you have separated yourself from your true Self. This is the price we pay for all attachments; we have substituted our attachments for our true identity and now we define ourselves by the relationships that we are in, and the things that we have.

When they are gone we feel an emptiness and a loss because it is as if we have lost a part of ourselves and who we thought we were. What we need to remember is that other people, outside conditions, and events do not define us. Further, we cannot control anything external to us and we certainly cannot control the events that already happened in the past. The best thing is to let them go. If your goal is peace and happiness, you must take the lesson from the experience that your happiness will never be found by trying to control people or things that are external to you, and let them go. Choose another way.

The only thing that you have control over is how you perceive the events that seem to be happening around you and your thoughts about it. When you do this you will find that your peace and happiness have always been within and you do have the power to control what thoughts you choose to think and, therefore, you have the power to experience peace and happiness. Choosing to see the love and peace in every situation and to not attach yourself to the thoughts of the ego, which always cause you to experience pain or anger, is to be right-minded.

Reality is the one constant. Reality is timeless, changeless and eternal. Becoming right-minded is the stepping stone to being restored to reality. Once you are restored to reality nothing that occurs in this world will ever have an effect on you again. Your peace and happiness will never be taken away by anyone's actions or words. Is changing your thoughts and changing your mind not worth it when you realize the importance of right-mindedness? Examine your attachments to the present and to the past and realize how worthless their true value is. These attachments are worthless if they can change and thus are not constant. They are worthless if they are external and they take your peace away.

Don't let your happiness and peace depend on anything external to you. We all have preferences. We all prefer certain foods, certain clothes, certain memories from our past and things that we would like to experience in the present. However, don't let your happiness depend on having or not having them. You will know that you have become attached to something if you feel angry or depressed when you are without it and have lost your peace. If that be the case, it should be dropped as soon as possible.

Take notice that the biggest attachment that you carry around with you is the past; past experiences, past disappointments and past errors. Drop the past because it is over, gone and finished. There is absolutely nothing you can do presently to change any of it. The best gift you can give yourself is to let it go. Have a last look at it, make peace with it, resolve any outstanding conflicts and move on. Don't live in the past. If you cannot let go of the past, you will always be experiencing the present in the past, and you will be using your past experiences to reference everything in the present. You will judge everything in this present moment from a past experience. That is not living, instead, that is being stuck reliving what has already occurred over and over again.

You have many memories from the past, some good memories, and some very painful memories. Memories that you hold onto could involve the loss of a loved one. You believe that you must also hold onto the painful memories in order to hold onto the good memories. You believe that it is like a package and that you must take the good with the bad. You believe that if you let go of the painful memories, you will also lose the good memories and that the suffering and pain of grieving actually connects you to the person who has passed away. We apply the same belief to relationships. If a relationship breaks up or if someone simply goes out of our lives, we are afraid to let go of the pain and suffering attached to the memories of this person or persons because we are afraid that we will lose them, or that we will lose our love for them.

So, we hold onto the pain and suffering as well as to the love. This is extremely painful. However, the opposite is true, as the pain and suffering that you are holding onto is cutting you off from the love that you feel for that person. You can only be connected to that person through love, not through pain and suffering. The more pain and suffering you are experiencing through the loss of a loved one, the more you are disconnecting yourself from them in love. Drop the attachment to the pain and suffering, and you will have a much deeper connection to that person through love and spirit. You will have a deeper connection to that person because, in reality, we are all one. The greatest moment in your life is right now. No matter what has happened in the past, you can start over right this second. What you do now will determine what your future will be.

The secret to letting the past go is this: you must take full responsibility for everything in your past. You see, your past is a collection of stories that involve you and someone else, usually someone very close to you. In each relationship you have, you have a story with that person. Within

You cannot keep little parts of each story in your past. If you keep a part of a story, you keep the entire story, good and bad.

that story you have with this person, you are playing a role, you could be the victim, or the victimizer. It is usually one or the other we all play. Therefore as long as you keep the story, you keep everything in the story. If you cannot let go of the role you played in the story, you keep the full story.

You cannot keep little parts of each story in your past. If you keep a part of a story, you keep the entire story, good and bad. If you perceive yourself to be a victim in the past, you must correct that before you can move into the present, here and now. The past keeps the present from you, and as long as you keep the past, you deny the present, here and now. It is only in the now that you will wake up, so you must find peace in this present moment, right here, right now. Peace does not exist in any other moment. And as long as you keep the past, you will never find peace in the present.

Only you can bring peace and happiness into your life. Only you can make the choice to wake up and remember who you truly are. Only you have the real power to do all of these things, no one else. Only you!

Heaven is a choice, and that means that love is a choice. To choose heaven, is to choose love, unconditionally. This world has yet, not only to practice what true love is, but has yet to truly understand what it is. If you cannot choose to love unconditionally in a relationship, then you are not free to choose Heaven. All God's relationships are unconditional, and if you cannot live an unconditional relationship in this world, then you certainly cannot live an unconditional relationship with God in Heaven. You are free to choose Heaven or hell, conditional or unconditional, selfishness or selflessness, that is the choice we have in all relationships. So, what are "Love and the Illusion of Love"?

CHAPTER 12

~~~

Love and the Illusion of Love

If you cannot ride a bicycle, changing bicycles is not going to help you ride. In the same way, if you do not know what a relationship entails, then changing relationships is not going to help you. Quite simply you must become the love that you seek. If you do not love yourself, then how can you expect someone else to love you? There is absolutely nothing wrong with having good looks, a nice house, fine clothes, lots of money or a good sexual relationship, but if you think that it is a necessity to have all of those things just to be happy in your relationship then you are going to be very disappointed in the end.

If you really want a relationship that is based on true love and not ego-based, you must work on the fundamental foundation stones required so that true love can emerge through you, to the other person, and back to you again, because what you give in a relationship is exactly what you will get back. True spiritual advancement is receiving by giving. Be careful though, it is not giving with the expectation that you will receive; there is a huge difference.

When you want something, like love, our spirit knows that we must give love first to receive it. Alternatively, the ego will give with the expectation to receive. This is not true giving, it is conditional, because you are only giving love with the expectation that you will receive it back. And when you do not receive it, just the way you want it, you are going to hate the person who failed to fulfill your needs. This is an ego-based relationship.

The foundations for a successful, loving, true relationship must be based on both loving and giving unconditionally. You will need to learn the true meaning of the following: trust, truth, honesty, gentleness, defenselessness, generosity, patience, faithfulness, joy, and finally, tolerance. In a relationship that is based on true love, nothing the other person would say or do would affect how you feel about them. This is what a true love-based relationship is really all about.

When you prioritize seeking a partner who supports you in your transformation into your higher spiritual Self, instead of fulfilling and enhancing your ego needs and desires, you have found your true soul mate; you have just found true love.

True love and happiness only comes when you stimulate your spiritual growth within the relationship, by extending it to your partner. As you grow spiritually taller, your partner will grow spiritually taller. When "two" become "One" the fires of passion will burn like you have never experienced before. Your "spiritual soul essence" is the ultimate key for true happiness and bliss in all relationships.

Relationships

The End of Needy Relationships

We have all had the experience of tremendous loneliness; many of us unnecessarily and unknowingly believe inwardly that we are lonely and empty. Most of us cannot face that emptiness and loneliness within, and so we run away from it and seek an escape from it. Dependence is one of the things we run to; we need to depend on people, possessions, and all kinds of things, because we cannot stand being alone with ourselves. We want to fill that void, that need for dependence, and we do it with people more than with anything else.

Whether you love to love, or love to hate, you still need people to do that. We also use sex, drugs, religions, drink, sport, fitness and a dozen other things to fill up this vast inner void of emptiness. Most people are also unaware that what you put into this void to fill it up, is simply energy for the ego; this is how the ego gets fed. The ego is very hungry, especially in relationships, and feeds on all conflict, war, guilt and fear that may arise in any relationship. In other words, the ego loves its relationships to be needy and dependent.

Relationships that are based on mutual needs being met can, and one day will, only breed conflict at best, and a deep fear at worst. We fear our needs not being met, and we will start a war until they are met once again. However interdependent we are on each other, we need to wake up and realize that we are only using each other for one purpose: to have our needs met. Then, when these needs are successfully met, even for a brief time, we become dependent on getting them met all the time.

Any relationship that has dependency built within it, will transform into a relationship based on loneliness, regret, abandonment, guilt and fear. We fear being alone, and now, to avoid that fear, we try to possess the

> *Any relationship that has dependency built within it, will transform into a relationship based on loneliness, regret, abandonment, guilt and fear.*
>
>

other person. Therefore, the relationship turns into a possessive relationship. From this possession arise emotions such as envy and suspicion, and the effects of this are constant conflict within the relationship. Such a relationship can never bring about peace, love and happiness for anyone involved.

Possessiveness arises within relationships because we fear that we may one day lose the person we have, which is really the fear that we will not have our needs met. The truth is that in all needy and dependent relationships, there is no relationship. When people cannot find another person to fulfill their needs, they seek for substitutes like drugs, alcohol, sex, food, fine clothes, new cars, jewelry, etc. All are designed to fool us into thinking that these things make us feel better. These attachments are the means we use for avoidance and escapism.

The ego mind-set being nothing in itself, is dependent upon attachments to give it its identity. You, your true Self, needs nothing, but as long as you align yourself with your ego self, you will have all the needs that the ego has. The solution is to get out of your ego self-identity, or risk spending the rest of your life seeking to get your needs met, and living a life of dependency trying to find the right people and possessions to complete you; always seeking, but never finding. It is the ego's fear of being nothing that becomes your fear of being nothing.

You are not your ego, and your ego is not you. To do nothing in regards to this is the ego's ploy. The ego will say, "This person is not good enough for you. Find another person who will love you the way you deserve." What the ego is really saying is, "Get another person who will meet *my* needs better", or just get a better person. Or maybe the ego will tell you to find a better drug, a better car, a better house or a better drink. The ego loves when you obey it, instead of stopping to question your thoughts, or its advice, by doing nothing – the ego just loves this. So long as you are willing to do nothing, which in fact you do most of the time by merely seeking a better attachment, you inevitably breed more pain, more conflict, more sorrow and more misery in your life. What I mean here by doing nothing is that you are doing nothing about your spirituality. You are indulging the ego and seeking outside yourself for what is in abundance within you. So, what is the answer? Is the answer breaking up the relationship and detaching?

The so-called experts say that detachment is the answer, but is it really? I often hear people say: "If it is not working, which is most of the time, try something else." When you react to any attachment by becoming "detached" from it, you are simply just going to become attached to someone, or something else. As long as you remain in the ego mind-set you will have attachments and detachments going on all of the time. This means that you will have unions and breakups going on all the time.

Detachment in this world's sense is not the answer because it means that you detach from one person, only to find another "better" person. If you are in hell – and you will be as long as you are aligned with the ego's self-identity

You don't detach from the person, you detach from your thoughts about the person.

– do you really want a better hell? If you detach from one person, automatically you will find another one just around the corner and off you go again, back into another union in hell. Unions and breakups, attachments and detachments are all forms of self-deceptions because you eventually become your possessions. The reason you do this is because you have no true identity and you need an identity. But, in reality, it is not you who has no identity – it is your ego. The ego, being an illusion itself, came from nothing and will return to nothing.

So how do you truly detach, truly? You don't detach from the person, you detach from your thoughts about the person. But first, let's be clear, if you are in an abusive relationship, whether it is verbal or physical abuse, both ultimately being the same, then you must leave that relationship. You are not asked to put yourself in harm's way in any relationship. You must detach from the ego in the relationship by taking full responsibility for everything in the relationship that you react to, including everything about the other person that you have a reaction to.

True forgiveness and self-empowerment are the two tools that one day will make this relationship very successful. It is really simple, but it is not easy to achieve because the ego-self will resist these choices. When you do this, when you detach from the ego in the relationship, you simply become the Observer in the relationship. What you observe are your demands, expectations, needs and desires. In other words, you are detaching from dependencies in order to live a life without judgment.

And to live a life without judgment is to hold unconditional love in your heart for everyone. It is impossible to love anyone while you hold onto judgment. Being the Observer frees you from judgment and allows love to enter. Detaching from the ego will automatically bring you to the level where you become the Observer.

However, be careful, because if you observe with judgment you are observing as an ego, meaning that you are still attached to the ego-self. The ego does this by denying that it is not in judgment. This is not being the true Observer, rather, it is the ego being clever. The ego-self cannot exist long without judgment, so by becoming non-judgmental you align yourself with your true Self, which is the same as your higher Self. When the ego-self is observed, there is a tremendous revolution that takes place in your thinking and in the feelings that you experience, and when that shift takes place, you become free.

You become free to live a life of true freedom from all dependency, neediness, fear, worries and conflict; you will be free from all doubts and suffering, and you will be finally free to love everyone universally and unconditionally. You can do this simply by making the decision not to attack anyone, and this is how you can love everyone unconditionally and universally. This is the map to Heaven. However, to get there you must first lose yourself, to find yourself.

Become a Nobody

You are nothing trying to make yourself into something. If this statement makes you angry and resentful, it is your ego's sense of self that is angry. It is the "you" who is the thinker who is resentful, but this is not the real you. The real "You", the Observer of life, could never take offence from that statement or from any other statement. Yes, you have a name, a family, a country, a religion, a set of beliefs, dreams and ambitions, and yet, in spite of all of this, you are nothing, experiencing something small, by pretending to be someone you are not, as each day passes by. You are asleep in a dream, where you seem to be making something out of nothing, and that includes yourself. To realize who you truly are you must become a *nobody* once again.

You might think that to become nobody is not that difficult. Try it and see just how easy it is, because it is our possessions that give us an identity. "Give up your possessions and follow me," said Jesus a few years ago. He was not talking about material possessions and wealth, what he was talking about was our false identity - the attachments we have to our thoughts. We cling on to these thoughts, because without them we feel empty; without possessing beliefs, people, concepts and ideas, we are empty and in that space we believe we are a thing of no great importance, we feel worthless without our attachments, whether they are good or bad.

We all have a drive deep inside us to become something, anything, and that is what we will spend our life trying to become; a somebody who means something. This is not going to be an easy concept to let go of, but you must if you wish to wake up and experience true love.

It will not matter if you are famous or infamous, either will do. We all want to be something, and to avoid the internal fear of being a nobody with nothing we then strive to belong to this or to that organization, to this or that ideology, to this church or that temple- this is the basis of our beliefs, why we hold so dear to a certain ideology, because it gives our life meaning, or so we believe.

But what we are really doing is exploitation; we are using organizations to give us an identity. To exploit is to be exploited. The desire to use others for our psychological necessities makes for dependence, and what we depend on, we must fear and possess, which turns into what we possess, possesses us. Through fear, the fear of being a nobody, you have become a prisoner in bondage to the need of your ego's self-image to be somebody.

All fears breed illusions, and all illusions breed contempt, conflict and disobedience. If your relationships are ego-based, then your life will be one where you will experience war and inner conflict against the world and all who live in it. The ego self that you have become so identified with is always seeking a better identity, and a better image for itself. Both you as an individual and humanity as a whole, have projected several images onto God through the countless religions of this world.

The purpose of those images that are projected is always to satisfy a self-image the projectors have of themselves. We also do this in our own personal relationships – we project an image onto our partners and now we want them to be that image at all costs. Every time you seek to force another person to change, especially to suit your needs, you will meet with the same level of resistance. This is the true cause of all war in relationships; trying to change someone else, which is force leading to resistance. These two forces will always clash.

The more you try to change another person; you will be met with equal resistance. This is force, and no one has the right to force anything on anyone – this is pure ego. You see, the ego works best when fed by either of two energies: force or resistance. Apply either and the ego will win on both accounts.

All relationships in this world are never between two people, but between two images. I have an image of myself, which is illusionary, and I have an image of you, which is also illusionary. And the better the image you make of each person the better the relationship will be. If one or both images are not satisfactory, then the relationship will fail. However, the truth is that the relationship will fail anyway, sooner or later, and have no doubt of that, because the image you seek is an illusion that does not exist.

It only exists within you, not in another person. You can believe it exists in another, but it does not and never will make it true for you. The reason this type of relationship will fail is that there is no real love within the relationship. How can there be when one or both people in it are exploiting each other for a better identity? Any love that is dependent upon two individuals getting their needs met is doomed to fail, because the ego has it set up that way from the very beginning.

To give up your possessions and become a nobody there is a very simple technique: just look at your partner. All relationships are mirrors of the separated self, and if you just look closely at your partner you will see very clearly everything about yourself that you, consciously and unconsciously, think you are but that in reality you are not. All relationships can give you the opportunity to undo the ego self-image that you have within. The ego has a plan for all relationships, which is war and conflict, but there is also another plan. Relationships can offer you a way to end all conflict, all fear, all loneliness, all doubts, all pain and all suffering once and for all. Relationships can serve as a process of self-revelation, and self-knowing.

This self-revelation is painful and demands constant vigilance. There will come a time when a choice must be made. It will be the choices you make that will determine the life you will have. When tension and conflict arises within it, as it inevitably will, it is then that great strides in spiritual growth can be made by one or both partners. Or else, when insecurity creeps in, as it inevitably does, then that particular relationship may be cast aside and a new one taken on in the hope of finding lasting security. However, there can be no security in relationships that are built on dependency, needs and desires. The ego will be in charge of your security and wellbeing in all your ego relationships, and God will be in charge in your higher Self relationship. One choice will bring you more pain, the other, bliss.

The tools you need are here right now, but the choice to use them or not is up to you. If you can grasp the concept of projection and forgiveness that is outlined in this book, then peace, love, and the joy of bliss will be waiting for you. The end of all needy, dependent, relationships can be yours right here, right now.

What Love Is Not

A Course in Miracles says, *"You project onto the ego the decision to separate, and this conflicts with the love you feel for the ego because you made it. No love in this world is without this ambivalence, and since no ego has experienced love without ambivalence the concept is beyond its understanding. Love will enter immediately into any mind that truly wants it, but it must want it truly. This means that it wants it without ambivalence, and this kind of wanting is wholly without the ego's 'drive to get'."[1]* When you say you love someone, what you are really saying is: I desire you, I want to possess you, I want to own you, I want to dominate you. The list goes on and on.

Then, because the desire to possess is there, fear is not far behind. Fear will arise, jealousy will swell, and envy will enter with anxiety and then, finally, depression. And this is what we call love? As long as we possess and try to own another person, love shall never be known.

We seek out a partner for a variety of reasons: we want someone to love, we want a companion because we are lonely, we want a sex partner, we want a person to make a home with, we want someone to keep us warm at night, we want someone to look after us when we are sick, etc. However, each of these reasons for wanting a partner come with needs and expectations that become an informal, often unspoken, contract, but this is not love, this is a job position. Yet we call this love. We romanticize our belief that another will make us whole, make us complete, and make us happy. And now, you see, we are back to beliefs again.

We feel so bad about ourselves when we are alone; we seek out another to avoid our own misery. But the problem then arises when we find a partner, the misery seems to leave, but does it? No, it comes back after a short time and now the real fun begins. Because the partner you say you love will be the first to get the blame for your own internal misery.

Now instead of love, it becomes hate, because it was hate right from the start anyway. The reason why it was hate and not love, is because love can never be owned, it can never be possessed, it can never be written on a piece of paper or in a contract. Look at the contract, or the vows of marriage, "I will love you and no other until death do us part. I will love, honor and obey you". A "vow" to love is a form of resistance, because you vow to love just one person, and no other, when in fact in Heaven, in the Reality of your Oneness, you love everyone. Most people will unconsciously resist this contract, and then this leads to the resentment of the one you are with in the relationship, which also then leads to deceit and betrayal in the relationship. Everything you resist with force will ultimately conquer you.

When there is true love there can be no duty, because duty implies a contract, and in all contracts there are expectations, demands, needs and desires.

In true love there can be no force, so therefore, there is no resistance. This equals, zero conflict. When there is true love, there can be no duty, because duty implies a contract, and in all contracts there are expectations, demands, needs and desires. If I have a duty to love you, and you have a duty to love me, then this is not an unconditional true love relationship. You will know if there is true love in the relationship, because without true love the relationship becomes boring; it becomes a routine habit of gratification.

All marriages fail because they become the very source of conflict you are trying to avoid, a battle between two egos that came together under a contract. It now becomes a battlefield for pent-up anger and emotions, and sexual problems arise in the bedroom. Sex often becomes the battleground because sex is the tool of escapism; you want to escape the pains and conflicts of the very thing you once thought was the answer to your own pain and aloneness in the first place.

So you may believe that being alone is the answer, and that not getting married or not seeking companionship will be the solution. There are those who set this concept as a goal, not to love, they do this to avoid the pains of love. They may have been hurt in a relationship and now believe that this is the

> *Love can only enter into your awareness when the concepts, ideas, and speculations of what love is become absent.*

way to avoid that pain. They may believe that to know God one must become celibate in order to be pure in heart. They begin a life of discipline and abstinence. But instead of becoming love, they live a life of inner conflict with themselves, always battling their inner needs and desires. Love can never be found in this way, because they are holding a concept of what love is, and again, love is not a concept or an idea, it is a state of Being. Their daily life is one of disciplined suppression, and a disciplined heart, a suppressed heart, cannot know what true love is.

True love can never be understood like a math equation, like a concept or like an idea can. True love cannot be formulated and forced upon another like a fine dress or a rich suit.-There is no such thing as "my love" or "our love", terms that are thrown around so freely. There can never be a "my", "I" or "our" in love. Love just is. You either encompass love within the Self, or you do not. Love can only enter into your awareness when the concepts, ideas, and speculations of what love is become absent. Love can only manifest when the idea or the image you hold of the self becomes absent.

When you say you love someone, what you are really saying is that you love what they give you. You love their image, you love the pleasures they bestow upon you, you love the comfort they bring you, you love that they remove the pain of your aloneness and your emptiness. You only love what you get from this person but you do not love what they are.

True love cannot be brought into a thought or an idea. It can only be experienced within, and without form. Love is different from what we know as emotional love, or feelings of love. True love is abstract, and, as such, it cannot be described in the literal sense, and to use words to describe it takes away from that pure unconditional feeling. Imagine being held and embraced by a hundred thousand angels, all at the same time.

As good as you may imagine this feels it still does not fully describe the bliss of true love. If you bring love into an idea, into a concept or speculation, there you will cover up love and you will lose the experience altogether. Hate is an idea, murder is an idea, and so are guilt, jealousy, revenge, fear and anger – they are all ideas, concepts and thoughts. If you dare to bring true love into this field of thought, you then associate love with hate, love with anger, love with murder, love with jealousy and love with revenge. Love becomes entangled with all of these thoughts and emotions and any sense of true love is then lost. True love can only be experienced in the now, without judgment, without thought, without past or future association of any kind; true love just is.

The conditions of the mindset that can bring this type of true love about can be described but not the experience itself. The conditions for love are forgiveness, trust and honesty. Love grows when there is complete open-mindedness. Love is learning what true tolerance and generosity really means, and in true love, there is an abundance of giving and sharing unconditionally. You cannot attain true love through bargaining because it is not a thing that you can buy. You cannot attain true love through sacrifice or abstinence because it is not a thing that is painful. You cannot attain true love by getting because it cannot be owned or possessed. True love can only be attained by giving it through Being it, because true love can only Be. The question then is to Be, or not to be. To Be is to be in a state of Being - here love is eternal, blissful and unending. To not be, is to be in the ego: here your love will be one of conflict, hate, specialness, revenge, betrayal, and suffering.

True love cannot be found when there are selfish vested interests, such as in positions of power, prestige or respectability. Love is not found in lust, in the passion for another, or in a beautiful image of another. Love can never be held within a thought; thoughts are ideas and love is much, much deeper than any idea, thought or concept.

You can say you are in love when you love everything negative about your partner, including when they become poor, when they become too fat or too thin, when they are angry, when they are depressed, when they are sorrowful and when they feel rejected.

If you can love this person then, you are on the way to experiencing what love is. However, keep in mind that if you hate just one person in this world, how can you say you love another? Where there is hate in your heart for one person, there can only be hate for everyone because we are all intricately connected and there

True love can never be understood, you can only understand what love is not. When you can eliminate everything that love is not, all you are left with is what love is.

is no separation among any of us. When there is love in your heart, there can only be love for everyone. Love is total and complete, and if it is not, it was always hate in the first place.

One must become the love one seeks; love can never be found in another person, another place, or another thing. True love can never be understood, you can only understand what love is not. When you can eliminate everything that love is not, all you are left with is what love is.

Dealing with Feelings and Emotions

There can be no feelings and emotions without thoughts. All feelings and emotions come from our thinking. All pleasures come from thoughts, not from anything external, nor from another person, and not even from your own body. Pleasure can be experienced in the body, but pleasure originates in the mind of the thinker. We are very confused in this world as to what pleasure really is. We believe that pleasure is pain, and pain is pleasure. We do this by believing that our special relationships bring us pleasure, while in truth all the bring us is pain.

Ironically, most people also believe that to sit and be still – to meditate – and enter into the true pleasure that is bliss within, is painful. It is painful because people rationalize it as too boring, or they might say, "I do not have the time to meditate". But who really believes that? Is it you, or is it someone or something else that lies within you and is telling you these thoughts? All thoughts of emotions and feelings derive from the false sense of self; they originate in the ego self-image, and are driven from the ego itself. And what feeds the ego is energy, your energy.

If you have feelings and emotions that are causing you discomfort and anguish there is a way to deal with them. What we normally tend to do with these feelings is get rid of them by denying them and then suppressing them. But they never do go away, and will always resurface once again. This is how we keep feeding the ego our energy; we use the ego's tools. Denial and suppression are two ways we feed the ego, and both never work, except for the ego, and so, instead, those negative feeling that keep resurfacing must be dealt with in another way. Take for example the feelings of anger. We all have this feeling at some time or other in our lives. Feelings of anger come from thoughts of anger. And because you energize the thought of anger, you literally now become that thought and the feeling now intensifies in itself into a strong emotion. Your next thought now takes you into determining why you are feeling this way. You search your mind to find out who is responsible because you believe that someone or something has made you feel this way. You have a database in your memory bank of everyone and everything that you have perceived has ever hurt you.

So into the database you go to find the culprit or culprits that you believe caused your pain. Remember, we do this unconsciously most of the time. Then, when you find the person responsible, you will either physically, emotionally or psychologically attack that person. It really does not matter which, because they are all the same. You project your anger onto this person in the hopes that it will make you feel better. And it does, just for a little while. The feeling, then, comes right back again in a day or two. It comes back because you do not really see that the anger is a part of you, and you, therefore, have not done anything about it that will enable you to truly let it go permanently.

Now, you are right back to where you started. With nothing changed off you go again and find another target. This is the true power of projection and judgment at work. Projection is the tool we use to get rid of the anger, and judgment is like a guidance targeting system that we all use to blame someone else for how miserable our lives are. When you are guided by your emotions it leads to despair and anguish because it leads nowhere, and it always comes back to you.

So how do you deal with your feelings and emotions? Once again, you become the Observer; you simply observe the thoughts and emotions that you are experiencing. You observe without judgment or putting blame on another or on yourself.

You literally become one with the "pain body", the pain that you are experiencing. Our natural reaction to pain is to try and get rid of it, but this only ensures that you keep it. When you become one with, let us say anger, the anger dissolves. You see, no one can make you angry, rather you feel angry because anger is a part of the

If we do not have people in our lives to hate, it means that we have to keep everything that is distasteful about ourselves.

ego self-image that you have chosen to be one with; an unconscious choice of course. And no one likes the feelings of their own anger so what we do is find someone to project it onto and get rid of it.

This is the true nature of blame and judgment; we want to get rid of everything that we do not like about ourselves and put it onto someone else. This is why we all love to hate someone; we use them as our garbage disposal system. If we do not have people in our lives to hate, it means that we have to keep everything that is distasteful about ourselves. We do this with our partners, with our own governments, with other governments, other countries, football teams, or just about anybody or anything we can get our hands on. We should never underestimate the incessant desire within all of us of how much we love to hate. This is the ego at work within.

In your relationships, if you can observe without judgment and you can look at the anger and hate without blame, it will simply dissolve and dissipate without you rationalizing it. You can remove the anger by removing what you think the cause is. You may think: I am angry because..., I hate you because..., You are to blame because..., etc. Remove your perceived cause and look very deeply into the thought, the feeling and the emotion, and say this:

This anger is mine. It is a thought that I have generated within myself to attack myself, and it is part of the false-self I perceive myself to be.

By owning the thought, the feeling and the emotion, now you are not attacking yourself through projection. At the same time you are also undoing judgment by becoming non-judgmental, which begins to chip away at the ego's self-image because it cannot survive without judgment.

The last step is when you look at your ownership of the thought and you say to yourself:

I do not want this thought; I do not want to feel this way. I release this energy, knowing that it is a part of my own self-image that I do not want to keep any longer.

You are once and for all undoing the ego's self-image that you have come to know so well. I have devised a technique to deal with the removal of all negative feelings and emotions, which I call ATF. See the Chapter 10 – *True Forgiveness* for a full step-by-step guide to deal with the removal of all thoughts of fear, guilt, anger, sinfulness, hatred and so on, in any and all of your love/hate relationships.

The pleasures of life should never be denied, however they should be seen for what they truly are. They are all forms of escapism, with the ultimate escape of all being sex. We use alcohol, drugs and sex as means of escaping the ugly truth of who think we are. If your life is preoccupied with any of the above, you are really trying to forget who you are, as well as forgetting who you are not.

Everything we do in life is centralized in giving emphasis to the idea of "me" - the false self-image. Beliefs, religion, gods, political views, sports affiliations to certain clubs, and social activities all strengthen the ego's self-image that is central to our identity. These attachments, after a while, become tiresome, they become a struggle, so we turn to sex for the ultimate escape. And in our sexual energy, just for a few moments in time we seem to forget everything; we forget ourselves, our existence here, just for those few seconds of bliss we seem merge into the seeming nature of our true self.

This is not heaven but, to the ego, it is as close as it gets. I am not saying that sex is right or wrong, or that it is good or bad. I am saying that sex is neutral and it only has the meaning that you give to it. The point that I am making is this: the ego makes love because it has never experienced the bliss of unconditional love. True love is never made, it can only be experienced, because it just Is. In all of our relationships, whether love or hate, we have a choice. We can settle for the little temporary pleasures of the body, which last the briefest of seconds, or we can choose a universe of true love that is so unconditional, all encompassing, eternal and immortal, that you will hardly have time to take your breath. This place, this mind-set, this love, is like experiencing a hundred million orgasms, all at the same time, and you have this for eternity. In my mind, there is no contest between these two choices in love; one will bring you nothing but pain, the other will bring you nothing but bliss. No contest, but you have to choose what you want.

Heaven is a choice.

So what happens when you do choose Heaven? What does your journey look like in regards to the different stages of awakening? The concept of ascension has been around for centuries, but there has been a great deal of confusion about how this process works. In this next chapter I would like to take you through the levels once again, and show you your journey home. This journey is up all the way home, which means that it just keeps getting better and better. Enjoy!

CHAPTER 13

~ ~ ~

Ascension

The Template of Creation

There are three types of people in this world. There are those who are asleep, those who are waking up and then there are those who are awake. Another way to describe this would be to say that there are those who live in darkness, those who are going into the light, and then there are those who are in the light. Ascension for many of those who are asleep may seem like an outrageous concept to even consider. But like many concepts that we have been led to believe, most people do not know what the true meaning of ascension really is.

Many people think that when they die, they will either ascend to heaven and meet with God, or go to hell. This could not be further from the truth. God, being Awareness, is at the very top level in the 7th Dimension of the higher Heavens as you can see in my diagram "Ascension" below. As Jesus once said, "No one goes to the Father except through me." In other words, no one goes to the Father except through the Christ Universe which is on the way up. No one can jump from the bottom – 3rd Dimension – to the top – 7th Dimension – in just one go; it is just not possible.

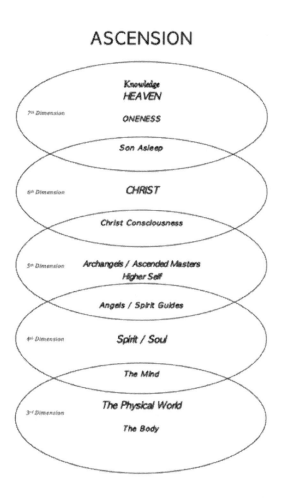

ASCENSION

Knowledge
HEAVEN

7th Dimension

ONENESS

Son Asleep

6th Dimension   CHRIST

Christ Consciousness

5th Dimension   Archangels / Ascended Masters
Higher Self

Angels / Spirit Guides

4th Dimension   Spirit / Soul

The Mind

The Physical World
3rd Dimension
The Body

An awakening must take place before you can ascend from the level you are on, to the next level which is always up, once you wake up. However, as long as you remain asleep, you will be up and down, and up and down to the Spiritual Universe. Why? You cannot take any thoughts of sin, guilt or fear any further up to the higher heavens, the Spiritual Universe is as far up as you can go, as long as you remain asleep. And once you reach the higher Heavens, very few indeed have returned to the lower level. Therefore, there are five awakenings that you must experience before you reach the top level. I will talk more on each of these awakenings later in this chapter.

We are all going to ascend at the end of this lifetime on Earth. Of that, there is no doubt! You cannot go down any lower than what this world is. This is as low as one can get. The concept of hell is just that, it is a state of mind that we can either choose or relinquish. And for most of us we all have been to hell and back in this lifetime, some maybe are still in it. However, the good news is that you can just as easily choose Heaven as you can choose hell. And if we bring free will into the equation, then that is the only true choice that you, I and everyone else truly has. All other choices are the illusions of free will. If you are constantly seeking outside of yourself, you are not using true free will. You have the illusion of free will, you have the illusion of choice.

However, if you are choosing between the internal and external, now you are using true free will. This is why we were given free will in the first place: you can choose to be separate, or you can choose oneness and unity. Those who are asleep are seeking and choosing the ego, choosing the external, and it is in making this choice that their choice to remain asleep and return here for another life is made. Those who have chosen to wake up are now choosing between the internal and external. Those who have awakened, seek nothing outside. So what does this mean when this lifetime is over for us?

If you look at the "Ascension" diagram, you will see the five different Universes. Each Universe, or each dimension, has its own level of consciousness. And it is so important to understand this: each Universe is a state of mind, it is not an actual place that is here nor there. In the 3rd Dimension you will see that our level of consciousness is held in the belief in the physical reality.

Then in the next level up, you will see the Spiritual Universe in the 4th Dimension. This level also has its own level of consciousness, called Spiritual Consciousness. And it is between these two levels that we all have ascended and re-incarnated back here many, many times since life began on this planet. And here is how ascension works for those who are asleep. Those who are asleep in this lifetime – at the time of death of their physical experience – will ascend to the Spiritual Universe. Their soul will wake up briefly there. They will do their life review, write another script for another life, and then their soul will go back to sleep and return here once again for another physical experience. When they return they will totally forget that they are in fact a spiritual being having yet another human experience.

For those who are waking up, there is another plan. When they ascend they will have a choice: to remain or return. And that choice is being made right here, right now, every day. And here is how this works. If you are continually seeking for something in the world, if you are constantly choosing outside of yourself, you will come back here again. Why? Because you are still attached to this world.

When Jesus said, "lead us not into temptation" he meant let us not seek outside ourselves for anything. Let us not be tempted to seek for anything from the ego. If you are seeking for peace in the world, if you are seeking for joy in the world, and if you are seeking for love in the world, you will only find pain, and you will come back and continue to be attached, until you detach. All attachments must be relinquished before you ascend this time in order to remain in the spiritual universe.

When Jesus said, "give up your possessions and follow me", he was not talking about any material attachments like your material wealth, your home or anything that is material in any way. He meant, give up your attachments to the body, give up your attachments to the world, give up your resolve to seek for things in the world that keep hurting you. If you think that you are your body and that the body and this world are real, then you should consider that there is a strong possibility that you are delusional. It is these attachments that keep us all separate, that keep bringing us back here lifetime after lifetime. This is what free will really is all about; you are free to keep your attachments and remain separate, or give them up and return home to God and the state of Oneness in the 7th Dimension. All other choices you make are illusions of choices.

So, what about those who have awakened? If you have awakened, you will ascend to the Spiritual Universe, and then move up to the next level, the 5th Dimension, which is called the Higher Universe. The Higher Universe is a place where there is no form, there are no bodies, neither physical nor spiritual. It is the highest form of knowledge that one can access while in a body in this world. The Higher Universe holds the Akashic records that are open to everyone, but that not everyone can access. This Universe is also just a state of mind. This is where your Higher Self's awareness resides. Everyone, and I mean everyone, in this world has a higher self, and if, and when, they access it, they will have access to all knowledge of everything that has ever happened and will ever happen in the future.

Therefore, the Higher Self and the Akashic records are in fact one and the same states of Mind, and this is the mind of Enlightenment. All those who have reached the state of Enlightenment have accessed the awareness of their Higher Self, and they will have access to all knowledge as well, them being one and the same.

When Jesus said, "no one goes to the Father, except through me" this is what he meant: the 6th Dimension is the Christ Universe. It is a place where we all join as one. Jesus also said, "It is only the solitary that will enter the gates of Heaven." Remember also, this is just another state of mind. Jesus has been the only man to date, who has reached the Christ state of mind on earth. There have been only a handful of human minds who have reached the Higher State of mind, but only he reached the Christ state of mind while still in the body.

This world is a game of illusion, delusion, perception and deception. Reality in the world sense is about the evolution of consciousness in the alchemy of time. Our purpose here is to experience everything that Heaven is not. Whenever you want, you can return home, but first you must know "*thyself*", and then, at any time that you choose, you will wake up and return home.

Ascension and awakenings are not related, they are identical. In each awakening you will ascend to a new level of awareness, and a new level of consciousness. Each awakening is solely an inside job. All transformations will occur within the mind first, and then after a little while, you will see these inner transformations manifest in your external life. It is just like when you change, how can your reflected shadow not change? So what are the stages of awakening?

STAGES OF SPIRITUAL AWAKENING

If you look at the diagram "Stages of Awakening" below, on Stages of Awakening you will see that there are, in fact, five awakenings that must take place. Also, there are five levels of consciousness that go hand in hand with each awakening. Consciousness, awareness and awakenings are relative to each other. At each awakening, you enter a new level of consciousness, which brings a new awareness.

Depending on your resistance to letting go, you could be delayed at each stage for a considerable time, or you could literally wake up through all five very, very quickly. Remember everything is under the law of cause and effect. The cause of your awakenings will be the direct result of you letting go of your attachments. Letting go of your attachments will be the cause, and your awakening will be the effect. It really is that simple to comprehend, but really not that simple to apply. There are so many little tricks that the ego uses to fool you, and you will have to be on your toes all the time to guard against thinking that you are on your way.

The first awakening, therefore, will be the self-awakening. This is where at some point in your life, you reach the stage and say something like this to yourself: "This world simply does not work, my relationships do not work. Nothing here makes any sense whatsoever, this is an insane world full of insane people".

Now, thinking or saying something like this which you truly believe in your heart, will have an amazing effect on you and this will be the beginning of great things that will begin to happen in your conscious and unconscious minds. It is usually pain that is the great motivator at this first stage of awakening.

We become so intolerant of pain that we say, "I have had enough, there has to be another way to live in this world". In *A Course in Miracles* it says: *"You can temporize...but you cannot depart entirely from your Creator, Who set the limits on your ability to miscreate."*[1] This line means that we will keep doing things our own way until the pain becomes so intolerable that we will surrender, and then look for another way. There is a limit on how much pain and suffering we will endure. It is only when we experience great pain in our lives that we begin the process of waking up. It is what you do next that is so important.

If you have reached this stage you have begun your journey to wake up. The next stage is this: *know thyself.*

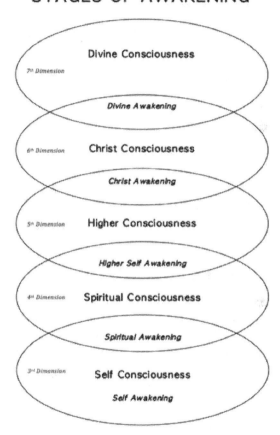

STAGES OF AWAKENING

7th Dimension
Divine Consciousness

Divine Awakening

6th Dimension
Christ Consciousness

Christ Awakening

5th Dimension
Higher Consciousness

Higher Self Awakening

4th Dimension
Spiritual Consciousness

Spiritual Awakening

3rd Dimension
Self Consciousness

Self Awakening

The Self Awakening

To know thyself is to know and understand the separated self that you think is who you really are. The truth is that you are not who you think you are, and this has been one of your greatest errors to date. And it is this grave error that is causing you all the pain and suffering in your life. The separated self contains three parts: the personality, the persona and the shadow. This is who you think you are, but not who you truly really are. It is not until you know who you are not, that you will remember who you truly are.

> **It is not until you know who you are not, that you will remember who you truly are.**
>
>

And you are not this separated self in a body waiting to die. Chapter 5 – *The Separated Self* explains this in more detail. At this point I will only reiterate that it is not until all three parts of the separated self are brought back into awareness that everything painful and untrue will dissolve.

The separated self also has a very sophisticated defense system, which uses many defense mechanisms that will keep you attached to this separated self that you are not. Freud was one man that we must thank, for it was he who showed us many of these defenses. However, I have re-interpreted many of Freud's theories because he fundamentally got the starting point fundamentally wrong. He was correct from the point of view that we need these ego defenses so as to exist here in the physical world, but he was wrong in believing or thinking that we need them at all.

All of the ego's defense mechanisms will keep you attached to the ego, and the effects of that will leave you in states of fear, terror and panic. You will suffer because of these defenses, and of this you are guaranteed. Remember what I keep saying, "pain is inevitable, suffering is optional". We will all experience some pain in life, some more than others. However, the whole point of waking up is to finally reach a place where pain and suffering are no longer attributes of life that you will ever experience again. That is the goal, and it is a very realistic goal to set for you. There is no one who sets their mind to reach this goal who cannot attain it. No one!

To become self-conscious is to know who you are as a person in this world. It is to know what makes you 'you', what makes you tick, what your defenses are, what it is that keeps you asleep. All of these you must come to know. If you do not know, you will not transcend your ego into your spiritual self. The work to transcend from your separated self into your spiritual self is now required by *you*. You can only transcend what you know. If you do not know yourself, you will not wake up into the higher Self. It is really that simple. So, go back to *Chapter 5 – The Separated Self* and begin to work on learning who you are. Know thyself.

The Spiritual Awakening

Your spiritual awakening will take place without you doing anything to make it happen. Remember, this will work under the law of cause and effect also. The cause of your spiritual awakening will be the effect of you undoing your ego defenses around your separated self. As long as you defend your separated self, you will keep your spiritual awakening in the distance. A spiritual awakening is the same as being truly right-minded.

So, let's say that now you have been able to undo your separated self, and you attained and experienced a spiritual awakening. What exactly does it mean to have a spiritual awakening? Being spiritual is not about wearing special spiritual clothing. It is not about reading special spiritual books. It is not about going to special spiritual talks, gatherings, or conferences. To be truly spiritual is to live at a level of spiritual consciousness. Being spiritual is a level of consciousness that you experience. This level of consciousness cannot be learned by someone who has not surrendered their ego's separated self. If they only have an intellectual understanding but it is not something that they have experienced in their hearts, they will be changing their behavior without first changing their minds.

A Course in Miracles tells us to never change your behavior without first changing your mind, unless your behavior is harmful to you or another. And for a good reason too - if you change your behavior without changing your mind first, you will be in conflict with yourself. One part of you will want something different from the other part. This is called the split mind. That is what the separated self is. It is those three parts that we all know so well by now: the personality, the persona and the shadow. The persona will want a spiritual awakening, the shadow will refuse it. So there you are, as the personality in the middle with two seeming warring factions on each side.

The only way to transcend this eternal internal war, is to become true right-minded. To be a truly spiritual is to be truly right-minded.

The Higher-Self Awakening

Very few will experience this level of awakening at this time on earth. There are no more than around a dozen people on the planet at this time who are awake at this level. At this level you will have full access to all knowledge which stems from the Akashic records, and you will be the bringer of a lot of new information and enlightenment to aid more and more awakenings for all of mankind. Remember, this is a state of mind, it is a level of consciousness that you attain through the awakening of your higher Self. A Course in Miracles describes all of these awakening stages in the section called the development of trust.[2] The higher Self is where the mind will now transcend the split mind completely and join into the mind of One. This will not be a comfortable journey, but the good news is this: you are not in charge.

This will happen when you are ready for it and not before. Why will this be uncomfortable? Remember I said that there are three parts to your mind: the wrong mind (or the ego), the right mind (or the Holy Spirit), and the decision maker (or personality), which is you. Well this is what is going to happen next: the wrong mind will disappear along with the right mind and the decision maker, your false self, because now there are no choices to make between what is true and what is false. When the split mind has completely dissolved, when the mind of right and wrong, good and evil, has dissolved, the higher Self moves into the formless state beyond all form where it merges now into the Christ awakening, and you become the Christ Self.

The Christ Awakening

Jesus said, *"No one comes to the Father except through me".*[3] What this means is that no one wakes up in Heaven, without being One with everyone here first in Christ. Jesus did not mean that he himself, the man, was Christ. Rather, Jesus meant that he was the symbol for all of us as Christ.

You will experience the Christ awakening for no more than a second. It will be the briefest of all of your experiences in the process of these awakenings. As *A Course in Miracles* tells us, you will look back on a forgiven world, and thank God that it was all just a dream. You are ready to meet God, the Pure Awareness of all creation. You are about to join God as Co-Creator of everything.

The Divine Awakening

What it is really saying is that when you wake up as Christ, in that very same instant you will wake up back in Heaven and the dream of separation will be over for good. You will now have remembered the state of Being, and entered into the Pure Awareness. There is no greater state of awareness than the Divine Pure Awareness of all Creation.

This is what the whole dream of separation was all about. You see, you have never been awake before. Not before the dream. You have never been aware in Heaven. You have

392

always been asleep. There are two states of the One mind in Heaven. One state is called "Being" and that is the state we have always experienced. There is another state called "Awareness", and that state is both in a state of Being and also in a state of Awareness, both at the same time. Our Creator has the experience of both states.

We, as His creation, have experienced only one up until this point, and we are all waking up into the second state which is Awareness. This is why we all have come here to this world; to wake up into Awareness and return as Co-Creators of everything there is. It is time to wake up to who you truly are. You are the living creation of the Creator of all life. And our Creator is called Awareness. You have an abundance of energy that you are simply denying. You deny this by relying on the ego's energy. The three baser chakras, are all ego identification. It is not until you transcend these energies, that all those lower baser thoughts will become detached. When you detach from level 1, and ascend to level 2, it is the same as transcending all three lower energies. Let me explain more in the section called The Chakras.

The Chakra Energy Fields

If you look at the diagram "Chakra Energy Fields", you will see that it is the very same template used as in every other metaphysical concept we have discussed. The reason being is that this template is the template of all creation. Everything fits into it, whether you are talking about actual universes, awakenings, consciousness, states of mind, or energy fields.

There are seven focal points of psychic energy in the body. These points are called chakras. Each center is associated with a different vibrational expression of the energy, from the first (base) chakra, which works with the densest form of this energy, to the seventh (crown) chakra which works with the energy in its finest form. Just as a personality profile can describe an individual's dominant personality characteristics, so a person can be described in terms of the chakras in which his energy is received and dissipated. There are certain labels which can be fixed to these chakras to define the dominant concern of an individual whose primary energy expression is fixed at that particular level. See diagram "Chakra Energy Field" below.

Thus the first chakra is associated with survival, a jungle or animal mentality of kill or be killed. The second chakra is associated with reproduction and sexual gratification. The third chakra concerns power and mastery. These lower three chakras are the focal points for most of the energy presently used by man in his worldly endeavors. These three chakras are primarily concerned with the use of energy for the maintenance and the enhancement of the ego. If you are fixated in using any of these three chakras, you are asleep, and will remain so.

It is only when you arrive at the fourth chakra, the heart chakra, that you enter into a realm which starts to transcend the ego. The fourth chakra is primarily concerned with compassion. The fifth chakra, located at the throat, is concerned with the seeking of God. The sixth chakra, located between the eyebrows, also sometimes referred to as the third eye, is concerned with wisdom. And the seventh, and last chakra in the body, is the crown chakra and it is concerned with full enlightenment or union.

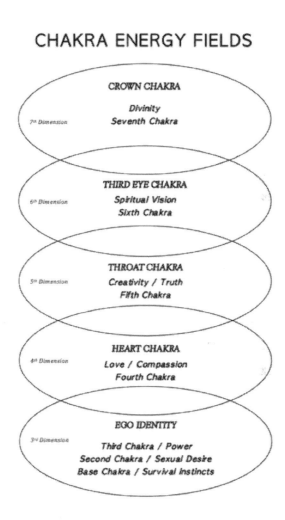

The spiritual path can be conceived, from an energy point of view, as the path up the spine that is the transformation of energy from the lower to the higher chakras i.e., the purification of energy. With this definition in mind, it is apparent that any use of energy which further strengthens the hold, or intensity, of the lower chakras interferes with the spiritual progress. The experience and habits associated with lust is the domain of the second chakra. The psychoanalyst, Sigmund Freud, was the master spokesman for the person who is fixated in the second chakra, just as Alfred Adler was the spokesman for the third chakra associated with power, and perhaps, the psychotherapist, Carl Jung, could be considered the spokesman of the fourth chakra of the heart, the seeking of Love chakra.

In our western culture there has been such an investment in the models of man associated with the second and third chakra (sex and power) that we have developed strong and convincing habits of perceiving the inner and outer universe in these terms. Though we may realize intellectually that the spiritual journey requires the transformation of energy from these preoccupations to the higher centers, we find it difficult to override these strong habits which seem to be re-enforced by the vibration of the culture in which we live in.

Thus it seems "normal" to have certain ego needs with regard to sex and power. Further, it is difficult for us to understand or assimilate that what is normal for a second chakra centered person is hardly normal for a fourth chakra centered person. A person whose energy is primarily centered around the second chakra, as so well described by Freud, thinks of everything as sexual in nature - political power is sexual potency, and so on.

A person whose energy is primarily centered around the third chakra sees it all in terms of power. Even his or her sexual activity is seen in that light. The first, second, and third chakras all maintain and enhance the illusion of separation. Every time you attach to these thoughts, your actions are driven by the energies of these three lower chakras, which then strengthen and reinforce your ego and you then therefore reinforce the illusion of the separation. You can avoid arousing these energies and simultaneously work from within to transmute these latent forces into spiritual energy. This involves taking the energy you might otherwise use in acts originating in the second chakra and move that energy up the spine to the higher chakras.

The purpose is to generate or collect energy which you can use in the service of becoming enlightened. By moving the energy up to the higher centers one will experience little of the sexual frustration that someone who is "celibate" in the usual sense might. From a habitual western vantage point it looks as if such a person is giving up something and must be suffering. But not only do you not suffer, but you will often experience far higher and more permanent states of bliss than can be experienced through the lower chakras.

The Illusion of Time

When you are in pain, time slows to a crawl. When you are in bliss time speeds up. When you are expecting something special, time seems to stop, and when you least expect anything, time flies. From the moment we are born we are living under the rules of time and space until the second we die. Can time be consciously slowed down and speeded up if we so choose at any second? Yes it can. Can we travel back in time, or can we travel into the future? Yes we can. We can because we can only truly travel anywhere, past present, or future in the mind.

To get into an airplane and, say, travel to the other end of the world, is an illusion of travel because you are not really going anywhere! I say that because all external travelling of the body through space and time is an illusion of travel. You are only truly going anywhere once you are in the mind. And then, it is only a matter of learning the rulebook as to where you go.

Most people do not realize this, but there is something in our psyche that automatically omits the present moment. Why? Because to the ego, the present moment is a very dangerous place for you to be.

Time in this world seems linear and that means that we are always travelling from the past into the future.

Most people do not realize this, but there is something in our psyche that automatically omits the present moment. Why? Because to the ego, the present moment is a very dangerous place for you to be. The ego only has control over thoughts in your past and future, however, when you come fully into the present moment you are outside of the ego and its influence on you. The ego will do everything it can, to keep you out of the Now.

The very moment you enter into the Now, into the present moment, you enter vertical time; you connect straight with the eternal timelessness and bliss of Heaven. This is one of the most difficult challenges for any spiritual seeker. What keeps everyone out of this wondrous and glorious blissful state is our allegiance to the ego itself; to the split mind of the ego; to the ego's self-image that we all carry within us.

The ego is held in our reputation, our achievements, our good family name; it is all around us, and we reinforce it within ourselves and get everyone else to play along with this game every day. To enter into this state of mind- the Now- you must become lost, because any old ego could access this eternal power within that we all have. Here is my point; as long as you hold onto you, the ego self-image, you are not going anywhere for you will stay as you are. You must let go of all attachments to the separated self to enter into the bliss of the Now. When you can do this, you will become lost, and then, bliss will find you.

You see, and I have mentioned this in this book several times, the two rooms that we are all attached to, have no space for the present moment – the Now. There is only past and future while you are attached to the split mind of the ego. In the good room, is your future, this is where you do all your planning and scheming, it is the persona. Then, in the bad room is everything you hate about yourself, your fears, and your past relationships, in short, in the bad room is your past.

So of the two rooms, past and future, where do we spend the present moment in this state of mind? Simply, we don't. In every second, and in every moment you are attached to this mind-set, you spend all of it, either in the past, or the future, but never in the Now. These two rooms cover up the Now, they cover up the present moment, entirely, in every second you experience this life. So, how can one access the Now? Simple, transcend up to a higher state of awareness, a higher state of consciousness, which is on level 2, and you will access the Now, which is on level 2. You cannot experience the Now from level 1, but you will on level 2.

Another cool thing is this, you can collapse time quite considerable by deep transcendence meditation. This is where you separate completely with the consciousness of the body, and enter into the vortex of timelessness, which is the Now. In the first two years I hardly slept at all, it nearly drove me crazy because my mind was so active. I just could not shut it down. Then, I learned a pretty cool technique, I learned to transcend my body, I already knew how from my past experiences, so it was no big deal. In the beginning, it was quite difficult, but I persevered and today, I can transcend my body for just twenty minutes and almost six hours will have passed here in this level of consciousness.

So, instead of lying awake all night going crazy with nothing to do, I would do transcendence, and the night would be over very quickly. The other cool thing was this, when I was out of my body, my body could sleep like a baby. Imagine if, say, someone who is in prison could do this, then a twenty year stretch would take very little time at all. Anyone can collapse time, if you put your mind to it. Once you enter the present moment, there are levels and degrees that you can access that will take you all the way to the top if you are ready and prepared for it. The higher you go in the temporal vortex, the further back in time you can travel, and also, the further your reach will be into future time zones as well. For those who are awake on level 3, the higher Self, they will have access to all knowledge that they have requested themselves. All that they have to do is ask, and the answers will be given. No one is refused at this level of consciousness.

As you can see on my chart there are five main levels of time, which also correlate to the levels of consciousness on each dimension. We are at the bottom in terms of the temporal structure of the five universes, or the five states of mind, because that is exactly what each level truly is; it is just a state of mind. So, if a thousand years go by on the third dimension, which is our physical experience, then that means that one year will only have passed in the spiritual universe, or the fourth dimension.

This also means that if you go even higher, into the fifth dimension a thousand years now become one day. That means that for every one day at this level of consciousness, a thousand years will have passed on earth. To go one step higher, into the sixth dimension you enter into Christ consciousness, which means that for every thousand years here, just one second passes in the real world.

At the top, the seventh dimension, you enter into the eternal bliss of Heaven's state of non-consciousness. You will see on my chart on the seventh dimension, a term called a Planck second. This is the smallest fraction of time that is possible. To give you an idea, a Planck second is a millionth, of a millionth, of a millionth, of a millionth of a second. And that is pretty small! In other words, the entire separation, the entire fall of man, the entire history of everything that has very happened from the second of the big bang to its end in the entire dream, lasted just one Planck second. It was literally over the second that it begun. So when you argue in this world about what is right and wrong, or good and bad, just think of this: nothing in this world matters once you are back and awake in Heaven. The conflicts that we all appear to have in our daily lives are just a distraction from knowing the truth of who we all truly are.

Ultimately, as we all raise our vibration up to the next higher level of awareness the physical universe will vibrate at such a high frequency of unconditional love that it will simply merge and become One with the spiritual universe just above us. The same will then occur when we have no use for our spiritual bodies. At that point the spiritual universe will merge and become One with the higher universe, and so on. When the higher universe merges into the Christ Universe, this is where we are all truly one with each other. When Jesus said, "No one comes to the father except through me", he was talking about this place, the Christ universe. *A Course in Miracles* calls this place *"The Real World"*. Once this is completed, the final merging takes place between us, as One, and God; the Christ universe merges once more with Heaven and God. Here Oneness is restored; the dream is over; we are awake in Heaven and co-creating with the Boss!

THE ILLUSION OF TIME

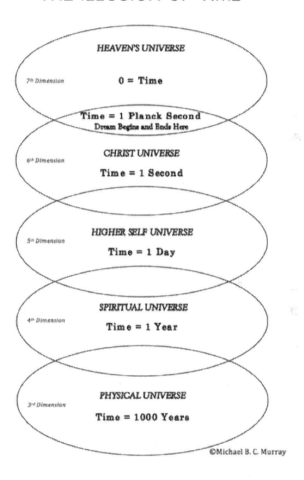

HEAVEN'S UNIVERSE

7th Dimension   0 = Time

Time = 1 Planck Second
Dream Begins and Ends Here

CHRIST UNIVERSE

6th Dimension   Time = 1 Second

HIGHER SELF UNIVERSE

5th Dimension   Time = 1 Day

SPIRITUAL UNIVERSE

4th Dimension   Time = 1 Year

PHYSICAL UNIVERSE

3rd Dimension   Time = 1000 Years

©Michael B. C. Murray

Everything in this world was made to blind us from the truth and fool us into actually believing what we see. All forms of seeing are forms of perception. However, ultimately, there are only two types of perception, and only one is true while the other one is false. As long as you are aligned with the ego and spiritually asleep, you are under the laws of the ego and seeing with false perception. This means that everything you think you see you think is real. However, remember that the thinker is the ego, and as long as you think that you are waking up, then you are doing it with the ego.

True perception sees through the ego's cunning plans and schemes. True perception is on level 2, while the false perception is on level 1. If you do not understand perception, you will not understand life!

The Illusion of Perception

You never see anything with your eyes, you only perceive. All manifesting is perceived within the illusion of time and space, or within the field of dreams that is the illusion in itself. But if you could just stand back outside of time and space and look from a higher level, you would perceive differently. If you are looking through a faulty looking glass, how can you see clearly? If you are looking with a limited lens, how can you see unlimited expansiveness of everything? If the way you see life does not make sense, it is insane to keep looking at things the same way. What you do not do, is try and fix the faulty glasses you are trying to look at life with, because that is what man has been

404

doing since the beginning of time, it can't be done, so stop it, look for another way. There is another way.

There is always another perspective to seeing everything, and if you can find a way to raise your awareness onto level 2, you will see for yourself that you will have a totally different perspective on the totality of everything. The person who can see this must be outside the illusion of thoughts. He must be looking at the illusion, not looking from within the illusion. You don't need eyes to see, you need vision and vision *You don't need eyes to see, you need vision and vision means understanding. You see everything differently because you understand everything differently.*

means understanding. You see everything differently because you understand everything differently – this is the difference between true and false perception.

This entire dream that we are all experiencing, right now, is just a dream of perception. Within the entirety of perception, there is wrong-minded perception, and there is right-minded perception. Wrong-minded perception is looking at everything in this world through the split mind of the ego. This is the mind of right and wrong, and good and bad. Right-minded perception in *The Course* is called the Holy Spirit; it is the correction for all wrong-minded perception, which means that the Holy Spirit is the answer to the ego. Or, right-minded thinking is the correction for wrong-minded thinking.

Another way to say this would be that the Holy Spirit is on level 2, while wrong-minded perception is on level 1. You cannot solve a problem from the same level of awareness where the problem is created. You must transcend to a higher level – level 2 – to solve the problems on level 1. Remember, there are five levels and that means that you perceive the dream from five different levels of consciousness, and you will experience each individual level yourself, as you wake up.

Right now you are experiencing false perception through the awareness of the body that you believe is you. This is the separated self perceiving the dream on level 1. Once you transcend to level 2, you will perceive everything from the true right mind, also called the Holy Spirit.

Once here, your work now begins in dissolving the separated self that you once believed was you. This means that you must begin to dismantle the three layers of the ego that defend the separated self, and then, you must reinterpret the two rooms, of right and wrong and good and bad, into what is true and what is false. All the information on how to do this is contained in this book. As long as you do not fall into the trap of right and wrong, or good and bad, you will remain on level 2. You must realize by now that you can only solve the problems that are on level 1, on level 2.

Then, once you have successfully separated from the ego wrong-minded thought system, on level 1, you will very soon find yourself awake on level 3. Here you will perceive everything through the eyes of your higher self. The higher self has two parts - one part of the higher self is still in the body and the world, the other part is connected wholly with Christ and God - and when these two parts become one, you will enter the Real world, or the Christ Universe. When the two become one at the higher self level, it means that the dream is over in a matter of seconds for you. You enter into Christ Consciousness on level four.

Now you will perceive the entire dream from the perception of Christ Consciousness. This will last about one second, and, as *The Course* tells us, this is when we look back on a forgiven world, where we have completely detached from everything that is not true. Then in the same instant, we will wake up in Heaven, and our perception now will be one of Oneness with God in the Creation of everything.

The World We Experience

So, what exactly will we create in heaven? Well, to start with we will be presented with our very own universe. Then each of us will be designated as the Creator of that world, and we will create everything we desire to put into it. We all have unlimited creative abilities to just about do and create anything we like, as long as it won't be another ego dream! To give you an example, consider the following.

Imagine that you are in charge of this world right now and you could change this world into anything you like. What would you do? How would you make everything in this world, and everyone in it, experience Heaven just about every day, for eternity? How would you create? What would you create? Try it.

But just to help you out a little, here is a little piece on this world and how it operates behind the veil. Everything in this world begins and ends with just a thought. So, let us look at thoughts themselves and how thoughts literally create the world that you are experiencing right now.

Today, in this modern world, physicists have proven beyond doubt that the physical world is one large sea of energy that flashes into and out of being in milliseconds, over and over again. Nothing in this world is really solid. Welcome, this is the world of quantum physics. In quantum physics everything begins and ends with just a thought. Physicists have proven that thoughts are what put together and hold together this ever-changing sea of energy into the objects and people that we see.

You think you see real people, but in truth, every person is just an aura of energy, that manifests as a person, created by just a thought. Everything here - people, plants and animals, all animate and inanimate objects – are all just energy that is manifesting and then dissolving, over and over, again and again. There are some people who can see this energy; it is sometimes called an aura. This is something I could see all my life, but I just never knew what I was seeing. So why do we see a person instead of simply the aura of energy that everyone is within the body? Our eyes deceive us, over and over again. *The Course* tells us that, "*Nothing so blinding as perception of form.*"[4] Do not believe everything you see!

Think of a movie reel that a projector would play in any cinema to show a movie. A movie is a collection of about 24 frames every second. Each frame is then separated by a gap.

However, because of the speed at which one frame replaces another, our eyes get deceived into thinking that we see a continuous moving picture.

Think of the old television sets of yesterday. They all had what are called "tubes". A television tube is simply a tube with thousands of electrons hitting the screen in a certain way, creating the illusion of form and motion. We all have the five physical senses: sight, sound, touch, smell, and taste. Each of these senses also has a specific spectrum; for example, a dog hears a different range of sound than we do, a snake also sees a different spectrum of light than we do, and so on. In other words, our senses perceive the sea of energy from a certain limited standpoint and make up an image from that perception. It is not a complete image, nor is it accurate; it is just an interpretation. Everything in this world is an interpretation, and as such, we must re-interpret everything.

What you think and the thoughts that you are attached to literally become your world.

All of our interpretations, while we believe that we are a body, are solely based on the ego's interpretations of reality. The thoughts we believe to be ours, in truth, come from the ego thought system. Once we believe these thoughts, they become our own, and by this belief we energize those thoughts and through them we shape the world we see all around us. It is like a soup mix, if you put a number of thoughts and ideas in a bowl, and then you energize it with the power of belief, you literally create the world you experience. What you think and the thoughts that you are attached to literally become your world. Thoughts empowered with our beliefs, literally cause this sea of energy to manifest into the forms that we see.

If you look around, everything you see in the physical world started as just a thought, then it became an idea. That idea then grew as it was fragmented, then shared, and finally expressed, until it finally grew enough to turn into a core belief that we all share. That idea was that we were all separate, not only from God, but from each other. You literally become what you think about most, and if you believe that you are separate, you will act accordingly because that is what you will experience.

> *Nothing in your world is going to change for you until you change your thoughts about the world.*
>
>

If you believe that you are sinful and guilty, then your life becomes what you have imagined and believed in most. The world is literally your unconscious mind reflecting back to you everything you need to re-interpret, which in this case is guilt, because that is the thought to which you have become attached. This world is literally showing you every belief that you are attached to, until you change it. You will know what you are attached to because you will react to it. And remember also, it is not people we are attached to, it is the thoughts we project onto people that we are attached to. Nothing in your world is going to change for you until you change your thoughts about the world.

At the European Organization for Nuclear Research known by its French acronym CERN, they are searching for the particle that gives mass to everything. The question is how could nothing become everything? How could the universe, with so many unbelievably large solid planets and stars, have come from nothing? So, at CERN, they are looking for what has been called the God particle and have spent billions upon billions of dollars looking for it.

Well, here it is for free: the God particle that gives everything mass is... *belief.* All gravity, all mass, all density is controlled and manifested by the belief we put into it. Let me explain - when I was having my out of body experiences at the very beginning, I remember several times returning from my weekly experiences, and finding my body suspended in mid-air - it was levitating. The reason was, because my belief that I was a body was temporally relinquished by me being out of body, the body then literally became nothing, even lighter than air, because my consciousness was elsewhere. My body was almost 170 pounds, and all of a sudden here it was, lighter than a feather. However, the very second my consciousness entered the body, and I could feel it, it collapsed onto the bed. In *The Course* we are reminded over and over again that we are not a body.

What you are is a thought, which has manifested as a body. What you believe in will manifest and become real for you. Quantum physics has shown us that the world is not the solid and unchangeable thing it appears to be. Instead, it is a galaxy of invisible energy that is like a *fabric* that runs through every bit of space that is in this universe. Anything can move through it, anything can sever it, and anything can manifest from it. Although most people do not see it, it is there.

However, we can and do manifest the world we experience with our individual thoughts, and the world is experienced as just one collective thought. Just like when you see a magician at a magic show, what you see with your eyes blinds you to what is really going on, because there is *never* nothing happening. Something magical is happening all around you in every second, but you are just not aware of it; you need to wake up because, otherwise, you will end up missing most of your life.

Just like the magician tricks you, you have tricked yourself into believing the thoughts that you think and therefore you believe that everything is true in this world. The key is that you do not think; it is only the ego that thinks. What you have yet to realize is that all thoughts that you attach yourself to will manifest in your world because once you attach yourself to a thought you energize it through your belief in it. Even the people that you think you see are just thoughts. What you think is true in this world is really an illusion, just like the magic trick.

Let us take a look at how energy manifests as a person. Energy is comprised of subatomic particles. These subatomic particles are then comprised of atoms, which are comprised of molecules. Molecules then make up cells, which make up all of our organs and tissues, including our skin. These then make the following systems that make a human body: cardiovascular, digestive, endocrine, excretory, immune, integumentary, musculoskeletal, respiratory, reproductive, and finally, the nervous system. There you have it, our journey from energy into a body. Next we need a personality, which will activate the thoughts that we choose to attach ourselves to the level of the mind.

Everything that you see here in this world – every body, animal, bird, plant, flower, fish and mammal – all have the same energy in its most beautiful and intelligent configuration. All energy is constantly changing beneath the surface and we control it all with our thoughts; that is how powerful our minds truly are.

If you could see beyond what they eyes show you, you would see that you, I, and everyone here are made up of just clusters of ever-changing forms of energy, that are simply ruled by our thoughts.

Quantum physics tell us that it is the act of observing an object that causes it to be where and how we observe it. We have also learned that an object does not exist independently of its Observer! So, as you can see, our observation, our attention to something, and our intention, literally creates that thing in our lives. This is the law of focus; what you focus on will expand for you. Let us take a closer look at this world and how everything here truly needs everything else to experience this entire event. The three dimensions that make this world a dualistic world are: the body, the world and the split mind. Your body needs the world to prove its reality to you, because you, in a body, will not exist without the world. And likewise, the world needs your body to confirm its reality.

If you were not in the body to perceive the world, then for you, there is no world. It is the body's five senses that prove that this world is real for you, because you can see it, taste it, hear it, touch it, and feel it. So, to your body, this world is truly real, and no more so than when you feel it – pain makes this world very real to the body. The body is attached to the world, and the world is attached to the body. When you break this union, as in death, from your perspective, both disappear.

Now, let us take it a little further because there is a third dimension – the split dualistic mind of the ego. This mind contains the two rooms of right or wrong, and good or bad. The body is attached to this mind-set, and so it projects this mind-set onto the world. *The Course* tells us that this world is neutral the same as the body, and that it is the split mind of the ego that we project onto a neutral world. As long as you remain attached to the split mind of the ego, you will always be arguing as to who is right or wrong, or judging who is good or bad.

> **As long as you remain attached to the split mind of the ego, you will always be arguing as to who is right or wrong, or judging who is good or bad.**
>
> ☯

There is no escaping this as long as you are unwilling to turn the other cheek as Jesus advised we do in Matthew 5:39. This is what he meant: look at this another way. When you turn your cheek you are looking at things from a different perspective. If we could just look in a different way at the seeming attacks that we experience from others, we will escape the pain that the attacks seem to bring. The only way to escape this mind-set is

414

first through transcendence, and then the re-interpretation of the two rooms of right or wrong and good or bad. You must raise your vibration and transcend to a higher state of consciousness to deal with this problem. So, how do we do that? There are tools in this book that will help you transcend to a higher level of consciousness. They are found in the *Chapter 10 – True Forgiveness*. Once you find yourself in that higher state of consciousness, you now must dissolve the image you hold of yourself as a body. You will discover how to do this in *Chapter 5 – The Separated Self.*

What you see and experience with your body is the physical world. The body can only experience and be experienced. Thoughts cannot experience or be experienced by just themselves: every thought needs a body to experience itself as something other than just a thought. Thoughts are merely concepts that need energy to become manifest and then are interpreted by a mind. And ultimately, thoughts need a physical world and a body to be experienced.

So, we had a thought of separation, and to experience that thought, we created a world and a body. The world is neutral, along with the body, as we have already discussed. That means that you can give a different meaning to both the world and the body, and the way you do that is by reinterpreting everything you see, from a higher level of consciousness.

From the perception of the true right mind you can look down on the world and the body and begin to let it all go. The way you let anything go is by reinterpreting it. Every thought has two meanings, right-minded perception, or wrong-minded perception. One is the ego's version of events, the other is the right-minded version. Only one of these versions is true, and you must decide which one, because the one you choose means the way forward for you. You must reinterpret everything as either true or false.

Be careful not to become confused in the levels when you begin the reinterpretation process, because each level has its own truths, which is true for that level, and does not necessary mean that it is true at another higher level. Let me explain - a truth at level 1 would be that we all believe that we are separate from each other. However, when you arrive at level 2, your experience of this form of separation will be much different, thus the higher you go, you will experience many different experiences of the separation at each level. You can use this information to understand how you learn to see and perceive the universe differently from the way you see it now so that you can create a world of peace, joy, love and bliss that you truly desire. You do not need everyone in the world to do this, you just need a very deep resolve that you want this, you need to convince yourself you want to wake up and take the necessary steps.

This is not an easy path, even though it is a simple path. It is not easy because you, as a separated self, just love being special but hate your separated existence as it is today. We all need to look at this very deeply. The need to feel special is ingrained within all of us, and it is causing us to create a world of pain. Someday soon you must realize that it is you, and only you, that is crucifying yourself and the way you are doing that is just by your thoughts. *It is never about any given situation, no matter how serious it is. It is always only your thoughts about a situation that makes life so painful. Change your thoughts, and you will literally change your world.*

Epilogue

Beginning in 2009, I have been studying, learning, applying and knowing what *The Course* says. I could only get to the knowing after first dedicating myself to relentless studying, incessant learning and devoted application. Then, and only then, I finally I came to knowing. Knowing will only come from application, not by thinking, or even from a life of continuous studying and learning. Ultimately, at some point you must let even the searching and seeking for knowledge go and just be. The seeker is the persona, and as long as you continue to seek, you will engage your shadow, sooner or later. That will not be a very nice experience for you. You see, the persona feeds the shadow, and together they both feed the ego.

When you have what you need, begin the process of detachment. Here is a devised code that was given to me to share with you: Everything you need is in this book for you to wake up.

Where does one begin with all this information? Let me try and bring all this together and take you through it step by step. I call this section the Ascension Code, because it is one of the many ways home; by ascension. And remember, it is just one of the ways home; there are countless others to choose from.

The Ascension Code

First Step

Choose which path you will take. To begin you have to choose one of the three options on how you will look at The Course from the perspective of waking up:

1. Holy book
2. Spiritual book
3. Psychology book

If you are on the journey to your awakening, which path are you on? Is it a holy path, is it a spiritual path, or is it a psychological path? If you are on a holy path, then your task is to use the Holy Spirit, which is on level 2. If you are on the psychotherapy path, then you must use, the true right mind, also on level 2. The true right mind is the mind that corrects the ego wrong mind. Each of these are just symbols, the Holy Spirit and right minded thinking are the same. If you are on a spiritual journey, then you will be on the path of detachment to attain complete emptiness, which means that you must do your detachment work on level 2, not level 1. In each of these, you must not reject or judge any or the other paths, each one is different but the same. They are different only in words, the symbol or concept they fit into are all the same. Words may differ, but symbols stay the same.

Second Step

Choose which story of the separation you wish to relinquish. You have four versions:

1. The Garden of Eden story
2. The Prodigal Son story
3. The Tiny Mad Idea story
4. The Hidden Truth – The Meaning of Life story

Decide which story of the separation you wish to detach from, one is not better or worse than any other. What this means is that if you choose the story of sin, guilt and fear, as in The Garden of Eden and The Tiny Mad Idea, then that is the story that you must forgive yourself for. To do this, you will be working with the Holy Spirit from level 2.

If you decide not to believe in that story, and you believe that this was all meant to be, just as it is, then you must detach from the ego itself. If you can do this you will see the story of separation from a different perspective, and now your path will not be one of seeing and undoing guilt, but rather, becoming aware of your attachments and detaching from them. You will be detaching from the true right mind on level 2. The choice is yours.

Third Step

Master the tools to get you to level 2. What are they?

1. Complete responsibility for *everything*
2. Complete acceptance of what is
3. Advanced True Forgiveness (ATF)
4. Complete Forgiveness
5. Simple Forgiveness
6. Self-Empowerment
7. Master a life of non-attachment

Most spiritual seekers fall into the trap of beginning their work on level 1. However, remember this common saying, "you cannot solve a problem at the same level the problem is being created." If you attempt this, you are only feeding the ego's persona. You must get to level 2, before you begin your work on level 1.

Fourth Step

From level 2, you must now begin the process of undoing the separated self. This process has three parts:

1. The persona must be recognized for what it is and it must be undone. This means that all seeking, searching, needing, wanting, planning, desiring, expecting and demanding must be relinquished

2. The shadow must also be recognized for what it is and it must also be undone. This means that we take responsibility and accept everyone and everything imaginable, and not only in your own personal world, but in this entire world including everyone and everything in it. There must be nothing and no one that you reject or judge either in their favor or against them.

3. You must revert back into your personality and accept that this is not who you are, but it is you until you wake up. You must reject nothing of your personality, or see any part as better than anyone else. If you cannot accomplish this, you will remain in the ego split mind. Be consistently content within yourself, and amazing things will happen. You now must come from the perspective of the personality access

Level 2, as often as possible. Using all the tools new Empowerment tools. Consistently using all the self empowerment tools found in Chapter 11 – *Self Empowerment* will help you do this.

Fifth Step

Relinquish your personal identity, which is the identity of the separated self. It is this identity that is keeping you spiritually asleep.

This process has five parts:

1. Relinquish all attachment to the body by relinquishing from its demands, expectations, needs and desires.

2. Relinquish the attachment to gender, which means that you will not defend pass any judgments based on either gender.

3. Relinquish the attachment to the family identity. Family becomes universal and the same process of relinquishment of demands, expectations, needs and desires applies.

4. Relinquish the attachment to religion. In addition to traditional religion, this also includes relinquishing any attachment to *The Course*. You make the course into a religion when you see it any differently from any other religion. Do not see any difference in any because there aren't any.

5. Relinquish the attachment to National identity. Why? Because it engenders separation and it is the source of all international conflict.

Sixth Step

You now must relinquish the three layers of the separated self. This process consists of three steps that, like the processes above, also consist of reinterpretation and relinquishment.

1. You must begin to relinquish all attachments to the external. You do not physically relinquish anything, instead, you must perceive everything and everyone from a right-minded perspective. At this point you will already be on level 2, so you will automatically see everything differently. Your task is to remain on level 2 and continue seeing and perceiving the world and your attachments from that higher perspective. Once you can do this, it will to relinquish everything. This is because your desires will be much higher coming from a higher state of consciousness and you will simply not value on level 2 the things that you valued on level 1.

2. You must replace all of the ego's coping mechanisms with the new empowerment tools, especially that of complete forgiveness and self-empowerment.

3. Lastly, you must recognize and disarm all of your defenses: denial, rationalization, intellectualization, displacement, sublimation, reaction formation, passive aggressiveness, etc.

Seventh Step

When you have reached this stage, what is left of your attachment to the ego will have retreated by now for its own safety. Now, you also change tactics and become the Observer. You now play the ego at its own game, if you are patient, it will show you exactly what you must detach from, if anything. When this happens, see this as is good rather than seeing yourself as having made an error, else, the ego will try to catch you out on that one.

At this stage, your life is now one of quietness, silence, contemplation, and total non-attachment. This will bring you into the present here and Now. And in the Now, your unlimited patience will win you an awakening, because the ego will come to you, if you are patient and remain in a silent state of mind. When the ego shows itself, recognize, correct, and release. This is simple forgiveness. There is not a need to go into any dramas, stories, or memories. At this point, just the three steps of simple forgiveness will take you home.

See you there!
Namaste!
Michael

Glossary

A

Awareness

Awareness – All Levels: Awareness is a state of mind. Each level of consciousness has its own state awareness. Awareness and consciousness are identical. Conscious awareness is awareness of your higher Self and above. Unconscious awareness is everything of the ego which abides in the lower levels of consciousness.

Pure Awareness – Level 5: Also known as Divine Heaven, Knowledge, Oneness, our eternal state of mind.

Awakening

Awakening – All Levels: When you experience any form of consciousness that is higher then the level you are on.

Self-Awakening – Level 1: When you realize that you are not you thought you were, and you now suspect that this world is not real.

Spiritual-Awakening – Level 2: When you experience a moment within in which you remember your spiritual divinity. This is an experience of level 2, or above.

Higher-Self-Awakening- Level 3: When you awaken on level 3 into your higher consciousness. Here you will have access to all higher knowledge that you will require to fulfill your script.

This knowledge will include profound insights and road maps for you to follow the journey within.

B

Being – Level 3 or above: A state of mind that is within non-consciousness. It is bliss without the awareness of bliss. This was our state before the seeming separation, and will continue after, but now along with Pure Awareness.

C

Consciousness

Consciousness – Level 3: When I refer to consciousness, I refer to a state of mind. Each level has its own state of consciousness and awareness. Consciousness and awareness are identical to each level.

Unconsciousness – Level 1: A state of mind where the person is spiritually asleep; they are unaware, or have forgotten their spiritual divinity.

Non-Consciousness – Levels 4, 5 & 6: A state of Being. This is a state that is experienced as there being nothing that is separate from anything else. In other words, there is nothing else to be conscious of. The state of Oneness and Non-Consciousness are identical.

Sub-Conscious – Level 2: The state of mind that is between the unconscious and conscious mindsets. It is between levels one and three. At this level your can still choose to be sub-conscious with the ego or sub-conscious with the true right mind (or Holy Spirit).

D

Dimensions

Physical Universe – The 3rd Dimension – Level 1: The physical universe is on the third dimension. This is the totality of the unconscious metaphysical separated mind, projected into form in physical consciousness. This is the thought of separation taking shape and then the body reinforces its reality.

Spiritual Universe – The 4th Dimension – Level 2: This is the universe of right-minded thinking. It still holds the illusion of a body, but that body is spiritual rather than physical. It is the home of the Holy Spirit. It is level 2 right-minded thinking. It holds spiritual truth and spiritual awareness for those who have awakened. It is the destination for all those who are still enjoying the cycle of life and death. It is the place where you will do your life review, and write your new script for your next life.

Higher Universe – The 5th Dimension – Level 3: This is beyond the form of the body or anything that is physical. This is a place of light, truth, higher awareness and a much higher level of consciousness.

Christ Universe – 6th Dimension – Level 4: This is the place where we all meet in Oneness, also known as the Real world in *A Course in Miracles*. It is the totality of the entire

Sonship. It is the place where remembrance of our true Christ self dwells while we experience the separation.

Heaven – 7ᵗʰ Dimension – Level 5: This is the state of Mind in our Oneness with God. It is a pure non-dualistic universe of everything that is. Being that it is eternal, it is the timeless state. It is the state of Awareness and Being.

E

Ego Defense Mechanism

Rationalization – Level 1: Rationalization is an external justification for an internal problem. When you rationalize you are not taking responsibility for what you are experiencing. Most often you will not be aware that you are doing this. For this reason you are never upset for the reason you think.

Passive Aggressive – Level 1: Suppressing your negative emotions such as anger, annoyance, frustration and irritation while you try to show that you are not upset. This is one of the highest contributing factors to the manifestation of cancer within the body. By storing this negative energy in the body, the energy then attacks the internal organs.

Reaction Formation – Level 1: This is when you hide your true feelings and take up the complete opposite emotions that you are feeling inside. People pleasing is a powerful reaction formation tool for the ego.

Sublimation – Level 1: This is where you take your internal negative energy, and you use it constructively. Musicians, artists, and sports people all use sublimated energy.

Displacement – Level 1: This is where you project your negative energy onto a less threating person or object.

Empowerment Tools

False Forgiveness – Level 1: When you attempt to forgive another person for what they have done.

Advanced True Forgiveness – Level 2: This is where you forgive yourself, but only for what you react to. It is detachment from your projections. This is detachment from level 1.

Complete Forgiveness – Level 2: The correction for the ego's tool of rationalization. This is where you become one with the body and bring all the emotional traumas to the truth, instead of rationalizing them with the ego. It is the undoing of the pain body, or the undoing of the totality of the ego emotional thought system.

Simple Forgiveness – Level 2: This is where you detach from all the stories and dreams of this world instantly as you recognize them. It has three steps: recognize, correct and release.

Self-Empowerment – Level 2: This is the correction for the totality of the ego false self, or the total separated self. Using this tool, you will increase your higher self awareness, this is this higher self way of dealing with any and all relationships. When you use self-empowerment, you align with your higher Self.

Responsibility – Level 1: At level 1 when you take responsibility you blame yourself and you put yourself into the bad room. This is the ego's version of you taking responsibility, this is false responsibility.

Complete Responsibility – Level 2: Where you bring everything down to truth or illusion; what is real or unreal; what is love and what love is not. Any time you see truth as true, or illusion as illusion, you are fulfilling and taking true responsibility.

L

Levels of Teaching and Learning

The Ego – Level 1: this is the ego split mind, the two rooms, the ying and yang, the persona and the shadow. It is also known as the mind of right and wrong, and good and bad.

The Ego – Level 2: This is the total thought of separation. It is the entirety of the ego thought system. This is everything that is unreal, false, untrue, illusion, and it includes all dreams.

Higher Self – Level 3: One mind without judgment.

Christ – Level 4: The sum total of every person, every animal, every plant, and just about everything you see, is all part of Christ. Christ is also known as the Son of God, which includes everyone and everything. Christ is the extension of the love of God. God Created Christ, while God is self Created. Christ is

432

also known as the state of Being, before the separation, and Pure Awareness after the separation.

M

Man

Neanderthal Man – Level 1: The totality of the unconscious ego mind projected onto an unconscious world and without the concepts of right and wrong, or good and bad.

Homo Sapiens Man – Level 1: The missing link has been so eagerly sought after, but it is not between apes and man, but rather, between Neanderthal man and Homo sapiens. It is the advent of the two rooms of right and wrong, and good and bad, that elevated Homo sapiens on the ladder of human evolution. When the brain of Homo sapiens was large enough to access the mind, this is when the mind of spirit became unconscious in an unconscious world.

Mind

The Ego Split Mind / Two Rooms – Level 1: The ego split mind is split at level 1 into the ego right mind and the ego wrong mind. It is the mind of right or wrong, and good or bad. It is also known as the two rooms, ying and yang, and the persona and the shadow.

The Ego Wrong Mind – Level 1: This is the shadow, which contains all our self-hate. This self-hate is then denied and projected onto all the people we do not like but hate. It is also known as, the bad room, the yang, or the victimizer.

The Ego Right Mind - Level 1: This is the persona which contains everything we like about ourselves and everything that we wish we could be. It is the mind of religious and spiritual specialness. It is also known as the good room, the Ying, and is the home of the victim.

The Split Mind – Level 2: This is the split mind where you will discern between what is true and real and what is false and illusion. It is discernment between what is illusion and what is reality? It is the discernment of the entirety of the ego thought system, and the correction for that thought is the Holy Spirit. It is the mind of true choice.

The Holy Spirit / The True Right Mind – Level 2: The correction for the entire ego thought system, which includes the ego wrong mind and the ego right mind. It is the mind of detachment and forgiveness. It is the voice for God.

P

Planck Second – Level 5: Named after Max Planck, the theoretical physicist who first recognized this physical constant that is the proportionality constant between the minimal increment of energy and the frequency of its associated electromagnetic wavy. It is the smallest fraction of time measured.

R

The Real World – Level 4: This is another name for the Christ Universe or the Universe of Oneness.

Reference Index

This index is organized by the chapters in which the reference appears. The first number represents the number of the footnote in the given chapter. For quotes from *A Course in Miracles*, the footnote number is followed by the standard designation of *The Course* reference code, chapter (or lesson), section, paragraph, and line number.

The Course reference code is as follows:

T: Text   **W:** Workbook for Students

M: Manual for Teachers   **CL:** Clarification of Terms

P: *Psychotherapy: Purpose, Process, and Practice* pamphlet

S: *The Song of Prayer* pamphlet

CHAPTER TWO – The Dark Night of the Soul

1. Report of the Tribunal of Inquiry – Set up Pursuant to the Tribunal of Inquiry (Evidence) Acts 1921-2002 into Certain Gardaí in the Donegal Division, (2006) Chapter 6, ¶6.09 pg. 264.

Available at: http://www.morristribunal.ie/SITECONTENT_172.pdf

CHAPTER THREE – The Surrender

1. Available at: http://www.goodreads.com/quotes/549821-there-is-no-coming-to-consciousness-without-pain-people-will

2. T-1.II.1:1-3 & T-1.II.2:1-2   **3.** T-1.II.5:1-2

CHAPTER FOUR – Spiritual Advancement

1. T-20.VIII.7:3-5   **2.** Luke 6:31 New Revised Standard Version

3. T-21.Intro.1:7

4. Available at: ttp://www.alberteinsteinsite.com/quotes/einsteinquotes.html

CHAPTER FIVE – The Separated Self

1. Available at: http://www.britannica.com/topic/persona-psychology

2. Available at: https://en.wikipedia.org/wiki/Big_Five_personality_traits#Sample_items

3. Available at: http://www.goodreads.com/quotes/549821-there-is-no-coming-to-consciousness-without-pain-people-will

CHAPTER SIX – Enlightenment

1. M-21.1:9-10

CHAPTER SEVEN – The Separation

1. T-2.II.3:6   **2.** T-13.V.1:1   **3.** W-189.7:1-5

CHAPTER EIGHT – The Root Cause of All Suffering

1. T-18.VI.3:1

CHAPTER NINE – The Illusion of Death

1. T-3.IV.7:12   **2.** T-24.VII.8:5

3. Available at: http://www.world-mysteries.com/sci_akashic1.htm

CHAPTER TEN – True Forgiveness

1. Eckhart Tolle (2004) *The Power of Now: A Guide to Spiritual Enlightenment*, Page 226, Novato, CA, New World Library

2. S-2.I.1:1   **3.** P-2.VI.6:3   **4.** W-190.5:2-5   **5.** W-5

CHAPTER ELEVEN – Self Empowerment

1. W-34   **2.** W-34

CHAPTER TWELVE – Love and the Illusion of Love

1. T-4.III.4:5-8

CHAPTER THIRTEEN – Ascension

1. T-2.III.3:3   **2.** M-4.I.A

3. John 14:6 New Revised Standard Version   **4.** T-22.III.6:7

Acknowledgments

Book Editor / Design
Gloria Hernández

This book would not have been possible without one person in particular. I would like to thank one person above all others and that is my Editor in Chief Gloria Hernández.
Without Gloria's dedicated endeavor and her ever persistent diligence with every detail, I would not have completed my task.
Thank you Gloria, you are forever in my eternal heart and you have my eternal gratitude. Namaste!

Book Editing / Proof
Rhodá Ui Choraine

I would like to also thank my very good friend and fellow Course student Rhodá Ui Choraine. I have known Rhodá for several years now and she has been a mighty companion with me on my journey.
Thank you dear friend Rhodá, and may the sun always be in your face, may the wind always be always on your back, and the may the winds of destiny carry you all the way home. Namaste!

Book Cover Design
Sharon Davitt

Last but in no way least, I would like to thank my very talented book cover designer and very good friend Sharon Davitt. I told Sharon the vision I had about the book cover one day, and that same night she sent me the exact vision on a picture, which turned out to be the cover of this book, and its cousin - the second title.
Thank you Sharon from the bottom of my heart, you are forever in my thoughts. Namaste!

Made in the USA
San Bernardino, CA
09 April 2018